MONEY MATTERS

CHARLES S.

MEEK

PROBUS PUBLISHING COMPANY
Chicago, Illinois

This publication is designed to provide accurate and authoritative information in regard to the subject matter covered. It is sold with the understanding that the publisher is not engaged in rendering legal, accounting or other professional service.

Library of Congress Cataloging in Publication Data Available

ISBN 1-55738-136-4

Printed in the United States of America
BC

1 2 3 4 5 6 7 8 9 0

Dedicated to L. K. Meek, my grandfather.

I wish I had known him better. . . . Thank you for your influence.

Special thanks to Cindy and Jeff, my family.

They are right. These short little projects aren't so short.

Contents

PROLOGUE

Test Your Financial Savvy

Test your financial savvy of real world investments and financial planning concepts. Try this short quiz:

1. I have a written plan for allocating my assets and planning for my financial future.
    - a. Yes
    - b. No
2. When federal government deficits are at their highest, interest rates can be expected to
    - a. Go up
    - b. Go down
    - c. No correlation
3. The price of gold has beaten inflation.
    - a. True
    - b. False
4. As a successful professional, leaving your spouse everything in your will could cost your kids how much in estate taxes?
    - a. $50,000   d. $600,000
    - b. $100,000   e. Nothing
    - c. $200,000
5. A living trust will save your heirs:
    - a. Federal estate taxes
    - b. Federal income taxes
    - c. Neither
6. Compared to beginning to save for retirement at the start of your working career, if you procrastinate until 10 years before retirement, you will need to save how much more *annually*?

      a.   Twice
      b.   5 times
      c.   10 times
      d.   15 times

7. Over the last 50 to 75 years stocks have historically returned
      a.   6%
      b.   10%
      c.   14%
      d.   18%
      e.   22%
      f.   26%

8. The top mutual funds have returned over the same 50 to 75 years
      a.   6%
      b.   10%
      c.   14%
      d.   18%
      e.   22%
      f.   26%

9. If you had put an equal amount into blue-chip stocks and also into bonds in 1925, and let all interest and dividends reinvest, the stocks would be worth how much more than the bonds today?
      a.   Twice
      b.   5 times
      c.   10 times
      d.   25 times
      e.   The bonds are worth more.

10. Stock market peaks are usually marked by
      a.   Low interest rates
      b.   High interest rates
      c.   Strong economy
      d.   Weak economy
      e.   Low cash positions by institutional investors
      f.   High cash positions by institutional investors

Correct Answers: 1. a   2. c   3. b   4. c   5. c   6. c
7. b   8. c   9. d   10. a, c, & e

Quiz Scorecard

Score (Number Correct)	Evaluation
0	Would you consider a vow of poverty?
1	Or maybe remarrying someone wealthy?
2	Don't leave that government job until you've read this book!
3	Better not listen to your father-in-law's investment advice anymore.
4	Better not listen to your best friend either.
5	In fact, you better buy them both a copy of this book.
6	If only they had had a couple of business courses in med school . . .
7	This book is just what you need to round out your vast storehouse of knowledge.
8	You're already on your way to fame and fortune.
9	*You* write a book and send me a copy.
10	Did you look at the answers first?

1

Introduction: Doctor, Lawyer, Merchant, Thief

This book is written for the college educated professional who wants to get his or her financial life in order. If you are the typical lawyer, architect, or whatever, you've spent your entire adult life learning all there is to know about your profession. Even if you are a successful entrepreneur, you know all about your industry. But have you managed your personal assets as well as your business?

Chances are that you have not taken the time to apply the formulas that you use successfully in your profession or business to your own financial planning. Somehow, you just don't get around to it. You've taken excellent care of your clients but maybe not of yourself. Your investments have been haphazard without a well-conceived plan and you know you need help. The "thief" referred to in the title of this chapter is the lost time you should have spent on your personal finances.

This Book Is For You, The Professional

This book is your ticket. It will get you off dead center. It will give you an easy and practical outline for your financial life . . .And do so without your having to dedicate the rest of your waking hours to this effort!

The Anthrax Connection

In this book, you'll get a real life lesson on finance. It has been suggested that Americans know as much about finance as they do about anthrax. In a recent survey, 72 percent of Americans said anthrax was better than powdered cleansers for removing bathtub rings, while another 12 percent said they would never buy any cough medicine other than anthrax. Anthrax is really an infectious disease of cattle and sheep. Humans get it only by talking to their commodities broker while sitting in the tub.

Can it be that, right here in America, our citizens are ignorant of finance? I would say, having been a broker for a national investment firm for 19 years, that 80 percent of investors profess absolute ignorance, 10 percent swear they know everything (but don't), and perhaps 10 percent actually have a realistic notion of what's going on in economics and finance. If these statistics are true, who's to blame? I put the blame right on the shoulders of our educators.

Many good things can be said of the American academic system. But the problems of coping with the real world of finance are not adequately addressed in our schools. You can go all the way through school, get a Ph.D., and still not know fundamental real world things like how to buy a house or how bond prices fluctuate. You can get a law degree and still not know how to settle an estate. Or, dear doctor, how many courses did you have in med school that taught you how to run a small business, which is what you are doing after all, isn't it?

And where are the school courses that expound the excitement, fun, and opportunity of the entrepreneurial spirit? Too many students today come out of school with no more ambition than to get lost in some big organization and retire on a pension. But, interestingly, Americans have a guilt complex about all of this. So many new clients say the same thing to me: "I must be your dumbest customer." Do you find yourself in this situation? The lack of formal education in finance is compounded by the incredible array of financial instruments available today. Even the most well-educated, successful professional gets a little queasy when the cocktail party chatter turns to the "accreted value of treasury investment growth receipts," or the "alpha" factor of mutual fund performance. Investment firms today can count 200 different investment products on their menu of delicious dollar delicacies. So what's one to do?

What This Book Is Not

This is not a get rich quick book. It is not about how to own $10 million worth of real estate for no money down. It is not about how the author made two million dollars in the stock market. Neither is it a textbook to explain all 200 investment vehicles available today.

If you want to be truly wealthy, you have two choices. The most efficient way is to inherit it. That's really the recommended way! (To paraphrase the TV ad: "We make money the old fashioned way. We inherit it.") Or, second, go start your own business, work 12 hours a day, 7 days a week, and provide a good service or product to the public.

What This Book Is

Experience is a good teacher. Having dealt for many years with people, their money, emotions, frustrations, and their dreams— perhaps this author can pass a few things along. There are some important concepts to be aware of when investing in the real world. Some of these concepts are obvious but overlooked. Some are mathematical, while some are simply common sense. Some are simple ideas, yet some are complex. Some are old and timeless; some are meant to be instructive about modern finance.

This book will shatter many of the myths about investing you may have held all these years. The primary purpose of the book is to discuss the most crucial ideas important to every investor. Some of these ideas have not been written anywhere else. Indeed, some may be too irreverent to be put in print by traditional authors. Some of them are available from other sources but have never been collected in one book before. We will talk about:

- How to be certain you'll be able to retire wealthy.
- Why to ignore what the majority are telling you about most investments.
- How to make your money grow without going out on a limb.

- How to make your savings work as hard for you as you have for it.

- How to preserve your capital in the volatile markets ushered in by the "Crash of '87".

- How to manage your money once you've "made it."

Together we will wade through the complexities of modern investing. We'll focus on investment returns that are realistic. We'll alert you to mistakes others have made. We'll stress the importance of financial planning for the future. We'll help you decide how to allocate your assets among stocks, bonds, real estate, and money markets.

One special section is devoted to concepts for the business owner. In another special section, we present a framework for dealing with the barrage of data and information about stock market cycles. In this section the problems of the ups and downs of our economy are explained, and an approach to potentially profit by them is presented.

The concepts are valuable to any investor. Whether you are busy running your own small business or climbing the corporate ladder, or even if you are approaching retirement age and want to learn more about how to protect your future, an understanding of the concepts in this book will help you.

This book was written to respect your valuable time. It is also different from other investment books in that it purposefully does not go into great detail on every subject. Instead, it focuses on concepts that do not become obsolete. It is designed to provide a framework for you to develop a meaningful financial plan. This book will tell you what you *really need* to know about successful investing.

If you're like most college graduates, you may have taken a basic course in college—Finance 101. Equally likely, though, you avoided it like the plague, being terrified of the idea of high finance. "Soshe" 101 (sociology) probably looked less threatening. This book is Real World 101. There is no prerequisite for this course. The final exam will be a self-evaluation "take home."We're going to start where the textbooks leave off. We'll dive right into the befuddling buzzword of the brokerage business: financial planning.

2

Why Financial Planning Is Important: Outlining Your Goals

"When one has had to work so hard to get money, why should he impose on himself the further hardship of trying to save it?"
Don Herold

"If you don't know where you're going, you're never going to get there."
Anonymous

Psychologists tell us that truly successful people tend to be goal oriented. They further tell us that putting a goal in writing has a powerful psychological impact of focusing one's attention to that goal and increasing the likelihood of achieving it. In a nutshell, that's the basis for financial planning. As a professional, you are no doubt rather goal oriented, or else you wouldn't be where you are today.

Most of the concepts are not particularly complicated. The primary purpose of financial planning is to formalize one's goals and get them down on paper. Let's take a look at some of the major concepts of financial planning.

There are five basic aspects to financial planning:

- Retirement planning.
- Estate planning.

- Family protection planning.
- Income tax planning.
- College planning.

Let's take them one at a time. First, retirement planning:

Retirement Planning

This is the most important aspect of the planning process. The goal: total financial independence (TFI). TFI is what it's all about. It's what we all dream about, but unfortunately the dream is about as far as most of us get. Recent studies have shown that nine out of ten Americans are not able to retire in the style they desire. That's really quite sad!

Chances are pretty good that you have never taken the time to commit a retirement wealth accumulation plan to writing. Perhaps one reason is that you haven't really been quite sure how to do it. So, in the next few pages, we're going to give you a method so simple yet so worthwhile that it will serve as your guide for years to come!

To start your retirement plan, you first have to ask: (1) When? and (2) How much? That is, when do you want to retire and how much annual income do you want to have? You then bring in all three legs of retirement planning, including: social security, company pension, and personal savings.

Let's say you're a lawyer making $100,000 a year. As a 40-year-old mature, and upwardly mobile professional, you are beginning to think a little more seriously about your future retirement. You would like to be financially able to retire early, say at age 60. Most people need 60 percent to 80 percent of their final salary to maintain their standard of living in retirement. This is true because one's expenses go down—your home is probably paid for, your kids are grown, and you have no daily commuting expenses, restaurant lunches, and so forth. I normally recommend using an 80 percent ratio to salary as a retirement income goal. One reason for using 80 percent instead of 60 percent is that most pension plans do not have inflation adjustment clauses. That is, if your company has a pension plan, it will probably stay fixed for the rest of your life (even though social security will increase with inflation). You may live 20, 30, or even more years after retirement (especially with modern health care breakthroughs). During that time, inflation could destroy your pension, which will probably be the primary source of your retirement income.

Another reason to shoot for the higher 80 percent figure is that for many people, expenses will be incurred in taking care of elderly parents. Longer life expectancies are affecting us financially in many ways. And a further thought: If you've been to Europe or Japan lately, you can appreciate the fact that a leisurely life of travel can be a bummer on your budget! So especially if you plan to travel a lot during retirement, you might need even more income than when you were working.

You, however, as a lawyer do not have a traditional fixed pension plan. You probably have, instead, a 401(k) plan. We will explain more about various types of plans later in Chapter 11. However, a 401(k) plan usually offers you the option of taking your accumulated lump sum at retirement, putting it into an IRA rollover, and investing it as you see fit. Therefore, you have the potential to make those dollars grow with inflation during retirement. So let's say that you decide to plan for 70 percent, or $70,000 of retirement income in today's dollars.

Be aware that this $70,000 is before taxes. But it is a pretty safe bet that your tax bracket won't change much during retirement, so we won't worry about adjusting for taxes for now. We should also note that your actual income needs will be far higher than $70,000 by the time you reach retirement age because of inflation. We are going to do our analysis net of inflation and, therefore, assume that our income and expenses will inflate at an even rate from today. But this $70,000 figure will be a moving target, so you should annually reevaluate.

Step 1: Estimate Social Security

The first step is to make an estimate of your social security benefits. There are various sources for this information. Your annual employee benefit statement from your employer is one source. Your investment firm may have financial planning software to help you. Or you can contact your local social security office. You may also call the Social Security Administration's toll free number (1–800–937–2000) and request form SSA–7004. This is a questionnaire that the government will use to prepare a list of benefits for you.

You may also get a rough estimate from the table below. The table is in 1990 dollars, and assumes pre-retirement income for one spouse in excess of $45,000. (Social Security benefits peak out at approximately $45,000 of working-year's earnings.) For someone with a salary under $45,000, benefits are less than shown. This task is an adequate estimate for our planning purposes, but those people near retirement age should request a benefit estimate from the Social Security Administration. Spouses who don't work outside the home will receive a benefit equal to half that of the working spouse. Working spouses may earn their own full benefit. Table 2–1 shows an individual and also a couple with a non-working spouse.

TABLE 2-1

Social Security Income Benefits Projected Annual Income At Normal Retirement Age In 1990 Dollars

Age In 1990	Individual	Couple
25	$12,000	$18,000
30	12,000	18,000
35	12,000	18,000
40	12,000	18,000
45	11,600	17,400
50	11,400	17,100
55	11,400	17,100
60	10,900	16,350
65	10,400	15,600

The normal retirement age, which is presently 65, will gradually rise after the year 1999, until it reaches age 67 in the year 2027. Normal retirement age will increase nearly one month per year after the year 1999. The table is adjusted accordingly to reflect future normal retirement ages. Retirement benefits can actually begin as early as age 62 currently, but your retirement check will be reduced permanently by as much as 20 percent. The amount of reduction depends on the number of months you get checks before you reach normal retirement age. If you start your checks early, you'll get about the same value in total benefits over the years, but in smaller amounts to take account of the longer period over which you'll get them.

By the way, up to one-half of your social security retirement benefits may be subject to federal income tax. This occurs if your adjusted gross income plus municipal bond interest plus one-half of your social security benefits exceeds a base amount. The base amount is $25,000 for an individual and $32,000 for a couple filing jointly. The amount of benefits subject to tax will be the smaller of:

- one-half the benefits, or
- one-half the amount of combined income (adjusted gross income plus municipal bond interest plus one half of total benefits) in excess of the base amount.

Since you want to retire at age 60, you'll need to make an adjustment in your calculations, as age 60 is before you can actually begin receiving social security. To keep it simple, let's assume, arbitrarily, that instead of receiving the $18,000 that you and your spouse would be entitled to at normal retirement age, you will receive an actuarially equivalent amount of about $13,000 beginning at age 60. (If you retired at age 62, you would be entitled to $14,400, that is, 80 percent of $18,000. Thus, $13,000 is a lesser amount just for planning purposes. All we really need is a figure to work with here.)

$70,000 retirement income goal
− 13,000 projected social security
$57,000 additional income needed during retirement

Step II: Estimate Your Pension Income

Since you will not have a fixed pension, this is not relevant. However, if you did, you would merely use the figure from your employer's annual benefit statement and add that to your social security.

Step III: Estimate Your Investment Capital Needed at Retirement Age,
the "Lucky 13 Rule"

This step simply says to multiply your required income needs by 13.
Thus,

$57,000 additional income needed during retirement
×   13 lucky 13 rule
$741,000 investment capital needed to generate $57,000
                    in income

Why 13? This is just my own rule of thumb. It's the arithmetic
reciprocal of a conservative interest rate. That interest rate is a bit
arbitrary, but works out to be 7.7 percent. Thus, 7.7 percent of
$741,000 equals $57,000.

$741,000   needed capital
× 7.7% interest rate
$57,000   required income

This formula essentially says that it will require $741,000 in capital
invested at a conservative pretax rate of interest of 7.7 percent that
won't invade your principal to generate the income you need in
retirement. In subsequent chapters we will analyze at length various
possible investment scenarios and show why this is a reasonable
interest rate to use for this purpose.

Step IV: Subtract the Future Value of Current Investments

Lump all of your present investments that could be used to generate
retirement income into a single basket. Those investments include
your 401(k) assets, IRAs, cash, stocks, bonds, mutual funds, investment real estate, etc. It does not include your home, since it does not
really have potential to generate income. One goal I think most people
should work toward is getting out of debt, and that includes having
your home mortgage paid off. Let's assume that these investments
total $50,000. The next step is to apply a conservative interest rate to
the investments and project the value at your age 60. This assumed
interest rate should be stated relative to, that is above, inflation so that

we keep everything in today's dollars. The interest rate I suggest using is 4 percent. By the time you've finished this book you'll see the rationale for this figure. Of course, with inflation, you'll be able to achieve an actual return far higher than this, but we want to keep everything net of inflation.

Here's where the compound interest tables come in. Look at Table 2–2, which shows the future value of one (dollar) at various rates of interest. Find the 4% column, then drop down to year number 20, since you want to retire in 20 years. The factor is 2.19111. Since we have $50,000, we multiply 2.19111 times $50,000.

> $50,000 current investments
> × 2.191111 factor from Table 2–2
> $109,555 future value of current investments

Okay. We now have $109,555 to apply against the $741,000 we need. Rounding this new figure to $110,000 here's where we stand at this juncture:

> $741,000 necessary total capital
> − 110,000 future value of current investments (age 60)
> $631,000 additional capital needed to retire

TABLE 2-2

Amount of 1 At Compound Interest

Year	2.0%	3.0%	4.0%	5.0%	6.0%	7.0%
1	1.02000	1.03000	1.04000	1.05000	1.06000	1.07000
2	1.04040	1.06090	1.08160	1.10250	1.12360	1.14490
3	1.06120	1.09272	1.12486	1.15762	1.19101	1.22504
4	1.08243	1.12550	1.16985	1.21550	1.26247	1.31079
5	1.10408	1.15927	1.21665	1.27628	1.33822	1.40255
6	1.12616	1.19405	1.26531	1.34009	1.41851	1.50072
7	1.14868	1.22987	1.31593	1.40709	1.50362	1.60578
8	1.17165	1.26676	1.36856	1.47745	1.59384	1.71818
9	1.19509	1.30477	1.42330	1.55132	1.68947	1.83845
10	1.21899	1.34391	1.48024	1.62889	1.79084	1.96714
11	1.24337	1.38423	1.53945	1.71033	1.89829	2.10484
12	1.26823	1.42575	1.60102	1.79585	2.01219	2.25218
13	1.29360	1.46852	1.66506	1.88564	2.13292	2.40983
14	1.31947	1.51258	1.73167	1.97992	2.26089	2.57852
15	1.34586	1.55796	1.80093	2.07892	2.39654	2.75902
16	1.37277	1.60469	1.87297	2.18286	2.54034	2.95215
17	1.40023	1.65283	1.94789	2.29201	2.69276	3.15880
18	1.42823	1.70242	2.02580	2.40661	2.85432	3.37992
19	1.45680	1.75349	2.10683	2.52694	3.02558	3.61651
20	1.48593	1.80610	2.19111	2.65328	3.20712	3.86966
21	1.51565	1.86028	2.27875	2.78595	3.39954	4.14054
22	1.54596	1.91609	2.36990	2.92524	3.60351	4.43038
23	1.57688	1.97357	2.46470	3.07151	3.81973	4.74050
24	1.60842	2.03278	2.56329	3.22508	4.04891	5.07234
25	1.64059	2.09376	2.66582	3.38633	4.29184	5.42740
26	1.67340	2.15657	2.77245	3.55565	4.54935	5.80732
27	1.70687	2.22127	2.88335	3.73343	4.82231	6.21383
28	1.74100	2.28791	2.99868	3.92010	5.11165	6.64880
29	1.77582	2.35654	3.11863	4.11611	5.41835	7.11422
30	1.81134	2.42724	3.24337	4.32191	5.74345	7.61221
31	1.84757	2.50006	3.37311	4.53801	6.08806	8.14507
32	1.88452	2.57506	3.50803	4.76491	6.45334	8.71522
33	1.92221	2.65231	3.64835	5.00315	6.84054	9.32529
34	1.96065	2.73188	3.79429	5.25331	7.25097	9.97806
35	1.99986	2.81383	3.94606	5.51598	7.68603	10.6765
36	2.03986	2.89825	4.10390	5.79177	8.14719	11.4238
37	2.08066	2.98519	4.26806	6.08136	8.63603	12.2235
38	2.12227	3.07475	4.43878	6.38543	9.15419	13.0791
39	2.16472	3.16699	4.61633	6.70470	9.70344	13.9947
40	2.20801	3.26200	4.80098	7.03994	10.2856	14.9743
41	2.25217	3.35986	4.99302	7.39193	10.9027	16.0225
42	2.29721	3.46066	5.19274	7.76153	11.5569	17.1441
43	2.34316	3.56447	5.40045	8.14961	12.2503	18.3442
44	2.39002	3.67141	5.61647	8.55709	12.9853	19.6282
45	2.43782	3.78155	5.84113	8.98494	13.7644	21.0022
46	2.48658	3.89500	6.07477	9.43419	14.5903	22.4724
47	2.53631	4.01185	6.31776	9.90590	15.4657	24.0454
48	2.58703	4.13220	6.57047	10.4011	16.3937	25.7286
49	2.63877	4.25617	6.83329	10.9212	17.3773	27.5296
50	2.69155	4.38385	7.10662	11.4673	18.4199	29.4567

TABLE 2-2 (*continued*)

Amount of 1 At Compound Interest

Year	8.0%	9.0%	10.0%	11.0%	12.0%	13.0%	14.0%
1	1.08000	1.09000	1.10000	1.11000	1.12000	1.13000	1.14000
2	1.16640	1.18810	1.21000	1.23210	1.25440	1.27690	1.29960
3	1.25971	1.29502	1.33100	1.36763	1.40492	1.44289	1.48154
4	1.36048	1.41158	1.46410	1.51807	1.57351	1.63047	1.68896
5	1.46932	1.53862	1.61051	1.68505	1.76234	1.84243	1.92541
6	1.58687	1.67709	1.77156	1.87041	1.97382	2.08195	2.19497
7	1.71382	1.82803	1.94871	2.07615	2.21067	2.35260	2.50226
8	1.85092	1.99256	2.14358	2.30453	2.47596	2.65844	2.85258
9	1.99900	2.17189	2.35794	2.55803	2.77307	3.00403	3.25194
10	2.15892	2.36736	2.59374	2.83941	3.10584	3.39456	3.70721
11	2.33163	2.58042	2.85311	3.15175	3.47854	3.83585	4.22622
12	2.51816	2.81265	3.13842	3.49844	3.89597	4.33451	4.81789
13	2.71961	3.06579	3.45226	3.88327	4.36348	4.89800	5.49240
14	2.93718	3.34171	3.79749	4.31043	4.88710	5.53474	6.26133
15	3.17216	3.64247	4.17724	4.78457	5.47355	6.25425	7.13792
16	3.42593	3.97029	4.59496	5.31088	6.13038	7.06731	8.13723
17	3.70000	4.32762	5.05446	5.89507	6.86602	7.98606	9.27644
18	3.99600	4.71710	5.55990	6.54353	7.68995	9.02425	10.5751
19	4.31568	5.14164	6.11589	7.26332	8.61274	10.1974	12.0556
20	4.66094	5.60439	6.72748	8.06228	9.64627	11.5230	13.7434
21	5.03381	6.10878	7.40023	8.94913	10.8038	13.0210	15.6675
22	5.43652	6.65857	8.14025	9.93354	12.1002	14.7137	17.8609
23	5.87144	7.25785	8.95428	11.0262	13.5523	16.6265	20.3615
24	6.34115	7.91105	9.84971	12.2391	15.1785	18.7880	23.2121
25	6.84844	8.62305	10.8346	13.5854	16.9999	21.2304	26.4618
26	7.39632	9.39912	11.9181	15.0798	19.0399	23.9904	30.1664
27	7.98802	10.2450	13.1099	16.7385	21.3247	27.1091	34.3897
28	8.62707	11.1670	14.4209	18.5798	23.8837	30.6333	39.2043
29	9.31723	12.1721	15.8630	20.6235	26.7497	34.6156	44.6929
30	10.0626	13.2676	17.4493	22.8921	29.9597	39.1157	50.9499
31	10.8676	14.4616	19.1942	25.4103	33.5549	44.2007	58.0828
32	11.7370	15.7632	21.1136	28.2054	37.5815	49.9468	66.2144
33	12.6759	17.1819	23.2250	31.3080	42.0912	56.4399	75.4845
34	13.6900	18.7283	25.5475	34.7519	47.1422	63.7771	86.0523
35	14.7852	20.4138	28.1022	38.5746	52.7993	72.0681	98.0996
36	15.9680	22.2510	30.9125	42.8178	59.1352	81.4369	111.833
37	17.2454	24.2536	34.0037	47.5277	66.2314	92.0237	127.490
38	18.6251	26.4365	37.4041	52.7558	74.1792	103.986	145.338
39	20.1151	28.8157	41.1445	58.5589	83.0807	117.505	165.686
40	21.7243	31.4092	45.2589	65.0004	93.0503	132.780	188.822
41	23.4622	34.2360	49.7848	72.1504	104.216	150.042	215.352
42	25.3392	37.3172	54.7633	80.0869	116.722	169.547	245.471
43	27.3663	40.6758	60.2396	88.8965	130.728	191.588	279.837
44	29.5556	44.3366	66.2636	98.6751	146.416	216.495	319.014
45	31.9201	48.3269	72.8900	109.529	163.986	244.639	363.676
46	34.4737	52.6763	80.1790	121.577	183.664	276.442	414.591
47	37.2316	57.4172	88.1969	134.951	205.704	312.379	472.633
48	40.2101	62.5847	97.0166	149.795	230.388	352.989	538.802
49	43.4269	68.2173	106.718	166.273	258.035	398.877	614.234
50	46.9010	74.3569	117.390	184.563	288.999	450.731	700.227

TABLE 2-2 (*continued*)

Amount of 1 At Compound Interest

Year	15.0%	16.0%	17.0%	18.0%	19.0%	20.0%	21%
1	1.15000	1.16000	1.17000	1.18000	1.19000	1.20000	1.21000
2	1.32250	1.34560	1.36890	1.39240	1.41610	1.44000	1.46410
3	1.52087	1.56089	1.60161	1.64303	1.68515	1.72800	1.77156
4	1.74900	1.81063	1.87388	1.93877	2.00533	2.07360	2.14358
5	2.01135	2.10034	2.19244	2.28775	2.38635	2.48832	2.59374
6	2.31305	2.43639	2.56516	2.69955	2.83976	2.98598	3.13842
7	2.66001	2.82621	3.00123	3.18547	3.37931	3.58318	3.79749
8	3.05901	3.27841	3.51144	3.75887	4.02138	4.29981	4.59496
9	3.51787	3.80295	4.10839	4.43544	4.78544	5.15977	5.55991
10	4.04555	4.41143	4.80682	5.23382	5.69467	6.19173	6.72749
11	4.65238	5.11725	5.62398	6.17591	6.77666	7.43008	8.14026
12	5.35024	5.93601	6.58005	7.28758	8.06423	8.91609	9.84972
13	6.15277	6.88578	7.69866	8.59934	9.59643	10.6993	11.9181
14	7.07569	7.98750	9.00743	10.1472	11.4197	12.8391	14.4209
15	8.13704	9.26550	10.5387	11.9737	13.5895	15.4070	17.4493
16	9.35760	10.7479	12.3302	14.1289	16.1715	18.4884	21.1137
17	10.7612	12.4676	14.4264	16.6721	19.2440	22.1860	25.5476
18	12.3754	14.4624	16.8788	19.6731	22.9004	26.6232	30.9126
19	14.2317	16.7764	19.7483	23.2143	27.2515	31.9479	37.4042
20	16.3664	19.4606	23.1055	27.3929	32.4293	38.3375	45.2591
21	18.8214	22.5744	27.0334	32.3236	38.5909	46.0050	54.7635
22	21.6446	26.1863	31.6291	38.1418	45.9231	55.2060	66.2638
23	24.8913	30.3761	37.0060	45.0074	54.6485	66.2472	80.1792
24	28.6250	35.2362	43.2971	53.1087	65.0317	79.4966	97.0169
25	32.9188	40.8740	50.6576	62.6683	77.3878	95.3959	117.390
26	37.8566	47.4139	59.2693	73.9486	92.0915	114.475	142.042
27	43.5351	55.0001	69.3451	87.2593	109.588	137.370	171.871
28	50.0653	63.8001	81.1338	102.966	130.410	164.844	207.964
29	57.5751	74.0081	94.9266	121.499	155.188	197.812	251.636
30	66.2114	85.8494	111.064	143.369	184.674	237.375	304.480
31	76.1431	99.5853	129.944	169.176	219.762	284.850	368.420
32	87.5646	115.519	152.035	199.627	261.517	341.820	445.789
33	100.699	134.002	177.881	235.560	311.205	410.184	539.404
34	115.804	155.442	208.121	277.961	370.334	492.221	652.679
35	133.174	180.313	243.501	327.994	440.698	590.665	789.742
36	153.150	209.163	284.897	387.033	524.430	708.798	955.588
37	176.123	242.629	333.329	456.700	624.072	850.558	1156.26
38	202.542	281.449	389.995	538.906	742.646	1020.66	1399.07
39	232.923	326.481	456.294	635.909	883.748	1224.80	1692.88
40	267.861	378.718	533.865	750.372	1051.66	1469.76	2048.38
41	308.040	439.313	624.622	885.439	1251.47	1763.71	2478.54
42	354.247	509.603	730.807	1044.81	1489.25	2116.45	2999.03
43	407.384	591.140	855.045	1232.88	1772.21	2539.74	3628.83
44	468.491	685.722	1000.40	1454.80	2108.93	3047.68	4390.89
45	538.765	795.437	1170.47	1716.66	2509.63	3657.23	5312.97
46	619.580	922.707	1369.44	2025.66	2986.46	4388.68	6428.70
47	712.517	1070.34	1602.25	2390.28	3553.88	5266.41	7778.72
48	819.394	1241.59	1874.63	2820.53	4229.12	6319.70	9412.25
49	942.303	1440.25	2193.32	3328.23	5032.65	7583.64	11388.8
50	1083.64	1670.69	2566.19	3927.31	5988.86	9100.36	13780.4

TABLE 2-2 *(continued)*

Amount of 1 At Compound Interest

Year	22%	23%	24%	25%
1	1.22000	1.23000	1.24000	1.25000
2	1.48840	1.51290	1.53760	1.56250
3	1.81584	1.86086	1.90662	1.95312
4	2.21533	2.28886	2.36421	2.44140
5	2.70270	2.81530	2.93162	3.05175
6	3.29730	3.46282	3.63521	3.81469
7	4.02270	4.25927	4.50766	4.76837
8	4.90770	5.23890	5.58950	5.96046
9	5.98739	6.44385	6.93098	7.45057
10	7.30462	7.92594	8.59441	9.31322
11	8.91164	9.74890	10.6570	11.6415
12	10.8722	11.9911	13.2147	14.5519
13	13.2640	14.7491	16.3863	18.1898
14	16.1821	18.1414	20.3190	22.7373
15	19.7422	22.3139	25.1955	28.4216
16	24.0855	27.4461	31.2425	35.5270
17	29.3843	33.7587	38.7407	44.4088
18	35.8488	41.5232	48.0384	55.5110
19	43.7356	51.0735	59.5676	69.3887
20	53.3574	62.8204	73.8639	86.7359
21	65.0961	77.2691	91.5912	108.419
22	79.4172	95.0410	113.573	135.524
23	96.8890	116.900	140.830	169.406
24	118.204	143.787	174.629	211.757
25	144.209	176.858	216.541	264.696
26	175.935	217.536	268.510	330.871
27	214.641	267.569	332.953	413.588
28	261.862	329.110	412.862	516.985
29	319.472	404.805	511.948	646.232
30	389.756	497.911	634.816	807.790
31	475.502	612.430	787.172	1009.73
32	580.113	753.289	976.093	1262.17
33	707.737	926.546	1210.35	1577.71
34	863.440	1139.65	1500.84	1972.14
35	1053.39	1401.77	1861.04	2465.17
36	1285.14	1724.17	2307.69	3081.47
37	1567.87	2120.73	2861.53	3851.83
38	1912.80	2608.50	3548.30	4814.79
39	2333.62	3208.46	4399.90	6018.49
40	2847.02	3946.40	5455.87	7523.11
41	3473.36	4854.08	6765.28	9403.89
42	4237.50	5970.51	8388.95	11754.8
43	5169.75	7343.73	10402.3	14693.5
44	6307.09	9032.79	12898.8	18366.9
45	7694.66	11110.3	15994.5	22958.7
46	9387.48	13665.7	19833.2	28698.3
47	11452.7	16808.8	24593.2	35872.9
48	13972.3	20674.8	30495.6	44841.2
49	17046.2	25430.0	37814.5	56051.5
50	20796.4	31278.9	46890.0	70064.3

Step V: Determine How Much You Need to Save Annually to Achieve Your Goal

Back to the compound interest tables. This time look at Table 2–3. This table shows the future value of one (dollar) invested every year at various rates of interest. Again, find the 4% column, then go down to year 20. The factor is 30.9692. We then divide our additional capital required by this factor:

additional capital needed $\dfrac{\$631,000}{30.9692}$ = $20,000 amount needed
factor from Table 2–3   to save annually

TABLE 2-3

One Dollar Per Annum (One Dollar Invested with One Dollar Added to the Fund at the Beginning of Each Subsequent Year, Compounded Annually)

Year	2%	3%	4%	5%	6%	7%	8%
1	$ 1.0200	$ 1.0300	$ 1.0400	$ 1.0500	$ 1.0600	$ 1.0700	$ 1.0800
2	2.0604	2.0909	2.1216	2.1525	2.1836	2.2149	2.2464
3	3.1216	3.1836	3.2465	3.3101	3.3746	3.4399	3.5061
4	4.2040	4.3091	4.4163	4.5256	4.6371	4.7507	4.8666
5	5.3081	5.4684	5.6330	5.8019	5.9753	6.1533	6.3359
6	6.4343	6.6625	6.8983	7.1420	7.3938	7.6540	7.9228
7	7.5830	7.8923	8.2142	8.5491	8.8975	9.2598	9.6366
8	8.7546	9.1591	9.5828	10.0266	10.4913	10.9780	11.4876
9	9.9497	10.4639	11.0061	11.5779	12.1808	12.8164	13.4866
10	11.1687	11.8078	12.4864	13.2068	13.9716	14.7836	15.6455
11	12.4121	13.1920	14.0258	14.9171	15.8699	16.8885	17.9771
12	13.6803	14.6178	15.6268	16.7130	17.8821	19.1406	20.4953
13	14.9734	16.0863	17.2919	18.5986	20.0151	21.5505	23.2149
14	16.2937	17.5989	19.0236	20.5786	22.2760	24.1290	26.1521
15	17.6393	19.1569	20.8245	22.6575	24.6725	26.8881	29.3243
16	19.0121	20.7616	22.6975	24.8404	27.2129	29.8402	32.7502
17	20.4123	22.4144	24.6454	27.1324	29.9057	32.9990	36.4502
18	21.8406	24.1169	26.6712	29.5390	32.7600	36.3790	40.4463
19	23.2974	25.8704	28.7781	32.0660	35.7856	39.9955	44.7620
20	24.7833	27.6765	30.9692	34.7193	38.9927	43.8652	49.4229
21	26.2990	29.5368	33.2480	37.5052	42.3923	48.0057	54.4568
22	27.8450	31.4529	35.6179	40.4305	45.9958	52.4361	59.8933
23	29.4219	33.4265	38.0826	43.5020	49.8156	57.1767	65.7648
24	31.0303	35.4593	40.6459	46.7271	53.8645	62.2490	72.1059
25	32.6709	37.5530	43.3117	50.1135	58.1564	67.6765	78.9544
26	34.3443	39.7096	46.0842	53.6691	62.7058	73.4838	86.3508
27	36.0512	41.9309	48.9676	57.4026	67.5281	79.6977	94.3388
28	37.7922	44.2189	51.9663	61.3227	72.6398	86.3465	102.9659
29	39.5681	46.5754	55.0849	65.4388	78.0582	93.4608	112.2832
30	41.3794	49.0027	58.3283	69.7608	83.8017	101.0730	122.3459
31	43.2270	51.5028	61.7015	74.2988	89.8898	109.2182	133.2135
32	45.1116	54.0778	65.2095	79.0638	96.3432	117.9334	144.9506
33	47.0338	56.7302	68.8579	84.0670	103.1838	127.2588	157.6267
34	48.9945	59.4621	72.6522	89.3203	110.4348	137.2369	171.3168
35	50.9944	62.2759	76.5983	94.8363	118.1209	147.9135	186.1021
36	53.0343	65.1742	80.7022	100.6281	126.2681	159.3374	202.0703
37	55.1149	68.1594	84.9703	106.7095	134.9042	171.5610	219.3159
38	57.2372	71.2342	89.4091	113.0950	144.0585	184.6403	237.9412
39	59.4020	74.4013	94.0255	119.7998	153.7620	198.6351	258.0565
40	61.6100	77.6633	98.8265	126.8398	164.0477	213.6096	279.7810
41	63.8622	81.0232	103.8196	134.2318	174.9505	229.6322	303.2435
42	66.1595	84.4839	109.0124	141.9933	186.5076	246.7765	328.5830
43	68.5027	88.0484	114.4129	150.1430	198.7580	265.1209	355.9496
44	70.8927	91.7199	120.0294	158.7002	211.7435	284.7493	385.5056
45	73.3306	95.5015	125.8706	167.6852	225.5081	305.7518	417.4261
46	75.8172	99.3965	131.9454	177.1194	240.0986	328.2244	451.9002
47	78.3535	103.4084	138.2632	187.0254	255.5645	352.2701	489.1322
48	80.9406	107.5406	144.8337	197.4267	271.9584	377.9990	529.3427
49	83.5794	111.7969	151.6671	208.3480	289.3359	405.5289	572.7702
50	86.2110	116.1808	158.7738	219.8154	307.7561	434.9860	619.6718

TABLE 2-3 (continued)

One Dollar per Annum (One Dollar Invested with One Dollar Added to the Fund at the Beginning of Each Subsequent Year, Compounded Annually)

Year	9%	10%	11%	12%	13%	14%
1	$ 1.0900	$ 1.1000	$ 1.1100	$ 1.1200	$ 1.1300	$ 1.1400
2	2.2781	2.3100	2.3421	2.3744	2.4070	2.4396
3	3.5731	3.6410	3.7097	3.7793	3.8498	3.9211
4	4.9847	5.1051	5.2278	5.3528	5.4803	5.6101
5	6.5233	6.7156	6.9129	7.1152	7.3227	7.5355
6	8.2004	8.4872	8.7833	9.0890	9.4047	9.7305
7	10.0285	10.4359	10.8594	11.2997	11.7573	12.2328
8	12.0210	12.5795	13.1640	13.7757	14.4157	15.0853
9	14.1929	14.9374	15.7220	16.5487	17.4197	18.3373
10	16.5603	17.5312	18.5614	19.6546	20.8143	22.0445
11	19.1407	20.3843	21.7132	23.1331	24.6502	26.2707
12	21.9534	23.5227	25.2116	27.0291	28.9847	31.0887
13	25.0192	26.9750	29.0949	31.3926	33.8827	36.5811
14	28.3609	30.7725	33.4054	36.2797	39.4175	42.8424
15	32.0034	34.9497	38.1899	41.7533	45.6717	49.9804
16	35.9737	39.5447	43.5008	47.8837	52.7391	58.1176
17	40.3013	44.5992	49.3959	54.7497	60.7251	67.3941
18	45.0185	50.1591	55.9395	62.4397	69.7494	77.9692
19	50.1601	56.2750	63.2028	71.0524	79.9468	90.0249
20	55.7645	63.0025	71.2651	80.6987	91.4699	103.7684
21	61.8733	70.4027	80.2143	91.5026	104.4910	119.7360
22	68.5319	78.5430	90.1479	103.6029	119.2048	137.2970
23	75.7898	87.4973	101.1742	117.1552	135.8315	157.6586
24	83.7009	97.3471	113.4133	132.3339	154.6196	180.8708
25	92.3240	108.1818	126.9988	149.3339	175.8501	207.3327
26	101.7231	120.0999	142.0786	168.3740	199.8406	237.4993
27	111.9682	133.2099	158.8173	189.6989	224.9999	271.8892
28	123.1354	147.6309	177.3972	213.5828	257.5834	311.0937
29	135.3075	163.4940	198.0209	240.3327	292.1992	355.7868
30	148.5752	180.9434	220.9132	270.2926	331.3151	406.7370
31	163.0370	200.1378	246.3236	303.8477	375.5161	464.8202
32	178.8003	221.2515	274.5292	341.4294	425.4632	531.0350
33	195.9823	244.4767	305.8374	383.5210	481.9034	606.5199
34	214.7108	270.0244	340.5896	430.6635	545.6808	692.5727
35	235.1247	298.1268	379.1644	483.4631	617.7493	790.6729
36	257.3759	329.0395	421.9825	542.5987	699.1867	902.5071
37	281.6298	363.0434	469.5106	608.8305	791.2110	1029.9981
38	308.0665	400.4478	522.2667	683.0102	895.1984	1175.3378
39	336.8824	441.5926	580.8261	766.0914	1012.7042	1341.0251
40	368.2919	486.8518	645.8269	859.1424	1145.4858	1529.9086
41	402.5281	536.6370	717.9779	963.3595	1295.5289	1745.2358
42	439.8457	591.4007	798.0655	1080.0826	1465.0777	1990.7088
43	480.5218	651.6408	886.9627	1210.8125	1656.6678	2270.5481
44	524.8587	717.9048	985.6386	1357.2300	1873.1646	2589.5648
45	573.1860	790.7953	1095.1688	1521.2176	2117.8060	2953.2439
46	625.8628	870.9749	1216.7474	1704.8838	2394.2508	3367.8380
47	683.2804	959.1723	1351.6996	1910.5898	2706.6334	3840.4753
48	745.8656	1056.1896	1501.4965	2140.9806	3059.6258	4379.2819
49	814.0836	1162.9085	1667.7712	2399.0182	3458.5071	4993.5213
50	888.4411	1280.2994	1852.3360	2688.0204	3909.2430	5693.7543

TABLE 2-3 (*continued*)

One Dollar per Annum (One Dollar Invested, with One Dollar Added to the Fund at the Beginning of Each Subsequent Year, Compounded Annually)

Year	15%	16%	17%	18%	19%	20%
1	$ 1.1500	$ 1.1600	$ 1.1700	$ 1.1800	$ 1.1900	$ 1.2000
2	2.4725	2.5056	2.5389	2.5724	2.6061	2.6400
3	3.9934	4.0664	4.1405	4.2154	4.2912	4.3680
4	5.7424	5.8771	6.0144	6.1542	6.2965	6.4416
5	7.7537	7.9774	8.2068	8.4419	8.6829	8.9299
6	10.0668	10.4138	10.7720	11.1415	11.5227	11.9159
7	12.7268	13.2400	13.7732	14.3269	14.9020	15.4990
8	15.7858	16.5185	17.2847	18.0858	18.9234	19.7989
9	19.3037	20.3214	21.3931	22.5213	23.7088	24.9586
10	23.3493	24.7329	26.1999	27.7551	29.4035	31.1504
11	28.0017	29.8501	31.8239	33.9310	36.1802	38.5805
12	33.3519	35.7861	38.4039	41.2186	44.2444	47.4966
13	39.5047	42.6719	46.1026	49.8180	53.8409	58.1959
14	46.5804	50.6595	55.1101	59.9652	65.2606	71.0351
15	54.7175	59.9250	65.6488	71.9390	78.8502	86.4421
16	64.0751	70.6730	77.9791	86.0680	95.0217	104.9305
17	74.8364	83.1407	92.4056	102.7402	114.2658	127.1166
18	87.2118	97.6032	109.2845	122.4135	137.1664	153.7399
19	101.4436	114.3797	129.0329	145.6279	164.4180	185.6879
20	117.8101	133.8405	152.1385	173.0210	196.8474	224.0255
21	136.6316	156.4149	179.1720	205.3447	235.4384	270.0307
22	158.2764	182.6013	210.8013	243.4868	281.3617	325.2368
23	183.1678	212.9776	247.8075	288.4944	336.0104	391.4842
24	211.7930	248.2140	291.1048	341.6034	401.0424	470.9810
25	244.7120	289.0882	341.7626	404.2721	478.4305	566.3773
26	282.5688	336.5023	401.0323	478.2210	570.5223	680.8527
27	326.1041	391.5027	470.3778	565.4808	680.1116	818.2232
28	376.1697	455.3032	551.5120	668.4474	810.5228	983.0679
29	433.7451	529.3117	646.4391	789.9479	965.7121	1180.8815
30	499.9569	615.1616	757.5037	933.3186	1150.3874	1418.2578
31	576.1005	714.7474	887.4494	1102.4959	1370.1511	1703.1094
32	663.6655	830.2670	1039.4858	1302.1252	1631.6698	2044.9313
33	764.3654	964.2697	1217.3683	1537.6878	1942.8770	2455.1176
34	880.1702	1119.7129	1425.4910	1815.6516	2313.2137	2947.3411
35	1013.3757	1300.0270	1668.9944	2143.6489	2753.9143	3538.0093
36	1166.4975	1509.1913	1953.8935	2530.6857	3278.3480	4246.8112
37	1342.6222	1751.8219	2287.2254	2987.3891	3902.4241	5097.3735
38	1545.1655	2033.2734	2677.2238	3526.2991	4645.0747	6118.0482
39	1778.0903	2359.7572	3133.5218	4162.2130	5528.8289	7342.8578
40	2045.9539	2738.4783	3667.3905	4912.5913	6580.4965	8812.6294
41	2353.9969	3177.7949	4292.0169	5798.0378	7831.9808	10,576.3553
42	2708.2465	3687.4021	5022.8298	6842.8646	9321.2471	12,692.8263
43	3115.6334	4278.5464	5877.8809	8075.7602	11,093.4741	15,232.5916
44	3584.1285	4964.2739	6878.2906	9630.5771	13,202.4242	18,280.3099
45	4122.8977	5759.7177	8048.7700	11,247.2609	15,712.0748	21,937.5719
46	4742.4824	6682.4325	9418.2309	13,272.9479	18,698.5590	26,326.2863
47	5455.0047	7752.7817	11,020.5002	15,663.2586	22,252.4752	31,592.7436
48	6274.4055	8994.3868	12,895.1553	18,483.8251	26,481.6355	37,912.4923
49	7216.7163	10,434.6487	15,088.5017	21,812.0936	31,514.3363	45,496.1908
50	8300.3737	12,105.3525	17,654.7169	25,739.4505	37,503.2502	54,596.6289

TABLE 2–3 (*continued*)

One Dollar per Annum (One Dollar Invested with One Dollar Added to the Fund at the Beginning of Each Subsequent Year, Compounded Annually)

Year	21%	22%	23%	24%	25%
1	$ 1.2100	$ 1.2200	$ 1.2300	$ 1.2400	$ 1.2500
2	2.6741	2.7084	2.7429	2.7776	2.8125
3	4.4456	4.5242	4.6037	4.6842	4.7656
4	6.5892	6.7395	6.8926	7.0484	7.2070
5	9.1829	9.4422	9.7079	9.9800	10.2587
6	12.3214	12.7395	13.1707	13.6152	14.0734
7	16.1189	16.7623	17.4300	18.1229	18.8418
8	20.7138	21.6700	22.6689	23.7124	24.8023
9	26.2738	27.6574	29.1128	30.6434	32.2529
10	33.0013	34.9620	37.0387	39.2378	41.5661
11	41.1415	43.8736	46.7876	49.8949	53.2076
12	50.9913	54.7459	58.7788	63.1097	67.7595
13	62.9094	68.0100	73.5279	79.4960	85.9494
14	77.3304	84.1922	91.6693	99.8151	108.6868
15	94.7798	103.9345	113.9833	125.0107	137.1085
16	115.8936	128.0200	141.4295	156.2533	172.6356
17	141.4413	157.4045	175.1883	194.9941	217.0446
18	172.3540	193.2535	216.7116	243.0327	272.5557
19	209.7583	236.9892	267.7853	302.6006	341.9446
20	255.0176	290.3469	330.6059	376.4647	428.6808
21	309.0453	355.4432	407.8752	468.0563	537.1010
22	376.0453	434.8607	502.9166	581.6298	672.6263
23	456.2249	531.7501	619.8174	722.4609	842.0329
24	553.2421	649.9551	763.6054	897.0916	1053.7911
25	670.6330	794.1652	940.4646	1113.6336	1318.4889
26	812.6759	970.1016	1158.0015	1382.1457	1649.3612
27	982.5478	1184.7439	1425.5719	1715.1006	2062.9515
28	1192.5129	1446.6076	1754.6834	2127.9648	2579.9394
29	1444.1506	1766.0813	2159.4906	2639.9163	3226.1742
30	1748.6323	2155.8392	2657.4035	3274.7363	4033.9678
31	2117.0550	2631.3438	3269.8363	4061.9130	5043.7097
32	2562.8466	3211.4595	4023.1287	5038.0120	6305.8872
33	3102.2544	3919.2006	4949.6783	6248.3750	7883.6090
34	3754.9378	4782.6447	6089.3343	7749.2251	9855.7613
35	4544.6848	5836.0465	7491.1112	9610.2791	12,320.9516
36	5500.2786	7121.1968	9215.2968	11,917.9861	15,402.4395
37	6656.5471	8689.0801	11,336.0451	14,779.5428	19,254.2994
38	8055.6321	10,601.8977	13,944.5655	18,327.8730	24,069.1243
39	9748.5248	12,935.5352	17,153.0455	22,727.8026	30,087.6554
40	11,796.9250	15,782.5730	21,099.4760	28,183.7152	37,610.8193
41	14,275.4893	19,255.9591	25,953.5855	34,949.0469	47,014.7741
42	17,274.5520	23,493.4901	31,924.1402	43,338.0581	58,769.7176
43	20,903.4180	28,663.2779	39,267.9224	53,740.4321	73,463.3970
44	25,294.3458	34,970.4190	48,300.7746	66,639.3758	91,830.4963
45	30,607.3684	42,665.1312	59,411.1828	82,634.0660	114,789.3704
46	37,036.1257	52,052.6801	73,076.9848	102,467.4819	143,487.9630
47	44,814.9222	63,505.4897	89,885.9213	127,060.9176	179,361.2038
48	54,227.2658	77,477.9175	110,560.9133	157,556.7788	224,202.7548
49	65,616.2017	94,524.2793	135,991.1534	195,371.6445	280,254.6935
50	79,396.8140	115,320.8408	167,270.3487	242,262.0792	350,319.6169

We thus must save $20,000 every year in addition to our present assets to accumulate the $741,000 we need to retire. This is the bottom line. It is the amount you need to invest every year. It includes all 401(k) contributions—both employee and employer amounts, as well as all other savings.

Wake up now! You'll need to save 20 percent of your income to reach your goal! Are you on track? A Merrill Lynch survey showed recently that 59 percent of 45 to 64 year olds want to retire before age 65. Yet only 18 percent save at least 20 percent of their income, a minimum for most people who want to retire early.

If you like, use the accompanying worksheet to calculate your own plan.

Retirement Income Plan Worksheet

For _____   Date _____

Present age _____   Expected retirement age _____

Note: All figures in today's dollars.

1. Annual retirement income goal
    (This is _____% of present income) $_____

2. − less estimated social security   (_____)

3. Necessary income from all sources
    except social security   _____

4. − less projected pension income   (_____)

5. Necessary income net of social
    security and pension $_____

6. × "Lucky 13"   × _____ 13

7. Total investment capital needed   _____

8. − less today's value of future inheritance (_____)

9.   Subtotal   _____

10. − less future value of all current
    investments

    Current investments × factor from Table 2–2
    $ _____ × _____ = (_____)

    (Use factor at the interest rate level you
    think you can achieve net of inflation)

11. Additional investment capital needed in
    today's dollars $_____

12. Divided by factor from Table 2–3   _____

13. Amount needed to save annually $_____

Now, the most important step is to execute the plan. The key to achieving your goal in the real world is to set up a monthly savings plan that is as automatic as possible. If your company offers a payroll deduction savings plan, take advantage of it. Another good way is to set up an automatic bank draft into a good mutual fund (or better, into several good mutual funds). This program allows the fund to charge your checking account every month. You may stop the investments any time you want. But you are far more likely to follow through with your plan if it is automatic.

This brings up part one of Meek's Reasonably Reliable Rags to Riches Recipe: The magic answer to investing, if there is one, is most certainly to invest *regularly* and *automatically*. I say again: regularly and automatically. (Parts two and three of the three-ingredient recipe will be found in Chapter 9.)

If you get nothing else out of this book, I hope it is a motivation toward thrift. If you think that things will just "happen" for you financially, think again. Even if you are covered by a company pension plan, many company pension plans are inadequate. And in our dynamic world economy, many companies that are on top of the world today will fail or become less profitable in the future and take much of the pension benefits down with them. Just ask employees of Eastern Airlines or LTV.

And social security is clearly in trouble. The original planners of social security anticipated that there would be about 30 workers for every retiree. Today there are only three workers for every retiree, and it's getting worse! Thus, there are fewer workers taking care of the elderly retirees. Though social security will continue to be with us, the system will just not be able to support the growing masses of retired Americans as envisioned. And there's another potential bugaboo. Many people today are counting on the equity buildup in their home to bail them out during retirement. The potential problem is that as the baby boomers reach retirement age, there will be a nationwide flood of aging houses hitting the market all at once. And this will hit just when zero population growth in the nation as a whole will also have a depressing effect on real estate. It is a real possibility that there will be a very depressed housing market just as the baby boomers are trying to sell. Don't rely on your home equity for retirement. Indeed, I recommend ignoring this source in a conservative retirement plan.

Let's dispel right here the myth that you don't have enough income to save. You will make a fortune in your lifetime. If you earn, let's say, $100,000 a year over your working lifetime of perhaps 35 years, you will earn $3,500,000! Don't you think you can cut loose a little of that?

Here's another fact. If you wait to begin saving until 10 years before retirement, you will have to save 10 times as much every year, compared to starting your savings at the beginning of your working life (to achieve the same goal)! If you doubt this, study the compound interest tables and see.

Another concept to look at here is that you want your retirement investments to have the greatest "time diversification" possible. The longer period you invest, the greater the predictability of the returns. In other words, some time periods are better than others as far as the investment climate goes. If you wait until the last few years before retirement to begin saving in earnest, you are taking a big chance. That period of time just might be a lousy one. This is a very big factor that is not often written about. Don't roll the dice with your future by waiting until the last moment.

This is a good time to discuss the notion of dollar cost averaging. The wonders of dollar cost averaging can be best illustrated by a simple example: Let's assume you invest $1,000 in a mutual fund periodically. Initially, the fund shares sell for $10. You therefore begin by buying 100 shares at $10 each. At your next buying point, the market has soared and the fund is selling for $20. You then buy 50 shares at $20 each for another investment of $1000. A few months later the market has corrected some of its advance and the fund's price falls back to $15, the midpoint of your two purchases. That puts you even, right? Wrong! You really have a nice profit! Your $2000 total investment has bought you 150 shares now worth $15 per share, or $2250. That's a 12 percent gain over your $2000 cost. Pretty nifty.

FIGURE 2-1

How long will the money last?

Before you start drawing on investments in retirement, a little advance planning may be required to ensure that the money will last as long as you do. The table below can help. It shows, for example, that if the value of your retirement account grows at a rate of 8% a year and you are taking out 15% of your original capital each year, the money will last nine years. Cut your withdrawals to 10% and the money won't run out for 20 years.

You can also use the table to gear your withdrawals to how long you want the money to last. Suppose you decide assets must last 15 years and you estimate that they'll grow at an annual rate of 10%. In that case, the table shows that you can withdraw roughly 13% of the value of your original capital each year. A dash means that at that rate of withdrawal, the money will never be exhausted.

If you think your account will grow at this rate...	And you are withdrawing your original capital at this rate...										
		6%	7%	8%	9%	10%	11%	12%	13%	14%	15%	16%
12%	Here's how many years your money will last					–	–	–	22	17	14	12
11%						–	–	23	17	14	12	11
10%		–	–	–	–	–	25	18	15	13	11	10
9%		–	–	–	–	26	20	16	14	12	11	9
8%		–	–	–	28	20	16	14	12	11	9	9
7%		–	–	30	22	17	14	12	11	10	9	8
6%		–	33	23	18	15	13	11	10	9	8	8
5%		36	25	20	16	14	12	11	9	9	8	7

THE AMERICAN FUNDS INVESTOR

SOURCE: American Funds Group, 333 S. Hope Street, 52nd Floor, Los Angeles, CA 90071.

Keep in mind that because of inflation as well as your changing situation, your retirement plan is a moving target. You should review it at least once a year. But don't wait to get started. Discipline is the key. Set a goal to get started the day after you've finished this book! . . .You have permission to feel guilty if you don't!

Estate Planning

The basic concepts of estate planning are simple. But only a few of the people who could benefit from estate planning understand these concepts. The primary effort in estate planning from a financial planner's perspective is to save on federal estate taxes.

Let's first look at what constitutes your estate at the time of your death. Basically, all property, both real and personal, is part of your estate for the purpose of federal taxes. Your *gross estate* includes:

- Fair market value of all your property interests.
- All property transferred by you during your lifetime with certain "strings attached," usually in the form of trusts.

Transfers subject to these provisions include:

1. Transfers under which you retained the use and enjoyment of the property during your lifetime, including the standard revocable living trust.

2. Transfers under which you retained the power to alter the time and manner of enjoyment or the identities of the beneficiaries.

3. Transfers under which the right to enjoy property is conditioned upon the beneficiary surviving you.

4. Custodial accounts for children in which you or your spouse is custodian.

- Annuities and pension benefits receivable by any beneficiary
- Life insurance proceeds, even if not paid to your spouse, unless all incidents of your ownership of the insurance policy was transferred more than three years prior to your death
- Joint tenancy property (i.e., with a right of survivorship, and not as tenants in common) and tenancies by the entirety.

Now, there are a few deductions that may be made from one's gross estate to arrive at the net taxable estate:

- Funeral expenses.
- Expenses of last illness.
- Expenses of administration.
- Claims against the estate.
- Mortgages and other indebtedness owed.
- Charitable contributions.
- Transfers to surviving spouse.

To calculate the federal estate tax, apply the net taxable estate to Table 2–4.

TABLE 2–4

(1) Taxable Transfer More Than Amount	(2) But Not More Than	(3) Tax on Amount in Column (1)	(4) Rate of Tax on Excess of in Column (1)
$ 0	$ 10,000	—	18%
10,000	20,000	$ 1,800	20%
20,000	40,000	3,800	22%
40,000	60,000	8,200	24%
60,000	80,000	13,000	26%
80,000	100,000	18,200	28%
100,000	150,000	23,800	30%
150,000	250,000	38,800	32%
250,000	500,000	70,800	34%
500,000	750,000	155,800	37%
750,000	1,000,000	248,300	39%
1,000,000	1,250,000	345,800	41%
1,250,000	1,500,000	448,300	43%
1,500,000	2,000,000	555,800	45%
2,000,000	2,500,000	780,000	49%
2,500,000	3,000,000	1,025,800	53%
3,000,000	—	1,290,800	55%

These tax rates also apply to gifts as well as estates. The term *unified credit* refers to an amount of money that is to be subtracted from the calculation of the taxes due from Table 2–4. That amount is $192,800 in 1987 and beyond. (Prior to 1987 it was a lesser amount.) Thus, as an example, assume an estate (or gift) of $750,000. The tax from the table is $248,300. Subtract from that the unified credit amount of $192,800, leaving a tax of $55,500.

$248,300 from table
−192,800 unified credit
$ 55,000 tax

There are a couple of footnotes to the table. First, beginning in 1993, amounts above $2,500,000 will be taxed at a rate of 50 percent. Also, for gifts made (or decedents dying) the benefit of the unified credit is phased out for table transfers in excess of $10,000,000. This is done in conjunction with a 5 percent surtax on estates over $10,000,000. The result is that a 60 percent rate is applied on transfers from $10,000,000 to $21,040,000. Beginning in 1993, the rate will be 55 percent on cumulative transfers from $10,000,000 to $18,340,000.

An important concept is the *unlimited marital deduction.* This means that one can pass 100 percent of his (or her) assets to his (or her) spouse without federal inheritance taxes. This is true whether your estate is 10 dollars or 10 billion dollars. It's very simple. However, your will should specify that you want this election. Some attorneys say that many wills written prior to September 1981 (when this law changed) may not adequately ensure that your family will get the benefit of the unlimited marital deduction. Your will may need to be rewritten to take advantage of it.

Every individual has, beginning in 1987, the ability to pass a total of $600,000 worth of assets, in addition to assets passed to your spouse, free of federal estate tax. This is referred to as the *exemption equivalent* amount. (Prior to 1987 the amount was lower.) Since gift tax and inheritance taxes are now unified, this $600,000 includes lifetime gifts as well as inheritances.

To clarify the $600,000 exemption equivalent, interpolate from Table 2–4 to determine the tax on an estate of $600,000. The amount would be:

$155,800 table (amt at $500,000)
+37,000 table (amt over $500,000,
              i.e., $100,000 times 37%)

$192,800 tax from table
−192,800 unified credit
      0 taxes due

A tax credit is an amount that directly offsets a tax, in this case $192,800. The $600,000 amount that is exempted from an estate is the value of assets that are thus not taxable because of the $192,800 tax credit.

Once you reach the $600,000 estate or gift amount, the effective minimum tax is 37 percent on every extra amount that is taxable, and the rate goes as high as 60 percent. The rates are high. Note that these taxes are not income taxes. Some estates may also pay income taxes. Many states also levy a state inheritance tax in addition to the federal estate tax.

In addition to the $600,000 lifetime exemption, anyone may give away $10,000 to any number of donees annually free of inheritance or gift taxes. Thus if you and your spouse have two children, you may each give each child $20,000 per year, thus getting $40,000 a year out of your estate, in addition to the $600,000 exemption equivalent. However, this $10,000 amount is not cumulative. That is, you can't make up the $10,000 for previous years.

A primary trick in estate planning is to maximize the benefit of the $600,000 exemption for each spouse. If, for example, your combined estate is larger than $600,000—let's say it's $800,000—you might pass without an adequate estate plan the entire $800,000 to your spouse. This results in what is referred to as "stacking" the estate of the second-to-die. When your spouse dies and the estate passes to the kids, everything over $600,000 will be taxed. Thus, assuming no appreciation or depreciation, $200,000 would be subject to the tax.

An alternative is to avoid estate stacking by having a two-part will. Such an arrangement would pass, at the death of the first spouse, up to $600,000 inheritance tax free to your children or to a family trust called an *irrevocable by-pass trust* (also called a *credit shelter trust* or *exemption equivalent trust*) with the balance left to the surviving spouse. Such a trust is usually a testamentary trust. That means it is provided for in the will and becomes operable only at death. This gets the first spouse's $600,000 exemption amount out of his/her estate. Then when the second spouse dies, *another* $600,000 can pass to the heirs free of federal estate tax. Thus, even if whatever is left to the surviving spouse has grown to $600,000 by his/her death, it too will pass inheritance tax free to the heirs, usually the children. Everything over

$600,000 in the surviving spouse's estate would be subject to federal estate tax.

An intriguing thing about this trust arrangement is that according to many attorneys, the surviving spouse can be the trustee or co-trustee and thus control the assets, at least to a degree. The surviving spouse can also use the income, and some reasonable amount of the principal, for "health, education, support, or maintenance" for life. If the spouse is not a trustee or co-trustee, the power of invasion of principal, in the discretion of the trustee, may be unlimited. The surviving spouse is referred to as the *income beneficiary*. When that spouse dies, the corpus of the trust assets goes to the children or other heirs, who are known as the *remaindermen*. If a child has not attained certain specified ages determined by you, the trust principal may be held in further trust until they reach the appropriate age. Even if the trust has grown to over $600,000 in value, there is no inheritance tax when distributed to the trusts' beneficiaries, as it had already been removed from the estate of the parent.

This technique is only for the benefit of the heirs. Remember, the surviving spouse never has to pay inheritance taxes. However, the savings for your children or other heirs can be substantial. The maximum savings occurs when the combined estate of a husband and wife is $1.2 million or more, as both parents can pass $600,000 to the children inheritance tax free. The savings in inheritance taxes for an estate of this size is at least $235,000 by this simple trust arrangement.

Don't let this sound too complex. Especially if the surviving spouse is trustee, it works very smoothly. From an operational standpoint, the surviving spouse just operates with two accounts instead of one. One account is in the individual's name as per usual, while a second account is in the name of the trust. You normally don't need a corporate trustee at all, except perhaps as a successor trustee if the surviving spouse should become unable to serve. Keep it simple.

There is one thing that defeats a two-part will. Any property that passes to heirs outside of the will is a problem. Such property that passes by "operation of law" does not go through probate, that is, goes directly to a named beneficiary regardless of what the will says. Such property includes life insurance paid to a named beneficiary (as opposed to being paid to the estate). It also includes pension benefits paid to a named beneficiary. Further, it includes joint property (except in Texas).

The amount that actually is dumped into the by-pass trust can vary. Ideally, in most cases, the amount should be as high as possible up to $600,000. But the amount that can go into the trust depends on who the legal owner of the property is at the time of death of the first spouse. Joint property is treated differently from separate property. And state laws vary on ownership of property of married individuals. Because jointly held property can defeat the purpose of a by-pass trust, often only a home or checking account should be held in joint name. One technique that can be used is a disclaimer provision in the will by which the surviving spouse may disclaim property for estate planning purposes.

The age and health of the couple should also be considered in ownership considerations of estate planning in order to take advantage of the stepped-up cost basis on property. At death, the cost basis on property for capital gains tax purposes is changed to the value as of the date of death. This offers another planning opportunity for families to save heirs income taxes as well as federal estate taxes.

It is important to consider all of your assets when doing estate planning. Your plan must be coordinated. There are nuances, especially in ownership provisions, that your local lawyer can help you with in your estate planning.

By the way, almost any decent general practice lawyer should be able to assist you in this area. However, don't assume that all general practice lawyers are competent in estate planning, or that just because your attorney recently reviewed your wills, things are as they should be. Be sure to specifically ask your lawyer about a by-pass trust. If necessary, find a lawyer who specializes in estate planning. Your state may have a procedure for certifying lawyers in various specialties. Check with the state board or look in the yellow pages.

Note that the wills must be properly written while both spouses are alive. There is no benefit to considering a two-part will if only one spouse is living. If arrangements aren't made prior to the death of the first spouse, the $600,000 exemption of the first spouse to die is lost. However, in theory, inheritance taxes could be avoided forever if every time one spouse dies, the remaining spouse remarries and leaves everything to the new spouse under the unlimited marital deduction! However, a properly written will or trust will assure that your ultimate beneficiaries receive your estate.

Many people today have large estates because of inflation. And many people don't realize how large their estate is until they sit down and start adding things up. Many families, when adding the value of home, life insurance, and pension benefits may easily be over $600,000. Every couple with assets over $600,000 should consider this technique.

Marital and *Q-TIP* trusts are variations on the two-part estate plan. Like the by-pass trust to which they are related, they are usually testamentary trusts but may be separate trust documents.

The marital trust is designed to help a surviving spouse manage assets. If used, assets not going into the by-pass trust would go into the marital trust. When used with the by-pass trust, the marital trust is sometimes called the "A" trust while the by-pass trust is referred to as the "B" trust. With a marital trust the spouse has broad control over the assets.

A Q-TIP (Qualified Terminable Interest Property) trust offers flexibility to the estate by allowing the executor to elect the marital deduction if beneficial. Compared to a marital trust, the spouse has less control over the assets and receives only the income from the trust. Either of these trusts has applicability when someone doesn't want to leave investment management burdens directly to a spouse. And especially with a Q-TIP trust, one may control future distributions of assets beyond the grave. For example, one may not want a spouse's future husband or wife to get at the assets in the event of a new marriage.

There are other types of testamentary trusts. One can have a trust in a will that has a purpose different from taking advantage of the unified credit. Such trusts are usually set up to have a trustee manage assets for a child until he or she reaches a certain age. This is a good idea as very few young adults can manage money well. In my own will, for example, I've specified that our son would not receive assets directly until age 25. At that age he gets one fourth of the assets in the testamentary trust. At age thirty, one third of the remaining assets are to be distributed to him. At age thirty-five he would get the balance of the trust.

There are also trusts called *living trusts*. These trusts are not testamentary trusts, but operational while the grantor is alive. These are usually revocable trusts that are really just management relationships. The text books say that these trusts are a way to "see your estate plan in action." Some lawyers say this is hogwash. There are no estate tax benefits. There are no income tax benefits. The only estate planning use for living trusts comes in certain community property states where the problem of property passing by operation of law by joint ownership may defeat the two-part will discussed earlier.

However, a living trust may have certain advantages. A living trust basically replaces your will. Thus it avoids any delay of probate. The trustee can settle the estate without court supervision. In addition to beneficiaries possibly receiving assets more quickly, there is the benefit of secrecy. The assets are not as accessible to public view as assets in a will (probate assets). Wills are on file at the court house and anyone can go look at them. This is not true for a trust document.

Another potential benefit of a living trust is to provide for your care if you become unable to do so. This is a valid reason for many people to consider a living trust. But in this case, it may be much simpler for you to assign a power of attorney to various family members to help you if you become disabled.

Also, some lawyers may ignore nonprobate assets such as are in a living trust when calculating estate settlement fees, so a trust may help your heirs save on lawyers fees to settle your estate. Proponents of living trusts say that significant cost savings can result from a living trust. This may well be true in states like California or Florida, which make estate settlement a legal nightmare. However, some states like Texas have very simple estate settlement procedures, negating this argument for a living trust. In fact, in some cases a living trust may be more expensive than no trust. First, it costs something to establish a trust, and there are trustees fees if you hire a corporate trustee. Further, after death, income taxes on the trust may be higher than without a trust, since an estate is a separate taxable entity that pays taxes at the 15 percent rate until its income rises above a certain point. The first dollars a trust earns are taxed at the beneficiaries' rates, which may be higher.

Further disadvantages of living trusts are that they may leave an estate open to creditor claims longer than probate does, and it may be hard to sell or refinance real estate to which a trust has title. Lenders don't like to deal in trust property because a trust's loan or mortgage is hard to sell on the secondary market. Revocable living trusts may be wasted effort unless you specifically want to provide a predetermined vehicle for managing your assets should you become disabled or have reason to believe your heirs will save substantially on lawyers' fees by using a trust. In these cases, a living trust is quite worthwhile.

Living trusts are often set up with you, the grantor, as the initial trustee. The corporate trustee takes over only when (and if) you become disabled. That way you avoid paying trustee fees until necessary, and you remain in complete control initially. Disability is sometimes defined as three doctors verifying such. At that time the corporate trustee takes over.

Another possible alternative to this arrangement is not having a living trust set up initially at all, but rather having a power of attorney containing provisions for a potential future living trust. For example, you may assign power of attorney authority to a trust company. In the event of disability, the trust company takes over and a living trust is set up at that time but not before. With this arrangement, you don't even have to mess with putting all your assets into a trust while you are still able to manage them yourself.

Compared to revocable trusts, irrevocable trusts may offer more distinct estate planning benefits. For example, if you give money to an irrevocable trust for an amount under the $600,000 exemption equivalent, you've gotten the assets and their future growth out of your estate. However, the gift is just what it says—irrevocable. If things turn sour for your finances, too bad. You can't get the money back.

The slickest use of an irrevocable trust is a life insurance trust. As previously indicated, life insurance proceeds are generally included in your estate for inheritance tax purposes. However, you can get life insurance out of your estate by assigning irrevocable ownership of your life insurance policies to a trust. You would remain as the insured. The trust would also be the beneficiary of the death benefit, in addition to being the owner. The estate planning benefit is that the death proceeds are excluded from your estate for inheritance tax purposes.

The trustee can be either an individual or an institution. The trust, as the owner, pays the premiums on the policy. The trust remains in force after the insured's death. Usually, the trust is set up to help support a surviving spouse until his or her death, similar to the by-pass trust, then passes to the children when the spouse dies.

There's one catch. If you die within three years of giving a policy to a trust, the proceeds are still included in your estate. And you must not retain any "incident of ownership" in the policy. Thus, you cannot simply use the trustee as a rubber stamp for your own insurance dealings. If you make out checks to the trustee and he simply endorses them over to the insurance company, for example, you may lose all the benefit.

Similar to the testamentary by-pass trust, irrevocable living trust assets can grow to an unlimited amount prior to the dissolution of the trust, and still incur no inheritance tax. Of course, when your children (or other heirs) die, these assets will be part of their estates.

You can specify in the trust agreement how assets are to be invested, just as you can in a testamentary trust. This may be advisable because at the death of the insured, the trust starts fresh with cash as the only asset. In my own insurance trust, I've specified that up to 50 percent of the assets may be invested in real property. The balance must be invested in mutual funds covered under the Investment Company Act of 1940, insurance policies/ annuities, interest-bearing time deposits, or fixed income securities. I've also established that various family members in succession should serve as trustees, starting with my wife, if living. In order to avoid paying trustees' fees to some institution (which may provide lousy investment management as well), I've named a corporate trustee only if all the eligible family members are unable to serve as trustee. I believe this arrangement provides the most prudent program with highest flexibility for my family at the lowest cost. Actually, a trust is not always even needed for the life insurance. If you have grown, reliable children, you could make them the owners and beneficiaries of the insurance policy. No need to even fool with a trust. The result is the same for estate planning purposes.

Life insurance is one way to prefund a federal estate tax liability with so-called discounted dollars. If both spouses are living, you can purchase surprisingly inexpensive insurance called "survivorship life" or "second-to-die life." It is usually about one third to one half as much as regular life insurance. A husband age 65 with a wife age 60 can buy $300,000 worth of insurance, payable at the second death, for only about $5500 annually, paid up in 8 years. The precise cost varies with a number of factors, but couples even in their 70s or beyond may find life insurance worthwhile. This is becoming rather popular and can be an excellent addition to an estate plan. Don't overlook it as a possibility. Life insurance to prefund expected federal estate taxes is a particularly good idea if you have a lot of illiquid assets that your heirs might be forced to sell at depressed prices to pay the tax. Your life insurance trust or your children should be the owner and beneficiary of the policy.

Yet another estate planning tool is a charitable trust. There are different types, but most common is a *charitable remainder trust*. The concept of the charitable remainder trust is fairly simple. The donor establishes a trust that will pay out an income during one of three specified time periods: usually the donor's lifetime, the lifetime of a designated person, or a period of years up to a maximum of 20. When the prescribed period ends, the trust terminates, and the trustee turns over the remainder of the trust fund to whatever charity the donor has named. You get an income tax deduction immediately and you retain a life interest in the income from the trust. You also get the recognition of the gift while still living. Gifted assets are removed from your estate for federal estate tax purposes.

How much income do you receive from a charitable remainder trust? There are several different ways the trust can be set up. For example, the income may be determined directly by the trust's investment income or by multiplying a fixed percent, selected at the outset, by the fair market value of the trust assets each year, usually with a minimum payment if the trust's value declines. This is called a *unitrust*. This approach allows for increases in the income received if the trust's assets appreciate in value. The charitable institution may either retain the donated asset or sell it and reinvest the proceeds. Another approach is where the donor may specify an annuity pay out of a guaranteed fixed amount. This is referred to as an *annuity trust*.

How much tax deduction is allowed? Of course, if you give a charity assets outright with no strings attached, you get a 100 percent deduction. However, when you structure such a gift with income back to you, the IRS allows only a partial tax deduction. The amount of the deduction depends on the age of the donors and the amount of income they retain. It is determined by the Treasury actuarial tables. For example, a donation with a guaranteed annuity pay out of 7 percent would provide a tax deduction of 40 percent to 70 percent of the asset's value, depending on the age of the donor.

How about capital gains taxes on gifting appreciated assets? Here again, it depends. The general rule is that there is no capital gains tax when appreciated assets are donated. (However, for donors who must pay alternative minimum taxes, the appreciated value of capital gain property donated to charity is a tax preference item. Alternative minimum taxes apply to only a few wealthy taxpayers who otherwise would pay very little tax.) But, if the IRS determines that the donor is receiving principal in addition to interest and dividends as income, a significant part of the capital gain is taxable. For example, annuity payments are considered partly return of principal. The IRS has developed standards to determine how much of a gain is taxable in these situations.

How is the income taxed? The rules are technical but generally it depends on the type of trust and on the source of the income the trust receives. Thus, if the trust's income is ordinary income, that's how it would be taxed to the donor. If the income is tax free municipal bond interest, that's how the donor is taxed. With an annuity type pay out, part of the income is tax free because it is considered a partial return of principal. In this latter case, the portion tax free is determined actuarily.

Here's an example of how one retired couple used a unitrust. They created the trust for the benefit of a favorite charity, depositing $300,000 worth of appreciated property. The couple escaped capital gains tax of about $56,000. They also earned an income tax deduction of $114,500 (worth $32,060 at the 28% federal tax bracket). Their estate will gain a tax savings of approximately $128,000. And the couple transformed an asset that was generating no income into a growing cash stream, starting at about $30,000 in the first year of the trust. They got the future growth of the asset out of their estate. And best of all, they were able to help their charity! What a deal!

Another type of charitable trust is the *charitable lead trust.* The name comes from the fact that the charity leads, rather than follows, the donor in getting money from these trusts. Donors who put assets into a lead trust can name a charity as the beneficiary of the income for a specific number of years. At the end of that time, the assets revert to the donor. The donor gets a deduction equal to the present value of the income that will go to the charity of the specified period.

An example might be a five-year lead trust in which $50,000 is deposited. The trust will pay a named charity $10,000 a year for each of the next five years. The donor gets an immediate deduction of $37,908, which is the present value of the $50,000. The donor remains liable for taxes on the income generated by the trust, because the donor is still the owner of the money. But taxes could be avoided by funding the trust with municipal bonds.

In order to preserve an estate for heirs, using a charitable remainder trust in conjunction with life insurance is sometimes recommended. In this plan, a life insurance trust, called an *estate preservation trust* or *wealth-replacement life insurance trust* can be established to accept annual gifts to purchase life insurance on the life of the donor. This may be a way for Dad or Mom to have their cake (the charitable donation) and the kiddos to eat it too (the life insurance). In summary, the charitable trust can be a great way to unlock appreciated assets, perhaps increase your income from those assets, get a charitable deduction, and help out your favorite charity.

A *generation-skipping trust* is rather interesting. The purpose of such a trust is to go one step further than a by-pass trust by helping grandkids minimize federal estate taxes at the death of their parents. Such a trust allows for income to be paid to the children, but the corpus is passed on to the grandchildren free of federal estate tax when their parents die. Each such transfer is still subject to the $600,000 gift/estate tax exemption limits. In addition, transfers over $1 million are also subject to a special generation-skipping transfer tax. Just like other transfers, the exemption amount is fixed at the time of transfer. So if $1 million in a generation-skipping trust grows to $10 million, there is still no tax when distributed to the grandchildren at their parents' death. By-pass trusts and irrevocable life insurance trusts can be set up as generation-skipping trusts.

One of the basic concepts of estate planning is one of *estate freezing*. The idea is that wealthy folks should get appreciating assets into the ownership of younger family members (or charities). The reason is obvious: If you've got more than you'll ever need, you don't want your estate to keep growing because that means higher and higher estate taxes. Get it out of your estate and let it grow somewhere else. Many of the techniques already discussed do just that. Recent law changes have limited other previously used estate freezing techniques, and future rules may limit these techniques further. This is an evolving area and by the time you read this, some details may have changed. I've attempted just to highlight the basics of estate planning. However, since we're pretty wound up on the subject, we might as well look at a couple of other more exotic techniques.

Here's one for a family really looking for all the loopholes! A parent and a child (or a parent and an existing by-pass trust) can jointly purchase an investment. The parent takes as his/her ownership interest a life estate in the property, that is the right to benefit from property during his or her lifetime. The child (or trust) takes as an ownership interest a remainder interest, which is the right to sole ownership of the property when the holder of the life estate dies. Thus, the parent's value for inheritance tax purposes is zero at death. IRS actuarial tables limit the amount the parent can invest relative to the total value of the investment, but this is a way to get more than the $600,000 exemption equivalent out of an estate. It's a good idea to write by-pass trusts and irrevocable life insurance trusts to specifically allow investments in remainder interests.

Another exotic technique is the *Grantor Retained Income Trust*, or GRIT. The grantor of the trust sets up a trust for younger generation family members and retains an interest income in the trust assets for a specified period of time. After the expiration of the retained interest, the assets will pass to the beneficiaries. The underlying assumption of the GRIT is that the grantor will survive the term of his retained interest. If the grantor dies prior to the expiration of the term, the trust assets are includable in the grantor's estate. If the grantor does survive, all postgift appreciation in the assets will pass tax free to the remaindermen (beneficiaries). An asset that is expected to substantially appreciate in value over the term of the GRIT is the ideal asset with which to fund the trust. . . .Oh boy, what will the lawyers think of next?!!

Caveat: Keeping up with current estate planning laws is like trying to nail Jello to a tree. Alas, this whole section on estate planning might be out of date by the time you read it. Do not take this information as hard and fast points of law, but rather as information to familiarize yourself with the general concepts. Even experts disagree on much of this. Check with your attorney.

Family Protection

We're concerned here with disability insurance and life insurance. First, disability. Statistically you are far more likely to become disabled in the next few years than to die. Will your family have adequate income if you should become disabled? Most Americans are underinsured. How much disability benefit is adequate? Most insurance companies will cover you to 60 percent of your working income, so from a practical standpoint, that is a good amount to carry.

When buying disability insurance, here are some of the things to check out:

1. Are the payments to you taxable or tax free? The rule is, if premiums are tax deductible (usually if paid by your employer), the disability payments are taxable to the recipient. If you pay the premiums, rather than your company, the payments would be free from federal income tax. This, of course, makes a difference in your planning.

2. How long do you have to be disabled before payments begin? You'll get a cheaper rate for a six-month wait than for a one-month wait, but do you have enough savings to get you by for the six-month waiting period?

3. Does the policy pay you if you are employable in another field, even if it is a much lower paying endeavor? Or will your disability be defined as being unable to get work in a job similar to your current one? Check it out.

With regard to life insurance, the message is to shop around. There is a big difference in cost. And especially if you have a policy issued before about 1980, let your financial consultant review it. Life insurance has gotten much better and you may even be able to get 50 to 100 percent more coverage for the same premium.

How much life insurance do you need? To some degree it's a personal thing. But many people do not have enough. According to

Consumer Reports (June 1986) the median amount of coverage for all adults who have any insurance was only $15,000 in 1984, including group insurance. That would barely take care of burial and other incidental expenses on the event of one's death, let alone provide for a family with children. There are many things to consider. Such things as funeral expenses, lawyers' fees, and uninsured medical expenses might run anywhere from $5,000 to $50,000 when one dies. In addition, federal estate taxes as previously discussed must be added to anticipated costs at death. Together these constitute immediate death expenses.

The first step then, is to have enough life insurance to cover immediate death expenses. The second step is to estimate how much capital it takes to generate the income your family will need if you die. Remember to include mortgage payments, children's college costs, and general living expenses.

Next, estimate what your spouse may be able to earn if he or she is working. Also, estimate what your family's social security survivor benefits will be. This is tricky. The benefits depend on many factors—including your spouse's earnings, your earnings and the consistency of them, your age at death, your spouse's age, your children's age, as well as certain minimums and maximums. To get an estimate, write the Social Security Administration, Office of Public Inquiries, Baltimore, MD 21235. As an example, the benefits may range from about $5,000 per year for someone who died with one child only and with annual income of $15,000 to about $19,000 for someone leaving a nonworking spouse with two kids. Let's say you estimate your family will need $40,000 in pretax income in addition to what your spouse may earn at a job, plus social security survivor benefits. Use the same Lucky 13 Rule:

$$\begin{array}{r} \$40,000 \\ \times \quad 13 \\ \hline \$520,000 \end{array}$$

Thus your family will need $520,000 plus immediate death expenses. If immediate death expenses including estate taxes are estimated at $25,000 (remember, a surviving spouse pays no federal estate tax), you'll need a total of $545,000 in income-producing assets:

           capital needed to produce family income $520,000
       + plus death expenses, including estate tax   +25,000
           necessary income-producing assets $545,000

If you already have, say $100,000 in income producing assets, subtract this from the above:

           necessary income-producing assets $545,000
       − less existing income-producing assets   −100,000
           amount of life insurance needed $445,000

There you have it. Is this more than you thought? Most people are advised to consider this process carefully. Don't go overboard on life insurance. But term insurance is cheap. Don't be caught dead without enough of it.

Income Tax Planning

> *"Next to being shot at and missed, nothing is quite as satisfying as an income tax refund"*
> F.J. Raymond

> *"The Eiffel Tower is the Empire State Building after taxes."*
> Anonymous

There are five broad categories of tax minimization strategies. All of the different tax strategies fall into one of these five areas. The list can serve as a guide or check list to use with your financial consultant and tax professional to be sure you are maximizing your allowed tax breaks.

1. Elimination. Eliminating taxes can be achieved through investments that generate income or appreciation that is free from income taxes. There are two primary ways to achieve this under today's tax laws: tax free municipal bonds and life insurance. Municipal bonds are the more obvious. But life insurance? Yes, modern life insurance policies can be excellent investments. Modern policies pay returns consistent with CDs, bonds, or stocks—all tax sheltered. However, on an insurance policy, if you pull the money out prior to your death, it may be taxable. Tax free withdrawals are no longer available on single premium policies. If you buy a policy that is a traditional, staged-in investment råther than a lump-sum single-premium investment, you still get the tax free withdrawal (loan) feature as well as tax free accumulation and tax free death benefit.

Municipal bond income is free from federal income taxes. However, for many people it is not as valuable now since the top tax bracket is now 28 percent (for some it can be as high as 31%). Prior to the 1986 tax act rates went as high as 50 percent. Here's the formula you can use to determine if muni bonds are valuable to you. If your top tax bracket is 28 percent, take the rate of interest you can get on muni bonds and divide it by .72. For example, if you can get a 7 percent muni:

$$\frac{7\%}{.72} = 9.72\%$$

If you can find a taxable bond, either a corporate bond or Treasury bond of equal quality and maturity with a yield better than 9.72 percent, buy it rather than the municipal bond.

If your top bracket is 31 percent, divide by .69. Thus, to compare a 7 percent muni:

$$\frac{7\%}{.69} = 10.14\%$$

You'd need a taxable bond with a yield of 10.14 percent to do better than the muni after tax.

2. Deferral.   Deferral involves legally putting off paying taxes until some later date. Some examples include annuities, IRAs, and appreciated assets. A significant feature of tax qualified retirement plans such as Keoghs, 401(k)s, as well as Individual Retirement Accounts (IRAs) and Simplified Employee Pension Plans (SEPs) is that tax on gains is deferred until you take it out, usually at retirement. Appreciated assets, such as real estate or stocks, no longer receive capital gains tax treatment as favorable as it was prior to the 1986 tax reforms. However, they still benefit from tax deferral as they aren't taxed, of course, until sold. If you hold an appreciated asset until you die, you effectively eliminate taxes for your heirs because of stepped-up cost. That is, at death, the appreciated asset's cost basis is legally changed to the value as of the date of death.

One may say about tax deferral: "So what? If I've gotta pay tax on it some day, I might as well pay it now." In the real world there is still a strong benefit to deferral, because in effect you retain the money that would otherwise have gone to Uncle Sam, which you can then invest. In other words, you can earn interest on the tax savings until some later date. To illustrate, let's say you invest $10,000 today at 8 percent interest compounded annually. In 25 years the money will grow to $68,485 in a tax deferred account. If you then take all the money out of the account in a lump sum and pay tax at a 28 percent tax rate, you're left with $49,309. However, if you invest 10 grand at 8 percent but pay taxes as you go at 28 percent, you'll only have $40,554.

$49,309   after tax value, Tax Paid at End
 40,554   after tax value, Tax Paid As You Go
$8,755   net benefit of deferral

Thus, the deferral benefit is $8,755, which is equal to 87.6 percent of your original investment.

3. Shifting. Shifting is a technique that allows you to take advantage of the lower tax brackets of other family members, usually by gifts. The 1986 tax reforms reduced the benefit of this technique by saying that in most cases the tax bracket of the donor applies. However, there is still a benefit to gifting money to children. This can be done through a Uniform Gifts to Minors Act (UGMA) account. These accounts are set up with a parent or grandparent as custodian for the child. Provided that the child is 14 or older, all of the income and profits are taxed in the child's tax bracket, which may be zero, or at least lower than that of the parents. Until age 14, the child can earn up to $1,000 of passive (unearned) income and be taxed at the lower rate. (The first $500 is tax free. The second $500 is taxable.) Above $1,000 in passive income for a younger child, the parents' bracket applies.

Any active income (wages) a child earns is taxed at his rate. If you put him to work in your business, the income is taxed at the lower rate and deductible to you. Just don't violate the child labor laws.

These accounts are irrevocable gifts and must be used for the child's benefit. And when the child reaches the age of majority (usually 18 years old), he becomes the sole legal owner. However, a UGMA account is still a good program, especially when used in conjunction with prefunding the child's college education. There is usually very little cost to establish a UGMA account.

Another alternative, if you prefer to defer the time the child can get the money beyond the age of majority, is by setting up a trust. There are a couple of different kinds that you may hear about. One is a 2503(c) trust (named after the IRS code section). Another is a Crummey Trust (named after the family whose trust was tested in court). Provisions of these can be tricky, but if your goal is to keep your kids from getting at the money too soon, ask your attorney to explain how these might work for you.

4. Adjustments and Deductions. Reduction of taxable income through depreciation deductions, interest expense, real estate taxes, and so forth is also an alternative. Included are deductions for contributions to retirement plans. Without dwelling here on the choices, the message is to take advantage of them as advised by your tax professional and financial consultant, but do not hamper your investment potential by doing so. Always look at the investment merit of tax oriented investments before the tax benefits.

5. Credit Management.   The source of your borrowing should be considered because of the phase-out of deductions for consumer loans in 1987. Prudent margin borrowing and home equity financing are sometimes advisable. Credit management means the proper use of these and other borrowing methods, which can make the after-tax cost of borrowing less expensive.

College Planning

Another important aspect to financial planning is planning for those youngsters' social life between the ages of 18 and 22—otherwise known as college. Here's what the average annual college costs for tuition, room, board, and fees in 1990 were:

Public university	$4,733
Private university	12,635
Ivy League university	19,262

And these are bare bones costs. Even a public university could cost $10,000 per year per child, including inevitable extras.

A good plan is to prefund these costs. This allows you to pay for part of the costs with investment earnings. One popular way to fund such an account is with zero coupon treasury bonds. These instruments can be bought to mature in the years the child will need the money. And interest rates are guaranteed. Let's say that you have a child age 6. Assuming the child wants to go to a private university, and assuming a 7 percent inflation of college costs (which is the current rate of increase for college costs) and also assuming zero coupon bond yields are available near 8 percent (rates as of this writing), here's how your plan might look:

Child's College Age	Estimated Annual Cost	Necessary Earnings before Taxes @ 28%	Cost if Funded Today with Zero Coupon Bonds
18	$28,456	$39,522	$10,628
19	30,448	42,289	10,413
20	32,580	45,250	10,142
21	34,860	48,416	9,931
Total	$126,344	$175,477	$41,114

If you can afford to put the entire estimated amount in an account today (or better, talk relatives into it!), and invest the money at 8 percent, you need contribute only approximately $41,114, compared to $126,344 if funded on a pay-as-you-go basis when the child is in college. This illustrates the benefit of prefunding. It costs less than one third as much, if planned in advance as in this illustration. Note that if your tax bracket is 28 percent, you would have to earn $175,477 before taxes to earn enough after tax to meet the $126,344 needed.

More realistically, you will need to set up a budget for your future college costs just as you do for your retirement. If you begin immediately contributing to the child's college fund, you will need to contribute approximately $5,915 each year. This assumes an annual compounded growth of 8 percent. Obviously, the higher return you can get, the less college will cost you.

You can construct a college plan for yourself with the compound interest tables similar to your retirement planning. However, it becomes a little tricky because there is not a single time of distribution of the money. It is spread out over the four (or more) years the child is in school. During this period you are earning interest on the declining balance in the college fund. You can get a little more accuracy by using a computer program designed for this purpose, as I did in the above illustration. Your financial consultant should be able to assist you.

Formal Financial Plans

There is a way to do financial planning on a more formal basis. It's through a "packaged" planning service. Most investment firms offer computerized programs that cover the above areas and more. My opinion is that some of these services are excellent values. They involve completing a questionnaire on your assets, income, and goals. The computer does the rest. The cost is low, usually around $200 to $500. The real benefit of such a plan is to see it all in writing in one package. The disadvantage is that there are differences in recommendations, depending on the various computer programs. Some such programs may be designed primarily to sell investments. Avoid these and look instead for the ones that are generic in nature. You and your financial consultant can then discuss alternative specific investments to put the plan into action.

There is one big drawback—taking the time required to fill out the questionnaire! Even if it takes only an hour, few people will spend the necessary time to do it. An alternative approach is financial planning modules on various needs as they arise—college planning, estate planning, retirement planning, tax planning, and so forth. In spite of potential shortcomings, the advent of low-cost planning services is a great service to American families. You may want to consider such a service.

3

Real World Questions and Answers: Answers to Some Questions You May (or May Not) Have Wondered About

Let's explore a few important finance and investment concepts. We'll use the question and answer format. The purpose is to stimulate your thinking on some things that are often underappreciated by most folks. This chapter will be a springboard to the rest of the book.

Q. What major political and economic trends effect the stock market?

A. These trends generally favor financial assets (stocks and bonds):

- low inflation
- peace and democracy
- low tax rates
- shrinking public sector and deregulation
- increasing confidence
- increasing population

These opposite factors tend to hurt financial assets:

- high inflation
- political instability
- high tax rates
- growing public sector and increased regulation
- increasing fear
- decreasing population

Q. A gentleman recently explained to me that he had achieved better than a 28 percent annual return on his investments for over twenty years. He showed me how he had put $100,000 into investments twenty years ago, never added anything to them, and today the investments are worth $670,000. Thus, he made a profit of $570,000 over his original investment.

$670,000 ending value
− 100,000 beginning value
$570,000 profit

$$\frac{\$570,000 \text{ profit}}{20 \quad \text{years}} = \$28,500 \text{ profit per year}$$

Dividing his profit per year by his original investment:

$$\frac{\$28,500 \text{ profit per year}}{100,000 \text{ original investment}} = 28.5\%$$

Was his annual return really 28.5 percent? Yes or No?

A. No way! This is a typical example of how figures can lie. Look at the compound interest table (Table 2–2, page 16) "Amount of 1 at Compound Interest." Begin at the left of the table and drop down to the 20 year line. Follow the line across to the right until you find a factor near 6.7 (6.7 is the ending value of the investments of $670,000 divided by the beginning value of $100,000). At the 10.0 percent column you'll see a factor of 6.72748. Thus, this person's true compounded return was really 10 percent—not 28 percent!

By the way, the man who told me this is chairman of the board of a small bank! True story. Misleading arithmetic can pop up anywhere. *Forbes* magazine caught one of the nation's largest real estate syndicators quoting past performance yields exactly the way this guy did— with averaged annual return instead of true compounded return!

Q. One very successful mutual fund, which we'll refer to as the Real World Example Fund Number One, was founded in 1954. (Note: I cannot mention the actual name of this fund because I cannot give every reader a prospectus, as required by law.) An initial investment of $10,000 in 1954 grew to over $1,200,000 by the end of 1989. What was the compounded annual growth rate over the 35 years?

12%   15%   18%   21%   24%   27%   30%?

A.   15%. This return is the single best of any mutual fund over that period of time. We all hear about fabulous returns from time to time of 20 percent, 30 percent, 40 percent and so on. However, rates like that are unsustainable in the long run. For comparison, the cost of living as measured by the consumer price index averaged 4.5 percent between 1954 and 1989, while the Standard & Poors 500 Stock Index averaged approximately 10.9 percent annually over the same period. An investment with a return exactly equal to inflation would have grown to $47,000 while an investment in the S&P 500 would have grown to $378,000. In the real world, if you can achieve returns of 12 to 14 percent over a working lifetime, you're a killer investor! It has been estimated that the fabulously wealthy Howard Hughes, based on the value of his original inheritance and on estimates of the value of his final estate, earned less than 12 percent per annum compounded over his lifetime.

Here's a little more on compound interest. Pretend your ancestors had set up a trust fund for you in the year 1492, the year Columbus discovered America. Given a choice, which would you have preferred your ancestors do for you?

a.   Set aside $100,000 a day for you without interest until today

b.   Put one penny in an account bearing 8 percent interest (compounded annually).

The $100,000 a day would have grown to $18 billion by 1990. Not bad. But the penny would have grown to $400 trillion. The latter is

22,000 times greater than the former! This, of course, is not the real world, but it does have implications for the real world. Compounded growth *is* a big deal.

Just for fun, here's another comparison—this time between simple interest and compound interest. Simple interest means essentially setting the interest earned aside and accumulating it without earning interest (thus earning interest on the principal only), while compound interest means that you earn interest on the interest previously earned as well as on the principal. If one of your ancestors in 1492 deposited $1 in a savings account earning 5 percent simple interest, the account would have grown to $25.00 by 1990. If that $1 had earned 5 percent compound interest the account would have grown to approximately $29 billion by 1990.

Q.   The way to predict the trend in interest rates is to follow several good economists. When they all generally agree you can be pretty sure that they will be reasonably accurate. You can invest accordingly. True or False?

A.   False. Ah! Very important concept. . . . A key aspect to investing is that unanimity of opiñion is usually wrong. This is true among professionals as well as amateurs. Take economists, for example, and their ability to predict interest rates. Every six months (early January and early July) *The Wall Street Journal* publishes the results of a survey of economists' projections on interest rates. In the July 1984 survey, for example, 24 respected economists were polled about their predictions on rates over the next few months. A strong consensus, 15 of the 24, expected an increase in bond yields. Only three predicted a significant drop. None correctly predicted the extent of the upcoming drop in rates. If you had taken the advice of the consensus, you would have missed one of the biggest bond market rallies in history, as Treasury bond yields dropped from 13.6 percent to 10.4 percent and subsequently lower still! (Remember, when interest rates decline, bond prices increase.)

In January 1987 the *Journal* reported that "Economists in Survey Also See Lower Rates in First Half." Treasury bonds at the time were yielding about 7.5 percent and the average prediction was for rates to drop to 7.05 percent by midyear. Only two were bearish enough to predict that rates would go as high as 8.0 percent. Well, as things have it, before the six months was out, bond yields had risen to over 9.0

percent and by October to over 10 percent—blasting bond prices to their most devastating losses since the horrendous bear market for bonds in 1980 and 1981! Moral: In the real world, the consensus even among the so-called experts is usually wrong. Believe it.

Q.   Real estate is the surest investment as it has always increased in value historically. True or False?

A.   False. Investment strategists, Stanley D. Salvigsen and Michael C. Aronstein, in a 1986 writing said

> . . . *a brief review of the cyclicality of property values since the turn of the 19th century reveals the following: The inflation experienced after the War of 1812 crested with a boom in real estate values that lasted until 1818. Between 1818 and 1820, real estate prices declined between 50 and 75 percent. Recovery from this trauma was relatively quick, and in a mere 15 years real estate had regained its former luster, fueled largely by speculation surrounding the construction of canals in the Midwest. (Location, location, location.) By 1835, property values throughout the United States were at record levels, particularly in the center of the canal town—Chicago. By 1841, prices softened—50–60 percent for high grade properties and 90 percent for the more speculative ones. The next flurry took place in California in the mid-1880's. Prices soared on plentiful mortgage money and easy payment terms (as little as 25 percent down). By the end of the decade, values were down 75 percent and no buyers were in sight. The real estate markets then remained relatively sane until the Florida land boom of the mid-1920s. When that craze peaked, those who were convinced that property was always destined to come back in value over the long term had a wait of nearly 40 years before prices recovered to their 1925 highs.*

Salvigsen and Aronstein also warned that

> . . . *the only difference between the present attitude toward property today and that prevailing prior to these historic peaks is the level of conviction and the degree of participation. At present, there are far more members of the society involved in the ownership of real estate than at any of the previous extremes. In addition, the leverage is greater, the real burden of mortgage costs is higher and the belief in the sanctity of the value runs deep.*[1]

Real estate has probably made more fortunes in recent years than any other investment medium. There will no doubt continue to be great opportunities to make money in real estate. However, history suggests that the greatest risk exists when confidence is the highest and when debt loads are high. Investors may say that things are different for real estate now than in the 1800s. When you hear that "Things are different now . . . ," skepticism is in order. The words of Salvigsen and Aronstein were little regarded when written, but they were predictive of the real problems now emerging nationwide.

Q. The answer to successful investing is to buy a diversified portfolio of stocks or a mutual fund and forget about it. True or False?

A. False again. Stocks, like other forms of investment, have their good times and bad as well. The average stock, as evidenced by the Value Line Index of 1700 stocks, during the six years between 1969 and 1974, dropped from 188 to 47—a whopping 75 percent drop! Interestingly, during this same period the economy, as measured by Gross National Product, increased from $900 billion to $1.4 trillion—a 50 percent increase!

Now, for mutual funds, it's not that simple either. Further, not many people realize that the fund with the best 15-year record as of this writing suffered losses of 42 percent and 28 percent respectively in 1973 and 1974. There is an incredible difference in performance from the best to worst performing funds. For example, take the period July 1982 through April 1986. This three-year-and-ten-month period was a roaring bull market for stocks. The five best performing mutual funds experienced a total increase in value ranging from 230 to 268 percent over this period. But during this same period the five worst performing funds actually lost money ranging from drops of −3 to −43 percent! Incredible! Interestingly, the worst performing fund on the list was once considered one of the best funds in the country. Well, nobody said it was going to be easy. The real world of investing can be pretty tough. Times change.

Q. Okay, as long as you stick with stocks that are thoroughly researched by professional investment analysts, the odds are in your favor. True or False?

A. Sorry. Out of luck. At least some evidence suggests that the answer is false—again. Neglected stocks seem to outperform closely followed ones. A study (*Medical Economics*, November 25, 1985,) of the performance of 2000 stocks from 1976 to 1981 shows that those covered by no more than two securities analysts averaged an annual compound return of 33 percent, compared with 14 percent for issues watched by at least nine experts. That's a return two to one in favor of the neglected stocks!

Another study by Avner Arbel and Steven Carvell, both professors of finance at Cornell University, found that since 1977, stocks followed by six or fewer analysts provided an average total return of 25.6 percent a year, while those tracked by more than 20 analysts returned 16.9 percent. Further, these neglected stocks have outperformed the Standard & Poor's index every year since 1980. Arbel and Carvell, who now write a newsletter called *The Generic Stock Investing Service* (P.0. Box 6567, Ithaca, NY 14851), explain that "Pension fund and mutual fund managers are not going to lose their jobs if they buy IBM and General Electric and then underperform the market, but they fear being fired if they buy unknown stocks that flop. As a result, under-researched stocks, taken as a group, are priced too low."

Yet another similar study was done by Mark Hulbert, editor of the *Hulbert Financial Digest,* which ranks the performance of investment newsletters. Hulbert noted in a *Barron's* article ("Negative Indicator? When Newsletters Pile Into a Stock—Beware!" *Barron's,* June 8, 1987) that there is an inverse relation between the number of newsletters recommending a stock and the performance of the stock. The more newsletters recommending a stock, the poorer it performs.

Buying and holding well-recognized growth stocks does not work especially well either. A study by investment advisor John Geewax of the firm of Geewax, Turber (in Phoenixville, Pa) tracked growth stock performance from 1966 to 1985. He concluded that the median growth stock fell behind the market averages by 0.77 percent a year. And about 60 percent of all growth stocks underperform the average, giving you a better than even chance of picking an underperformer.

With yet another twist to this concept, studies have found that stocks of companies recognized as being "excellent" seem to underperform "nonexcellent" ones. Oklahoma State University professors W. G. Simpson and Timothy Irelands (*Barron's,* October 5, 1987) found that during 1974 to 1980, nonexcellent companies produced higher monthly returns 47 times, compared to 37 times for excellent ones. Similarly, another study by Michelle Clayman (*Barron's,* October 5, 1987, Also Michelle Clayman, "Managerial Excellence and Shareholder Returns," from *The Journal of American Association of Individual Investors,* August 1987) reported stocks of nonexcellent companies outperformed the S & P 500 index two thirds of the time, while two thirds of the companies perceived to be excellent underperformed the index.

This phenomenon is not too hard to explain, really. Companies that are fully studied or are recognized as excellent will tend to reflect a fair market valuation. If everyone knows about a company and its successes, its stock is less likely to be inaccurately priced in the market place. Bargains are most likely to be found in what is called the "inefficient" segment of the market. Money manager John B. Carl of Austin, Texas, likes to say: "Look for the stocks that are unwanted, unloved, or ignored."

Here's something else to chew on. Even given that you find an investment firm with a truly superior research department, it may not help you. Here's why. There are several assumptions you have to make. First, you assume that each individual securities analyst is as competent as the research staff as a whole. Second, you assume that the information the analyst has will get to your broker in a timely fashion. Third, you assume that you will get the information in a timely fashion. Fourth, you assume that you will act on the information in a timely fashion. . . . Ah, but somewhere along the line, the chain may break down. These four assumptions are not too bad, but there are dozens of reasons why any one of them may not work at any given moment.

Q. Which approach to picking stocks is apt to produce the better results?

a.   buy stocks near their low point, or

b.   near their high point

A. Again, contrary to apparent logic, at least some studies suggest that (b) buying high may actually be better. One study (*Barron's,* September 23, 1985, 31) found that a portfolio of stocks selling at their peaks for the previous five years would have outperformed the market by about 4 percent from 1971 through 1981. In comparison, a portfolio of stocks bought at their lows would have produced returns only 1 percent better than the market as a whole.

The term *relative strength* is an important concept that we can mention at this point. Evidence supports the idea that there are trends in business that are reflected in stock price moves. Stocks that are outperforming the rest of the market, i.e., demonstrating good relative price strength, tend to continue to do so. We'll get into even greater detail on this topic in the Chapter 6.

The real world message for now is that value is related to things other than price alone. Corporate earnings and dividends, industry trends, economic conditions, supply and demand, and other factors should be considered when analyzing the value of an investment. A stock can appear high priced but still be a good value.

When relating this general idea to the market as a whole, another point can be made. Many investors thought that the stock market was too high in 1950 when the Dow Jones Industrial Average was at 200, as that was the highest it had been in over 20 years. In the next 16 years, the Dow increased fivefold, reaching 995 by 1966. And many investors thought the market was too high in 1985 at 1300. These same people thought it was too high in 1986 at 1800, but it marched on to 2700 before falling back. Remember this: Markets climb a "wall of worry." Good investments always seem to go much higher than one thinks.

Q. What is earnings momentum?

A. Let's say that a company has historically been growing its earnings at 10 percent a year. Then its earnings accelerate to perhaps 15 percent growth. Spotting such earnings acceleration has been a proven way to identify stocks that have beaten the market. It seems that it takes quite some time—weeks or even months—before the price of the stock fully reflects the change in the underlying fundamentals. There is adequate time to get in before the upward move in the stock is over. A couple of mutual funds have used this technique almost exclusively to beat the market by a wide margin for many years.

Q. Are there any other proven techniques to beat the stock market?

A. There is no one single method that works all the time. We'll be discussing various approaches throughout the book. We've already touched on three methods: stocks that are not well known (the *neglected stocks*), stocks that are demonstrating *strong relative price strength,* and stocks that have *increasing earnings momentum.* Another approach is selecting *low P/E* (price to earnings) ratio stocks. The P/E

ratio is simply an arithmetical calculation that divides the price of a
stock by its earnings per share.

The P/E of the average stock has been about 14, as you can see from
the chart, Figure 3–1, which shows the P/E for the Standard and
Poor's 500 index going back to 1939.

FIGURE 3–1   Price-Earnings Ratios for the S&P 500

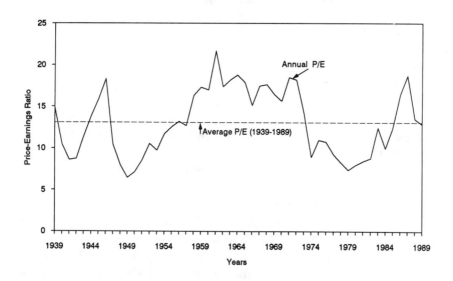

SOURCE: *AAII Journal,* March 1990.

FIGURE 3-2

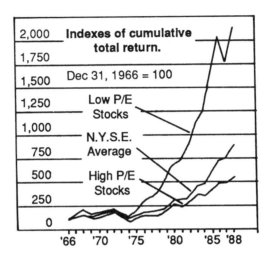

2,000	Indexes of cumulative total return.
1,750	
1,500	Dec 31, 1966 = 100
1,250	Low P/E Stocks
1,000	
750	N.Y.S.E. Average
500	High P/E Stocks
250	
0	

'66 '70 '75 '80 '85 '88

SOURCE: The *New York Times*, August 9, 1989.

One study, commissioned by the regional brokerage firm of Legg Mason Wood Walker, showed some dramatic results for low P/E investors. For the 22 years from 1967 through 1989, stocks with low price/earnings ratios averaged returns of 15 percent a year, compared with 8 percent for high P/E stocks. The cumulative results are shown in Figure 3-2.

Marc Reinganum, professor of finance at the University of Iowa, reported results of an analytical study in the September 1989 issue of *AAII Journal.* His study analyzed companies in "The Greatest Stock Market Winners: 1970–1983," published by William O'Neill & Co. To be considered a great winner, a company generally had to at least double in value within a calendar year. In addition to confirming the importance of the relative-strength ranking of a stock and its earnings momentum, his study showed other variables as correlating to superior stock market performance. These include:

- *A price-to-book-value ratio of less than 1.0.* (Book value is the accounting cost of all the company's assets on a per share basis. It is calculated by taking all assets, subtracting liabilities, then dividing by the number of shares of common stock outstanding.)
- Fewer than 20 million shares outstanding. This suggests that *smaller stocks* tend to outperform larger stocks.
- *High and/or increasing pretax profit margins.* (The pretax profit margin of a company is the percentage of total sales that becomes profits after all expenses other than taxes. In other words, it is the pretax profits divided by sales.) The rough cut-off point was 11 percent. Thus, a majority of the successful companies had 11 percent or higher margins and they were improving still further. (Note: This ratio varies a lot from industry to industry so it may be less useful.)

In Chapter 4 we'll discuss small stock performance more in detail. We'll also discuss the value of selecting stocks with high dividends, which is another way to win in the market. Yet another concept is investing in companies that have something new in the works. At least one study has shown that stock market winners often have new products or services, new management, or a new and dynamic change in an industry. And then in Chapter 6, we'll put it all together to show you how to use all this great new-found information to manage your own portfolio!

Q. At retirement, the investor's goal usually changes from growth to income with safety. The best way to achieve the highest income with safety is to invest all your funds in bonds and CDs or other fixed income investments. True or False?

A. False. Trick question. Though most financial advisors would recommend putting a portion of one's retirement dollars into bonds and CDs, there is another overwhelming side to the argument. Preservation of capital is of course of utmost importance to a retired person. However, true safety of principal implies preservation of purchasing power.

If inflation rises at just 4 percent a year, it will take twice as much income in 20 years to live on as it does today. If inflation rises at 6 percent a year, it will take three times as much income in 20 years as it does today. That $5 hamburger will cost you $15 in your lifetime! This author witnessed what can happen to fixed income retirees. I saw retirees 15 years ago insisting on putting all of their money in "safe" fixed income investments. But what has happened since then? First, there have been emergencies that have necessitated dipping into principal, such as hospital bills, a new roof for the house, and so forth. Compounding these problems, investments in high yielding, long-term bonds have declined in market value in the last 15 years, as the general level of interest rates has increased since the time of purchase (making the old bonds worth less because of higher yields available on newer ones). Because of inflation, these investors can no longer make ends meet on a limited income. What looked like a great income back then, doesn't cut it today. And because of increased longevities, many people will spend 30 or even 40 years retired, possibly outliving their fixed incomes! Safety is not always what it seems.

One large investment management firm likes to tell the story of two fictional couples, the Boones and the Klausens. Both couples retired in 1957 with $100,000. The Boones, believing safety was important, put the $100,000 in a fixed income investment paying 8 percent. (In reality banks and savings and loans were paying about 3 percent back then.) They concluded that with the $8,000 annual income they were set for life with no worries about inflation. Indeed, $8,000 was a pretty good annual income back then.

The Klausens, on the other hand, invested their $100,000 in the Real World Example Fund Number Two. (Again, I am prevented by law from mentioning the fund's actual name, since I am in the securities investment business.) They understood that the only safe investment was one that would protect purchasing power. They gave up income to start, as the first year they received only $2,695. However, the mutual fund was able to increase the income every year. By 1976 the annual income was $11,624 per year. By 1986 the annual income was $33,892, while the Boones, on the other hand, were still receiving only $8,000 per year.

By the end of 1987, the value of the Klausens' fund had grown still further to $1,108,566. During 1987, of course, the market witnessed one of the greatest financial panics in world history—the Crash of 1987. Yet this fund, like many others, actually increased in value during 1987 in addition to paying its dividend.

	The Boones	The Klausens
Original investment	$100,000	$100,000
Total interest received	$240,000	$365,720
Value of investment 12/31/86	$100,000	$1,090,036

Now, don't run out and put everything you've got into a mutual fund! But, in the real world a 6 percent inflation rate will double prices every 12 years. Prudent investing demands planning for the future. It may be prudent for retirees to invest for a combination of growth plus income. If need be, profits on the growth portion can supplement the interest earned on the income portion. One way to do that is to begin a *systematic withdrawal plan* from a mutual fund. Through such a plan, the fund can send you a regular check either monthly, or less frequently, for any amount you desire. Of course, if you take a very large amount, you will eat into your principal. If you take a reasonable amount, there will be some years where the fund's total return will be below your withdrawal amount, but some years where the total return will be greater than your withdrawal amount so that remaining value can continue to grow over time.

The founder of the Real World Example Fund Number One gives the following advice about total return to younger and older investors:

> Young people want capital growth. Retired people want income. But really, after 45 years of advising thousands of investors, I believe that every person is seeking and should seek the maximum total return net after taxes and after inflation.
>
> Total return means the total of the dividends and interest plus the capital gains. And if you seek out a well-managed mutual fund that is trying to provide the maximum total return, then the young person can obtain capital gains by reinvesting automatically each year all the distributions that are paid by the mutual fund. On the other hand, the older person desiring high income can enter into a cash withdrawal agreement with the mutual fund very easily. The fund will send that person 8 percent a year or 10 percent a year or whatever income is requested—which will be taken out of their total return.

This is a true wise man speaking. We have to admit that it makes good sense.

I did a study on how such a withdrawal plan would have worked out with the Real World Example Fund Number Two for the 30 years beginning 1957. Figure 3–3 shows an initial $100,000 investment in the fund on January 1, 1957. We initially begin an $8,000 annual withdrawal, that is 8 percent, to give a direct comparison to the Boones' return. The plan is to readjust the withdrawal to 8 percent of the remaining account value at the end of each 10-year period.

As you can see from the illustration, by the end of the first 10-year period (12/31/66), the account had grown to $143,813 (in addition to having withdrawn $8,000 per year). So let's give ourselves a raise to 8 percent of the new value of $143,813.

$$\begin{array}{r} \$143{,}813 \\ \times \quad 8\% \\ \hline \$\ 11{,}505 \end{array}$$

Thus, for the second 10-year stretch, we withdraw $11,505 per year. That's a pretty handsome raise.

By the end of the second 10-year period [12/31/76, Figure 3–3 (continued)] the total value had risen to $154,775. This is particularly impressive because this 10-year period included the worst bear market for stocks since the depression. Let's now give ourselves another raise to 8 percent of the then accumulated value of $154,775.

$$\begin{array}{r} \$154{,}775 \\ \times \quad 8\% \\ \hline \$\ 12{,}382 \end{array}$$

Thus, for the third 10-year period we withdraw $12,382 per year from the fund. That's better than 50% more income than our original income amount of $8,000.

FIGURE 3-3

Hypothetical Illustration—Real World Example Fund Number Two

Date	Initial Investment	Offering Price	Sales Charge Included	Shares Purchased	Net Asset Value per Share	Initial Net Asset Value
1/1/57	$100,000.00	$4.89	3.50%	20,449.898	$4.715	$96,421

Systematic Withdrawal Plan
Dividends and Capital Gains Reinvested
Annual Withdrawals of $8,000.00 (8.0% Annually) Beginning 12/31/57

| | Amounts Withdrawn | | | | Value of Remaining Shares | | | | |
Date	From Income Dividends	From Principal	Annual Total	Cumulative Total	Annual Cap Gain Distrib'n	Remaining Original Shares	Capital Gain Shares	Total Value	Shares Held
12/31/57	2,722	5,278	8,000	8,000	5,245	71,936	5,029	76,965	20,307
12/31/58	2,591	5,409	8,000	16,000	3,850	92,430	10,992	103,422	20,141
12/31/59	2,577	5,423	8,000	24,000	7,754	90,800	19,297	110,097	20,598
12/31/60	2,788	5,212	8,000	32,000	6,198	82,096	24,995	107,091	20,855
12/31/61	2,672	5,328	8,000	40,000	6,831	88,359	35,451	123,810	21,146
12/31/62	2,731	5,269	8,000	48,000	4,817	66,390	33,028	99,418	20,952
12/31/63	2,666	5,334	8,000	56,000	5,033	71,038	43,128	114,166	20,948
12/31/64	2,773	5,227	8,000	64,000	7,602	70,858	53,872	124,730	21,358
12/31/65	2,948	5,052	8,000	72,000	9,519	77,734	72,600	150,334	22,092
12/31/66	3,585	4,415	8,000	80,000	11,528	66,567	77,246	143,813	23,121
Totals	28,051	51,949	80,000		68,378				

FIGURE 3-3 (continued)

Date	Initial Investment	Offering Price	Sales Charge Included	Shares Purchased	Net Asset Value per Share	Initial Net Asset Value
1/1/67	$143,813.00	$6.22	0.00%	23,121,062	$6.220	$143,813

Systematic Withdrawal Plan
Dividends and Capital Gains Reinvested
Annual Withdrawals of $11,505.00 (8.0% Annually) Beginning 12/31/67

	Amounts Withdrawn				Value of Remaining Shares				
Date	From Income Dividends	From Principal	Annual Total	Cumulative Total	Annual Cap Gain Distrib'n	Remaining Original Shares	Capital Gain Shares	Total Value	Shares Held
12/31/67	4,018	7,487	11,505	11,505	8,752	164,838	9,021	173,859	23,337
12/31/68	4,645	6,860	11,505	23,010	7,351	173,007	18,845	191,852	23,642
12/31/69	4,903	6,602	11,505	34,515	11,584	134,084	25,770	159,854	24,202
12/31/70	4,933	6,572	11,505	46,020	7,019	120,999	31,541	152,540	24,348
12/31/71	4,799	6,706	11,505	57,525	3,231	128,511	38,501	167,012	23,876
12/31/72	4,702	6,803	11,505	69,030	5,719	134,016	47,963	181,979	23,773
12/31/73	4,930	6,575	11,505	80,535	4,007	98,164	41,708	139,872	23,331
12/31/74	7,128	4,377	11,505	92,040	0	71,058	32,211	103,269	22,304
12/31/75	6,120	5,385	11,505	103,545	801	86,072	42,234	128,306	21,546
12/31/76	5,238	6,267	11,505	115,050	2,541	100,074	54,701	154,775	21,072
Totals	51,416	63,634	115,050		51,005				

The period covered is not necessarily representative of the Fund's results during different market periods. Past results are no guarantee of future results.

FIGURE 3–3 (continued)

Date	Initial Investment	Offering Price	Sales Charge Included	Shares Purchased	Net Asset Value per Share	Initial Net Asset Value
1/1/77	$154,775.00	$7.35	0.00%	21,072,157	$7.345	$154,775

Systematic Withdrawal Plan
Dividends and Capital Gains Reinvested
Annual Withdrawals of $12,382.00 (8.0% Annually) Beginning 12/31/77

	Amounts Withdrawn					Value of Remaining Shares			
Date	From Income Dividends	From Principal	Annual Total	Cumulative Total	Annual Cap Gain Distrib'n	Remaining Original Shares	Capital Gain Shares	Total Value	Shares Held
12/31/77	5,232	7,150	12,382	12,382	3,028	135,356	3,051	138,407	20,459
12/31/78	5,393	6,989	12,382	24,764	0	142,986	3,378	146,364	19,541
12/31/79	6,215	6,167	12,382	37,146	1,759	156,313	5,728	162,041	19,064
12/31/80	7,536	4,846	12,382	49,528	3,813	173,401	10,665	184,066	19,074
12/31/81	8,963	3,419	12,382	61,910	12,589	151,612	21,688	173,300	20,058
12/31/82	10,545	1,837	12,382	74,292	11,032	179,344	40,102	219,446	21,535
12/31/83	10,054	2,328	12,382	86,674	9,691	196,036	55,280	251,316	22,319
12/31/84	10,447	1,935	12,382	99,056	11,383	190,229	65,470	255,699	23,245
12/31/85	10,862	1,520	12,382	111,438	11,390	233,684	95,009	328,693	24,330
12/31/86	12,199	183	12,382	123,820	63,225	227,597	160,151	387,748	29,397
Totals	87,446	36,374	123,820		127,910				

The period covered is not necessarily representative of the Fund's results during different market periods. Past results are no guarantee of future results.

How do we look by December 31, 1986—the end of the third 10-year period? As you can see [Figure 3–3 (continued)], the value had increased again, this time to $387,748! This 10-year period was an exceptionally good period for stocks. We could easily increase our income again substantially.

Note that over the 30 years the total value fluctuated. Some years were up, some years were down. I started the analysis in 1957 to illustrate this. The very first year took the value down from $100,000 to $76,965! That year, 1957, was a sharp bear market year for stocks. But it didn't hurt the program over the long run.

Subsequent to this period studied, the Crash of 1987 came around. But not only was 1987 a year of positive results for the fund, but so were 1988 and 1989. The strategy continued to work equally well into the future.

This approach is an excellent one and is one way to have your cake and eat it, too, during your retirement years. The Klausens never had less in income than the Boones had. They were able to give themselves periodic raises to offset inflation. And the value increased handsomely over time!

Q. Fixed income investors have the choice of investing in short-term instruments or long-term instruments. Short-term investments include Treasury bills, certificates of deposit (CDs), money market funds, short-term notes, and so forth. Long-term instruments are bonds, with maturities ranging to as long as 30 years. A valid way to choose which alternative to invest in is to pick the one with the lowest yield. True or False?

A. True. This is sometimes referred to as the *minimum yield strategy.* Let's look at the last few years. In early 1978 one could have invested in one-year CDs yielding 7 percent. At the same time, you could buy long-term U.S. Treasury bonds with a yield of 8.25 percent. The yields on the bonds looked especially attractive in comparison to CDs as well as historic yields on bonds, which had generally been below 8.25 percent. However, those who bought the bonds were sorry later as the general level of interest rates went much higher. By late 1981 one-year CDs were 18 percent and Treasury bond yields reached 14.5 percent (briefly to 15 percent).

By then, the values of bonds had dropped precipitously. Not only had bond investors seen the market value of their holdings drop, but they were still getting only a paltry 8.25 percent interest. By comparison, the CD investor was getting increasingly higher yields each time his CD matured—and no loss of principal value. Having reached for the higher yielding bond in 1978 was a mistake—big time.

Now, if you were an investor in late 1981, would you rather have had the 14.5 percent T-bond or the 18 percent CD? Most investors were petrified of the bond market. Indeed, an informal poll of investors I spoke with showed a nearly unanimous opinion that interest rates were going even higher, perhaps to 20 or 30 percent! "Why buy bonds when you can get 18% risk free?" they asked. An article in our local business journal (Fig. 3–4) evidenced the public fear of higher interest rates and weak financial markets.

Let's see why the bond was a better investment than the higher yielding CD. By 1986 interest rates had returned to their 1978 levels. CDs were back to 7 percent and bonds back to 8.25 percent. Investors who had bought bonds in 1981 locked in very high yields and realized, to boot, huge gains in the value of the bonds. For example, the 10 percent T-bonds due in 2010 in 1981 could have been purchased for 70 percent of face value. That is, a bond with a $1,000 face amount was selling in 1981 for $700. The 10 percent coupon yield on the bond ($100 per year in interest), plus the potential capital gain at maturity ($1,000 face value less $700 market value, or thus $300 discount), yielded an effective *yield to maturity*[2] of 14.5 percent. This same bond in 1986 was selling for $1,170. That is, every $1,000 bond had a market value of $1,170. Thus the bond had appreciated from $700 to $1,170, a whopping 67 percent increase in value!

Not only had the 1981 bond investor received a tremendous capital gain, but in 1986 he was still receiving the same high level of income from the coupons ($100 per year) he got in 1981. The CD investor, even though he received much higher income for awhile, really made the wrong decision in 1981. The bond with lower current yield in 1981 was by far the better deal.

Now, this period was something of an anomaly in recent U.S. history because of the high level that interest rates reached. But it does prove a point. The minimum yield strategy is a valid approach to fixed income investing. Investors need to be flexible in their thinking about investing—in the real world.

FIGURE 3-4

Prime Interest Could Escalate High as 30% by Year's End

Remember Chicken Little and the "sky is falling" theory?

That famous prognosticator would have felt right at home among some of the nation's top money managers in mid-September at the annual investment conference of San Francisco-based Montgomery Securities.

Attended by about 400 managers from throughout the country, with assets of approximately $350 billion, the overwhelming consensus was that the decline in the Dow Jones industrial average isn't over yet—and in fact will sharpen into panic selling in the stock market between now and the first of November.

Despite the stunning drop of over 150 points in the D.J.I.A. already since mid-June . . . and despite signs of some downticks among banks' prime lending rates (following a slight softening by the Federal Reserve in the discount-rate surcharge) . . .

. . . some of the leading money managers at the conference predicted that the Dow will plunge all the way to 750 . . . or even, more incredibly, to around 650 (a drop of roughly 200 points more!) within the next month or so.

Among those forecasting a drop as steep as the latter—almost 25%—is David Polak.

Although his position is more extreme than the majority in attendance, his track record leaves little to be desired: Over the last seven years, Polak, who runs Argus Investors Counsel West, is in the top one percent in performance among 4,000 funds tracked by A. G. Becker.

Polak believes we're sitting on the brink of a credit crisis of truly major proportions.

Contrary to other avenues of thought, he predicts a major surge upward in short-term loan rates. His thinking is that mushrooming government borrowings ahead will crowd out the corporate sector—and foresees the prime rate escalating all the way up to 25 percent . . . and possibly as high as 30 percent before year-end. (No, those numbers are NOT misprints!) . . .

Admittedly at the extreme end in his forecasts, Polak's views were basically identical to those of Joseph Reed, Jr. However, Reed, one of three managers of about $500 million of equity assets for Alliance Capital Management Corp., sees the Dow plummeting "only" a hundred points or so, to the 750 level, within the weeks ahead.

He shares the major fear that government borrowing will force a relentless upward pressure on interest rates.

FIGURE 3–4 *(continued)*

Additionally, "the technical picture is collapsing and nobody's doing anything about it," Reed feels. He's referring to items such as the low level of odd-lot public short selling, poor advance-decline numbers in stocks, a breakdown in the Dow's transportation average, and the lack of any kind of market leadership.

As a result, Reed predicts extremely high volume days featuring large number of stocks opening (after trading delays) several points lower than their previous day's close. The largest declines, he projects, will be among the smaller, younger companies with mountains of high debt on their balance sheets.

In this panic selling scenario, highest risk of all is in the technology sector. Reed is joined by many in predicting that—despite their already significant declines—technology stocks are at the top of the "danger list," due to their generally higher price-earnings ratios. Disappointments over earnings, in a recessionary setting, are expected to hasten their plunge.

Amidst all these heavy gloom-and-doom clouds, where is sunshine to be found?

Money-market funds were the clear top choice as the favorite "resting place" for these money manager's money.

Again in an extreme position, Polak has increased his cash reserves from about 25 percent in early summer to an extraordinary 70 percent now!

As he said, "There isn't a day that goes by when I don't do some selling of equities, because I think we're in a major bear market."

• • •

You think the United States economy is alone in its difficulties?

Not exactly.

In France a few weeks ago, the central bank cut the key interest rate "to help spur the flagging economy".

Meanwhile, at the same time, Switzerland raised two key rates—to record levels—"to cope with inflation".

According to the Swiss central bank, these increases were to emphasize a restrictive monetary policy, with the goal of "stabilizing price levels".

The lending fee to financial institutions was boosted a full percentage point by the Swiss central bank . . . to 6%.

SOURCE: Maurice Olian, *Austin Business Journal*, vol. 1, no. 9, October 1981, pp. 1, 4.

Q. Why is it that when federal government deficits are at their highest, interest rates haven't gone up as most people expect?

A. In the 1980s, the number one economic fact on the minds of investors (by far) was the federal government deficits. Yet interest rates went down. The table below shows the annual federal deficits as a percentage of gross national product and also shows net federal debt outstanding as a percentage of gross national product. (Total debt is the result of accumulated deficits. Net federal debt is gross interest-bearing debt of the U.S. government less amounts held by federal

government agencies and the Federal Reserve. Gross national product
(GNP) is the sum of all goods and services produced in the country
during the year.) The table also shows interest rates on 10-year
maturity Treasury bonds. Incidentally, the *Economic Report of the
President,* from which this information is derived, is available annually
from the U.S. Government Printing Office. I recommend that serious
investors get each annual issue. You may obtain it by phoning
202–783–3238. The period shown is that of the big rise and subsequent fall of interest rates from the mid-1970s to the mid-1980s.

TABLE 3–1

Year	Annual Federal Deficits ÷ GNP	Net Federal Debt ÷ GNP	Treasury Bond Yields
1976	4.3	24.1	7.6
1977	2.8	23.9	7.4
1978	2.7	23.4	8.4
1979	1.6	22.1	9.4
1980	2.8	23.1	11.5
1981	2.6	23.3	13.9
1982	4.1	27.0	13.0
1983	6.3	30.8	11.1
1984	5.0	32.9	12.4
1985	5.4	36.0	10.6
1986	5.3	37.3	7.7

SOURCE: *Economic Report of the President,* February 1990.

As you can see from Table 3–1, deficits and debt were generally
declining in the late 1970s while interest rates were increasing!

However, deficits and debt were increasing in the early 1980s while
rates were declining from their 1981 high. Also, here's another
interesting fact. Britain has been pretty close to a balanced budget in
recent years. Yet interest rates there have been over 12 percent. The
United States, on the other hand, has experienced big federal deficits,

yet rates have been near 8 percent. In fact, if there is a relationship between deficits and interest rates, it is an inverse one. How can that be? Because of the national concern and investor focus over the problem, the question deserves a closer look.

First, general perceptions of economic facts are often wrong. This is one of the main themes of this book. As far as interest rates are concerned, the public has tried inaccurately to pin sole blame on the federal deficit. According to economist A. Steve Holland:

> Government borrowing represents an increase in the total demand for loanable funds. This suggests that real interest rates rise as the size of the government budget deficit increases in real terms. One rarely sees a positive correlation between the size of deficits and the level of interest rates, however. This is probably because they respond in opposite directions to changes in economic conditions; deficits tend to rise during business recessions and fall during expansions (because tax revenues and outlays for transfer payments are sensitive to the state of the economy), while interest rates typically fall during recessions and rise during expansions.[3]

Okay, if the federal government is not the Simon Legree of high interest rates, who is to blame? Other possible culprits include: consumer debt, energy prices, the state of the economy, taxes, the supply of money, inflation expectations by the public, and the international currency exchange markets—just to name a few. My opinion is that nobody really yet understands the interrelationships of all the factors that affect inflation and interest rates.

In my almost 20 years in the investment business plus several years studying economics in college, I've never seen or heard of anyone who could consistently predict the course of interest rates and inflation. Entire books have been written on this subject. It is a fascinating field. My best advice to the reader is not to worry much about all this. In Chapter 5 we'll outline an asset allocation strategy that will work for you without having to predict interest rates! On the subject of debt, here's a word of warning. Government debt is somewhat high compared to most of the past. However, if there is a debt problem today, it more likely lies in the private sector. Private debt is historically very high. Some of the more serious potential problems in this sector lie in real estate mortgage debt and consumer debt. The rise in debt in these sectors of the economy is shown on the following table.

Year	Consumer Installment Credit ÷ Disposable Personal Income (%)	Mortgage Debt Outstanding ÷ GNP (%)
1950	7%	25%
1960	12	40
1970	15	47
1980	16	54
1990	18	65

SOURCE: *Economic Report of the President*, February 1990.

Here's another telling statistic: the ratio of the par value of bonds compared to the market value of equity (stocks) for companies listed on the New York Stock Exchange has increased dramatically over this same period. In the 1950s it was as low as 20 percent. By the 1980s it had increased to 70 percent!

Notice the various charts on debt (Figures 3–5, 3–6, 3–7, and 3–8). One word of explanation: Economists often speak of nonfinancial debt. Financial debt is banking system debt, primarily bank deposits, which are in reality liabilities (debts) of the banks.

FIGURE 3–5   The Debt Surge: Total U.S. Nonfinancial Debt as a Percentage of GNP

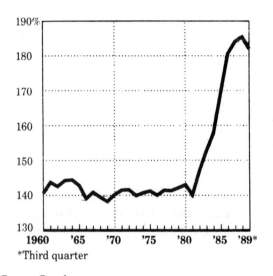

*Third quarter

SOURCE: Federal Reserve Board.

FIGURE 3–6   Government Budget Deficit and Foreign Saving as Shares of GNP

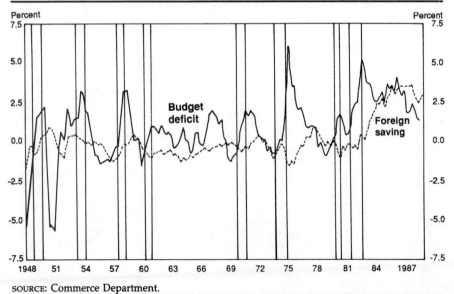

SOURCE: Commerce Department.

FIGURE 3-7   Nonfinancial Debt

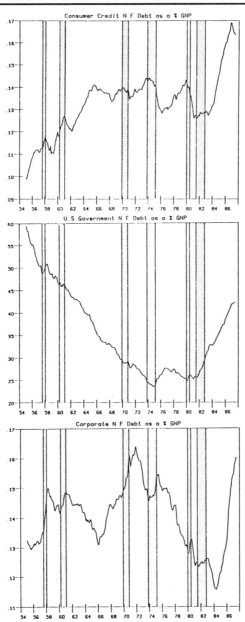

Note: Shaded areas represent N.B.E.R. designated economic recessions.

FIGURE 3–8   The Rise of Debt

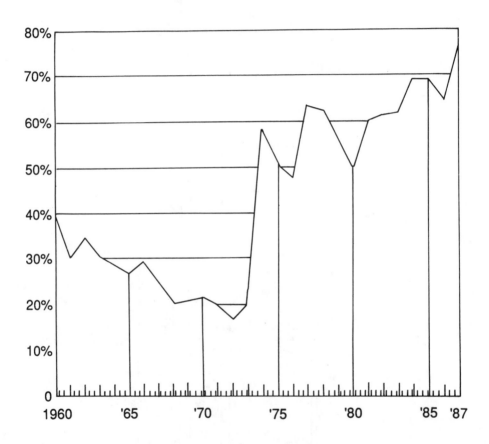

Ratio of par value of bonds to market value of equity
for NYSE-listed issues, in percent

SOURCE: New York Stock Exchange.

Here's the message from these statistics on private debt: We have greatly increased our debt relative to our ability to pay that debt. And the question becomes: How much more debt can we handle? No tree grows to the sky. We are most certainly near the saturation point on debt accumulation.

What excessive debt does to a nation is exactly what it does to a family. It improves one's standard of living in the short run at the expense of the future. If our economy goes through a period of debt reduction, consumers will be using available cash flow to pay off debts rather than buying houses and cars, etc. This could have serious implications for the economy. The increase in our standard of living will slow. Further, instead of higher interest rates, a slowing economy might suggest lower interest rates. The big surprise of the next few years could be an eventual return to the levels of interest rates of the 1950s and 1960s—i.e., 4 to 5 percent interest rates on CDs and bonds! . . . Oops. Just when I said nobody can predict interest rates, I let slip something that might look like a forecast! Well, right or wrong, it is rather fun to think about the future.

Endnotes

[1]Stanley D. Salvigsen and Michael C. Aronstein, "The China Syndrome," Merrill Lynch, May 1, 1986. Stan Salvigsen was rated the number one investment strategist on Wall Street by *Institutional Investor* magazine while at Merrill Lynch in 1986. As of this writing Salvigsen and Aronstein are principals of the investment management firm Comstock Partners, New York.

[2]*Yield to maturity* is a calculation that figures in both the annual coupon interest and any discount in market value to face value (or minus any premium over face value). The calculation assumes a compounded rate of increase or decrease in the market value, and also assumes that the coupons paid are reinvested at the yield to maturity rate. Accurate calculation of yield to maturity should be done on a computer or taken from a bond yield table.

[3]A. Steve Holland, "Real Interest Rates: What Accounts for Their Recent Rise?" in *Review*, The Federal Reserve Bank of St. Louis, December 1984, pp. 18–29.

4

No Return Policy: The Truth About Historical Investment Returns

Let's look a little harder at some historical returns on various investment classes to see what we can learn. If you are one that hates numbers, you may already be a bit bewildered. But hang in there. You should find this chapter interesting—unless you have a "no return policy" on your investments. The information in this chapter will be the foundation of our investment strategies developed in the upcoming chapters.

Figure 4–1 shows the long-term results of stocks versus Treasury bills and gold. All returns are after inflation. As you can see, the return for stocks has been far superior. Indeed, stocks have been so incredibly ahead of other types of assets that it is important to stop here for a minute to reflect on why this is true.

Businesses reflect the fact that mankind constantly strives to better itself. Corporations are dynamic entities that tend to create their own value by technological change, creating their own markets, products, and services. Human progress is a fundamental truth that is reflected in share prices. The serious investor has to appreciate this notion. The future is never exactly the same as the past. But the argument for stocks is that unless the course of human nature itself changes, the long term trend for stocks will continue to be upward.

Digging deeper, Ibbotson Associates (8 South Michigan Ave., Suite 700, Chicago 60603, phone (312) 263–3435) is a recognized authority on such data. Based on information from their annual *Yearbook*[1], here's

FIGURE 4-1 Stocks, Treasury Bills and Gold; Total Returns after Inflation 1871–1988

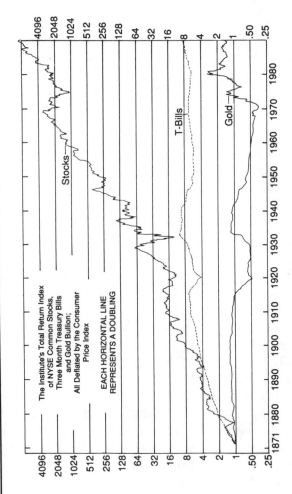

After adjustment for inflation and reinvested dividends, but ignoring income taxes, the purchasing power of each dollar invested in the stock market has grown approximately 9,000-fold in the past 119 years (8% per annum compounded). An investment in U.S. Treasury Bills, also adjusted for inflation and the reinvestment of earnings, appreciated about eightfold (1.8% per annum). Finally, after inflation and a modest 0.4% annual storage and insurance charge, an investment in gold would have less than doubled (a 0.3% per-annum return) in more than a century.

SOURCE: Reprinted by permission from the January 26, 1990 edition of *Market Logic*, $95 per year, published by The Institute for Econometric Research, 3471 North Federal Highway, Fort Lauderdale, Florida 33306, telephone 800–327–6720.

how various types of financial assets have performed over the 64-year period from 1926 through 1989. The following are compounded annual returns for inflation (the Consumer Price Index), three-month U.S. Treasury bills, long-term U.S. government Treasury bonds, long-term corporate bonds (Salomon Bros. High Grade Corporate Bond Index), large blue chip stocks (Standard & Poors 500 Index), and small-company stocks.

Inflation	3.1%
T-bills	3.6%
Long-term government bonds	4.6%
Long-term corporate bonds	5.2%
Big-company stocks	10.3%
Small-company stocks	12.2%

Figure 4–2 shows how these indices have performed through the 64-year period. It shows how much an investment of one dollar made in 1926 in various assets would have been worth at the end of 1989. Unlike the previous chart, growth by the various investment classes is the actual total return before subtracting the effects of inflation.

Small stocks in the Ibbotson study are basically defined as those New York Stock Exchange companies having a market capitalization in the lowest one fifth. Market capitalization (often just called "market cap") of a stock is the total value of its shares. It is figured by multiplying the stock price by the total number of shares outstanding.

Small stocks, you will note, have performed even better than large stocks. The reason appears to be that it is simply more difficult for a large company to grow. However, note that this is not always true. The chart reveals that during the 1950s, big companies tracked closely to small stocks. And small stocks tend to be more volatile, thus more risky. During the crashes of the 1930s and 1970s, the small stocks got hit much harder.

Even for blue chip stocks returns can be extremely variable from period to period. For example, the best five-year period was 1950 to 1954, when stocks returned 23.9 percent annually. For the five-year period 1928 to 1932 the average return was an average annual loss of 12.5 percent.

Stock returns were positive in more than two thirds of the years (45

FIGURE 4–2   Wealth Indices of Investments in the U.S. Capital Markets; 1926–1989 (Year-End 1925 = 1.00)

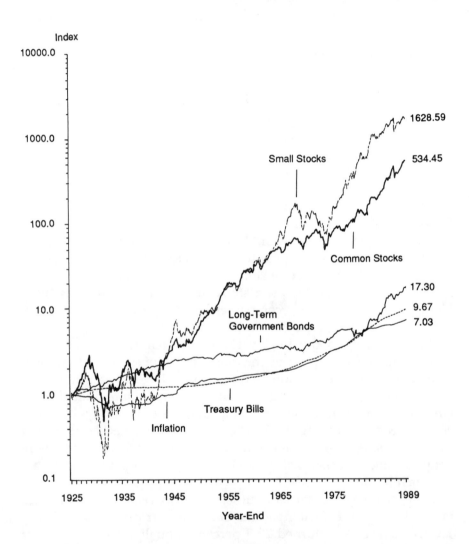

SOURCE: SBBI 1990 Yearbook Ibbotson Associates/Chicago

out of 64 years). The longest period over which the blue chip index would have earned a negative return was the 14-year period 1929 to 1942. Interestingly, the longest period an investor would have earned a negative return after inflation was during the 18 years and four months from June 1964 through September 1982. (In nominal terms, that is, before subtracting inflation, an investor would have more than tripled his investment, however, during this 18-year period.) Figure 4–3 illustrates the variability of stock returns. The first graph on the chart shows government bond returns, month-by-month from 1926 to 1988. The second graph shows common stock likewise. In both graphs, each mark above the horizontal line is a month in which stocks or bonds increased. Each mark below the line was a decreasing month. What you can clearly see is that the number of up months about equals the number of down months. However, the longer the holding period, the fewer the down periods for stocks. For example, there has been only one down 10-year period for stocks and no down 15-year periods. Time is your lever when investing in stocks.

Another interesting fact about stocks is that while the total return for common stocks over the 62 years was 10.3 percent, including dividends reinvested, if dividends were excluded, the return would have been reduced to 5.3 percent per annum. Reinvesting dividends represents half of the total return. Dividends are thus an important element of stock market investing, perhaps more than many people recognize. Figure 4–4 shows how dividends have grown over the years. Focusing on this consistent growth can take some of the worry out of stock investing, it seems to me. Recognizing this underlying trend should reduce the investor's concern over the short-term ups and downs in share prices.

Here's even more evidence of the importance of dividends. A study by John Slatter (an analyst with the Cleveland brokerage firm of Prescott Ball & Turben) and Harvey Knowles (a Merrill Lynch broker in Cincinnati) was reported in the January 1990 issue of *Money* magazine. According to the study, if one had kept his portfolio in the 10 Dow Jones Industrial Stocks with the highest dividend yield between 1968 and 1988, he would have produced a total return of 1,557 percent compared to only 426 percent for the Dow Jones 30 stocks as a group! (The term *total return* means dividends received plus capital appreciation.) I personally manage portfolios for some of my

FIGURE 4–3 Common Stock Returns

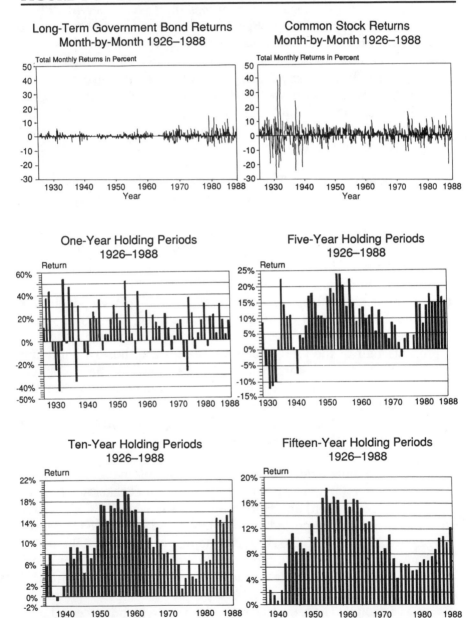

FIGURE 4-4 Dividend Growth for the Stock Market

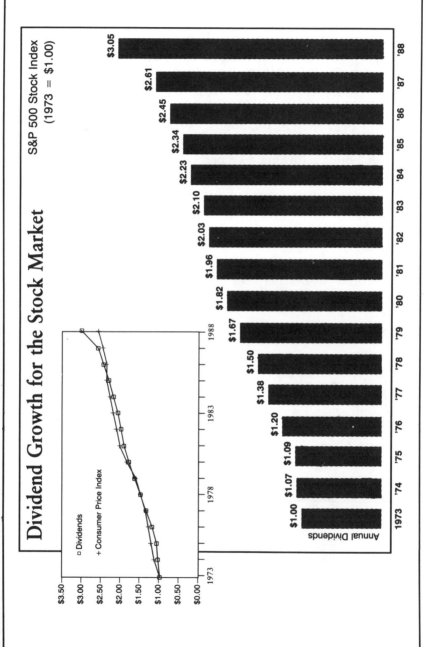

clients based primarily on this concept alone, expanded to include high dividend stocks not necessarily limited to the Dow Jones Industrial group. It is a simple but viable approach.

The return on bonds is also very interesting. Generally the returns have been more stable than stocks. However, in recent years the bond market has been volatile. The year 1981 marked the bottom of a very long-term bear market for bonds, comparable perhaps to the bear market low in stocks of 1932. In 1982 bonds began their reversal with corporate bonds returning 43.8 percent including interest plus appreciation—the best year ever. Figure 4-5 shows the long term trend in bond yields. Remember that bond prices move inversely to yields. Thus, during most of the post World War II period, interest rates were rising, taking bond prices lower. That accounts for the low long term total return of bonds. Since 1981 bonds have been performing quite well relative to other assets.

Here's how. assets perform annually during each decade of the Ibbotson study.

TABLE 4-1

	1920s*	'30s	'40s	'50s	'60s	'70s	'80s
S&P 500	19.2%	0.0%	9.2%	19.4%	7.8%	5.9%	17.5%
Small companies	−4.5	1.4	20.7	16.9	15.5	11.5	15.8
Long-term gov't.	5.0	4.9	3.2	−0.1	1.4	5.5	12.6
Long-term Corp.	5.2	6.9	2.7	1.0	1.7	6.2	13.0
Treasury bills	3.7	.6	.4	1.9	3.9	6.3	8.9
Inflation	−1.1	−2.0	5.4	2.2	2.5	7.4	5.1

*Based on the period 1926–1929.

The following charts show an even longer perspective on bond yields and inflation. Figure 4-6 shows long-term U.S. government bond yields and inflation from 1798 to 1985. Figure 4-7 shows a history of wholesale prices and real interest rates. The bottom portion specifically shows a five year moving average of real interest rates on long-term U.S. government bonds. "Real" interest rates means taking the actual yield and then subtracting the rate of inflation. The value of this chart is to show that each time real interest rates reached a high

FIGURE 4-5 Long-Term Bond Yields

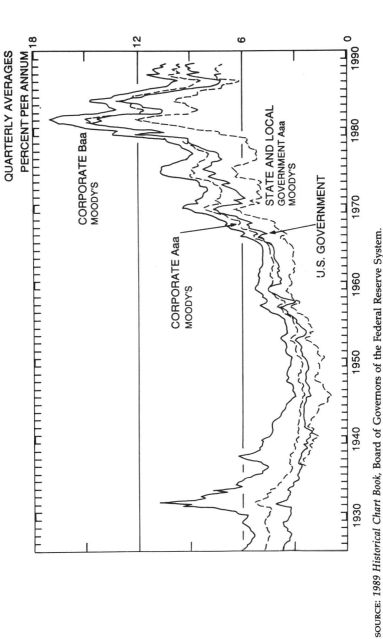

LONG-TERM BOND YIELDS

QUARTERLY AVERAGES

PERCENT PER ANNUM

CORPORATE Baa
MOODY'S

CORPORATE Aaa
MOODY'S

STATE AND LOCAL
GOVERNMENT Aaa
MOODY'S

U.S. GOVERNMENT

SOURCE: *1989 Historical Chart Book*, Board of Governors of the Federal Reserve System.

FIGURE 4-6 Inflation and Long-Term Bond Yields

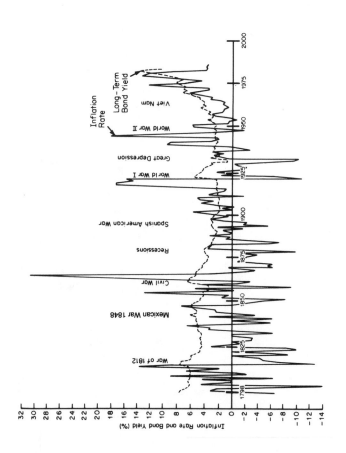

SOURCE: Bond Yields from Sidney Homer, "Long-Term Bond Yields from Medieval Time to 1975," in *A History of Interest Rates.* Copyright 1977 by Rutgers; the State University. Updates from Roger G. Ibbotson and Gary P. Brinson from their book *Gaining the Performance Advantage* (New York. McGraw-Hill, 1987).

**FIGURE 4–7   A History of Wholesale Prices and
Real Interest Rates**

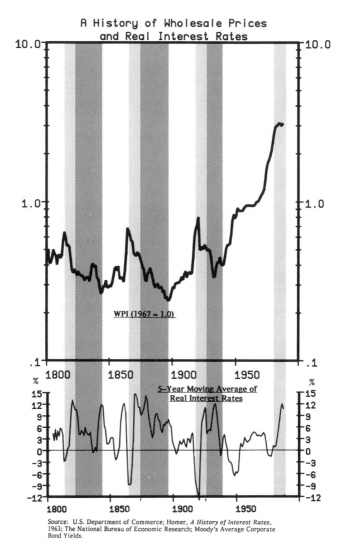

A History of Wholesale Prices
and Real Interest Rates

WPI (1967 = 1.0)

5–Year Moving Average of
Real Interest Rates

Source: U.S. Department of Commerce; Homer, *A History of Interest Rates*,
1963; The National Bureau of Economic Research; Moody's Average Corporate
Bond Yields.

Chart provided compliments of Comstock Partners, Inc./New York, N.Y.
SOURCE: U.S. Department of Commerce: Homer, *A History of Interest Rates*, 1963; The
National Bureau of Economic Research; Moody's Average Corporate Bond Yields.

point similar to the 1980s, a subsequent decline took rates much lower over many years to follow.

On the top part of the chart, the lightly shaded areas indicate early phases of secular depressions, and the darker shadings indicate the later and more severe stages. The chart was provided compliments of the investment management firm of Constock Partners, Inc., New York. They point out that the 1980s truly deserve the term *depression.* Witness the collapse of the oil and farm economies, as well as real estate in some areas of the country. As you ponder these various charts, hopefully you will begin to develop a sense of history about economics and the investment markets.

How about real estate? The real estate market is larger than the bond and stock markets. Figure 4–8 indicates that in the mid-1980s real estate made up about 55 percent of the major U.S. investment assets, while stocks and bonds accounted for less than 45 percent. Of interest, owner-occupied, single family homes make up over 60 percent of the market value of real estate.

Figure 4–9 shows how unleveraged real estate performed over the approximately 40 years between the mid-1940s and mid-1980s. This chart shows that unleveraged real estate has done extremely well, second only to common stocks over this period. When leveraged, as is often the case, real estate has done even better than this chart indicates.

For comparison, Figure 4–10 shows how short-term interest rates changed from the late 1920s to the mid-1980s. (If a picture is worth a thousand words, this chapter will be like reading the Old Testament.)

And finally, how about precious metals and collectibles? According to Ibbotson and Brinson, gold has an expected real return near zero.[2] That is, it should track inflation. In Britain, the compound real return from gold over four centuries was 0.1 percent per year. In the United States it was 0.7 percent per year over two centuries. However, Figure 4–11 is very interesting. It shows various assets over the one, five, ten, and twenty years ending 1990. U.S. coins are at the top of the list over twenty years, while foreign exchange is at the bottom! But note also that different time periods show much different annual performance rankings for various assets. The moral here is that, in the short run, anything can happen! And what happens to be the best performer in one period may not be so hot in another.

FIGURE 4-8 Composition of U.S. Investment Assets

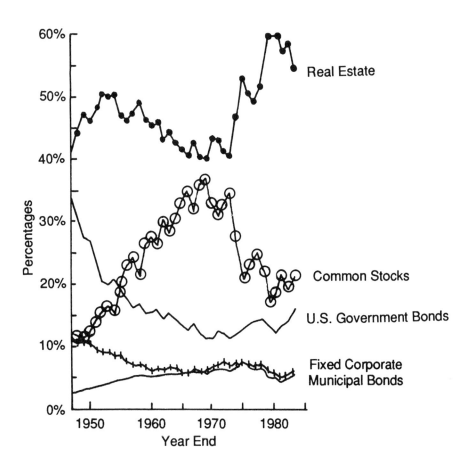

SOURCE: Roger G. Ibbotson and Gary P. Brinson, *Gaining the Performance Advantage* (New York, McGraw-Hill, 1987).

FIGURE 4–9   Performance of U.S. Investment Assets

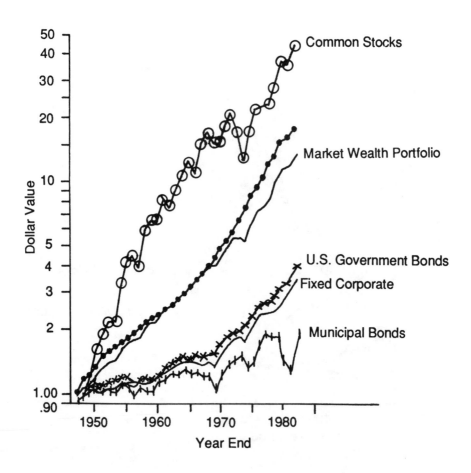

SOURCE: Roger G. Ibbotson and Gary P. Brinson, *Gaining the Performance Advantage* (New York, McGraw-Hill, 1987).

FIGURE 4-10 Short-Term Interest Rates: Business Borrowing (Prime Rate, Effective Date of Change; Commercial Paper, Quarterly Averages)

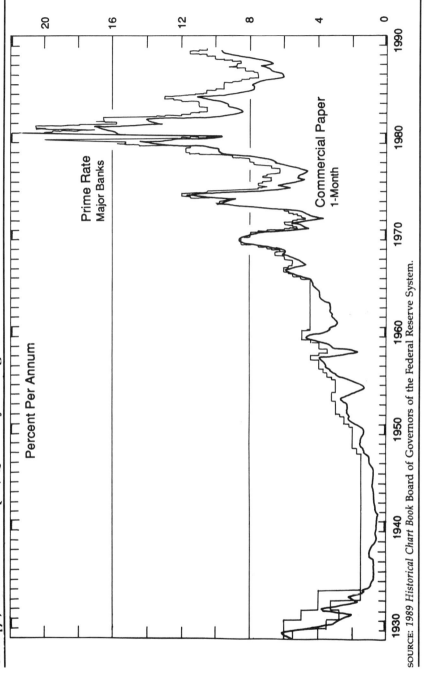

SOURCE: *1989 Historical Chart Book* Board of Governors of the Federal Reserve System.

FIGURE 4-11 Financial and Tangible Assets–Compound Annual Rates of Return

	20 Years	Rank	10 Years	Rank	5 Years	Rank	1 Year	Rank
U.S. Coins	17.3	1	7.3	6	15.0	3	14.6	4
Chinese Ceramics[a]	14.4	2	7.6	5	14.6	4	18.0	2
Stocks[d]	12.7	3	17.3	1	17.7	2	15.4	3
Old Masters[a]	12.7	3	12.3	3	23.9	1	44.5	1
Gold	12.3	4	-4.3	13	3.0	11	0.5	12
Diamonds[c]	10.7	5	6.4	7	11.8	7	5.5	8
Bonds[d]	9.6	6	12.6	2	12.0	5	7.5	7
Oil	9.0	7	-3.8	12	-7.0	14	-0.7	13
3-Mos. Treasury Bills[b]	8.6	8	9.5	4	7.0	8	8.3	6
Housing	7.4	9	4.7	9	5.0	9	2.4	11
U.S. Farmland	6.5	10	-0.6	11	-0.6	12	3.9	10
CPI	6.2	11	4.8	8	3.8	10	4.4	9
Silver	5.4	12	-10.2	14	-4.0	13	-2.9	14
Foreign Exchange	4.4	13	1.5	10	11.9	6	10.5	5

[a] Source: Sotheby's
[b] Stock returns assume quarterly reinvestment of dividends. Bond returns assume monthly reinvestment.
[c] Source: The Diamond Registry.
CPI Consumer Price Index.
Note: All returns are for the period ended June 1, 1990, based on latest available data. Information provided by Salomon, Inc./New York, N.Y.

The goal of most investors is to beat the market. It is not easy to do. Some mutual funds have succeeded in doing so, however. We noted earlier how the Real World Example Fund Number One, a growth fund, for instance, returned approximately 15 percent annually between 1954 and 1989, after all commissions (8.5 percent load) and expenses, while inflation was about 5 percent over the same time period. Of note, long term corporate bonds returned about 6 percent during the same period, and the S&P 500 returned 11 percent. Thus the fund outperformed inflation by approximately 10 percent annually, the bond market by 9 percent, and stocks by 4 percent.

We also looked at the Real World Example Fund Number Two, a growth and income mutual fund. This fund has an even longer record, going back to 1934. Over its 54-year history between 1934 and 1987, it returned nearly 13 percent annually after all commissions (8.5 percent front end load) and expenses compared to 4 percent for inflation, 5 percent for corporate bonds, and 11 percent for the S&P 500 stocks. Thus, the fund returned a premium of better than 8 percent over inflation, 7 percent better than corporate bonds, and 2 percent better than stocks.

Relative Long-Term Performance Of Top Mutual Funds

	Return over Inflation	Return over Bonds	Return over the S&P 500
Real World Example Fund No.1	10%	9%	4%
Real World Example Fund No.2	8%	7%	2%

Thus a reasonable long term goal of professional management appears to be 2 to 4 percent better than the stock market as a whole or 8 to 10 percent over inflation. Is 2 percent better performance worth the effort? Indeed it is. Each incremental increase in return becomes very significant in the long run, as these tables indicate:

$1,000,000 Lump Sum Invested at Various Compounded Annual Returns Grows To:

	10 Years	25 Years	40 Years
10%	$2,600,000	$11,000,000	$ 45,000,000
12%	3,100,000	17,000,000	93,000,000
14%	3,700,000	26,000,000	189,000,000

$30,000 Invested Annually at Various Compounded Annual Returns Grows To:

	10 Years	25 Years	40 Years
10%	$530,000	$3,200,000	$15,000,000
12%	590,000	4,500,000	26,000,000
14%	660,000	6,200,000	46,000,000

Many stock mutual funds fail to exceed the returns of the market as a whole. Figure 4–12 shows all mutual funds in existence for the entire 30-year period ending 1988 for which information is available.

FIGURE 4-12

Equity Mutual Funds in Existence for 30 Years (Period Ending 1988)

Growth or Growth and Income Objective, in Order of Fund Performance	30 Year Total Return (%)	Annual Rate of Return for 30 Years (%)
Fund Number 1.	7734.2%	15.6%
2.	2743.5	11.8
3.	2727.2	11.8
4.	2642.1	11.7
5.	2592.8	11.6
6.	2569.2	11.6
7.	2371.5	11.3
8.	2302.4	11.2
9.	2219.9	11.0
10.	2136.3	10.9
11.	2012.9	10.7
12.	1972.5	10.6
13.	1964.2	10.5
14.	1884.1	10.4
15.	1868.6	10.4
16.	1867.2	10.4
17.	1755.4	10.2
18.	1728.6	10.2
19.	1706.6	10.1
20.	1638.4	10.0
21.	1619.5	9.9
22.	1575.1	9.9
Standard & Poor's 500 Comp.	1567.4	9.8
23.	1549.9	9.8
24.	1546.4	9.8
25.	1537.0	9.8
26.	1522.4	9.7
27.	1502.9	9.7
28.	1474.7	9.6
29.	1473.6	9.6
30.	1433.3	9.5
31.	1400.1	9.4
32.	1384.5	9.4
33.	1370.7	9.4
34.	1337.2	9.3
35.	1330.3	9.3
36.	1272.3	9.1
37.	1255.3	9.1
38.	1255.3	9.1
39.	1252.1	9.1
40.	1243.7	9.0
41.	1207.4	8.9

FIGURE 4–12 *continued*

Equity Mutual Funds in Existence for 30 Years (Period Ending 1988)

Growth or Growth and Income Objective, in Order of Fund Performance	30 Year Total Return (%)	Annual Rate of Return for 30 Years (%)
42.	1177.0	8.9
43.	1160.4	8.8
44.	1159.9	8.8
45.	1158.4	8.8
46.	1152.4	8.8
47.	1151.4	8.8
48.	1150.8	8.8
49.	1146.8	8.8
50.	1123.8	8.7
51.	1103.0	8.6
52.	1095.8	8.6
53.	1066.6	8.5
54.	1055.0	8.5
55.	1031.5	8.4
56.	1008.6	8.3
57.	966.8	8.2
58.	948.3	8.1
59.	923.5	8.1
60.	888.3	7.9
61.	840.5	7.8
62.	812.1	7.6
63.	793.4	7.6
64.	740.5	7.4
65.	697.8	7.2
66.	679.3	7.1
67.	677.7	7.1
68.	607.9	6.7
69.	584.8	6.6
70.	577.2	6.6
71.	77.2	1.9

Wow! What a difference in performance! The top mutual fund was up 7,734 percent while the bottom fund was up just 77 percent. Approximately one-third of all funds beat the market. The Real World Example Fund Number One was the top performer on this list. The Real World Example Fund Number Two was in position number 4. (Remember, these are not the actual names, which I must omit because it would require a prospectus with each copy of this book.)

A closer look at the long term record of a fund like Real World Example Fund Number Two is very instructive. There have been many years of difficulty. Studying Figure 4–13, one can gain a great feel for history.

Notice that there were many, many times when you could have bought this fund and two or even more years later you would still have had a loss! But if you were patient, you would have eventually been rewarded. This is a very important point. The long-term for common stocks and well managed mutual funds is very good. But, it takes patience. The long-term uptrend is frequently interrupted with downswings. Short-term performance is always uncertain and subject to volatility. Superior returns can be achieved in stocks, *but only if you recognize that there will be ups and downs and you are able to hold on for a few years.*

Figure 4–14 is instructional. Notice the chart on the left hand side entitled "15 Years of Building." It shows the results of accumulating $250 per month for every 15-year period in Real World Example Fund Number Two's history between 1934 and 1989. Notice that there was a significant difference in the ending value, but in every time period a significant profit resulted.

Figure 4–14 also shows how a mutual fund can be turned into an income vehicle as needs arise, such as during retirement. Figure 4–14 (continued) shows 10, 20, and 25-year comparisons of regular monthly investing.

I track mutual funds and have developed an index of growth funds and an index of income/balanced funds (Figure 4–15). These indexes consist of a maximum of 20 mutual funds in each category considered to be among the best managed funds. The growth funds are primarily common stock funds. The income funds are fixed income and/or balanced funds that invest in bonds but may also include stocks. Annual returns are the performance of net asset values, assuming reinvestment of dividends and capital gains, but excluding commissions. Though past performance is no guarantee of the future, here is how the index has faired. The growth funds have produced a total result almost double that of the Standard & Poors 500 Index over the 17-year period shown. And the income funds have more than doubled the total of the Consumer Price Index, i.e., inflation.

FIGURE 4–13   Real World Example Fund Number Two

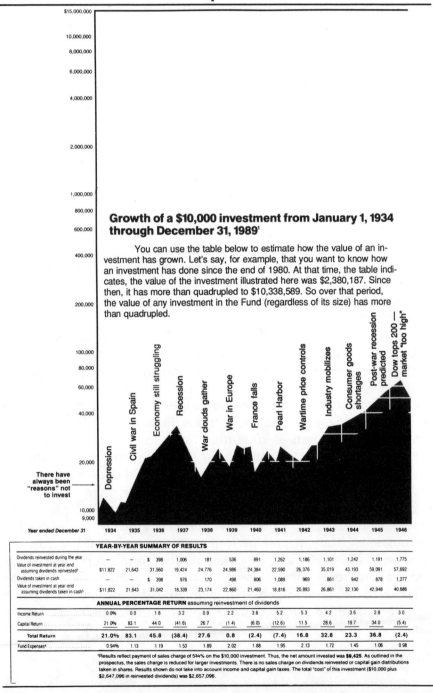

Growth of a $10,000 investment from January 1, 1934 through December 31, 1989[1]

You can use the table below to estimate how the value of an investment has grown. Let's say, for example, that you want to know how an investment has done since the end of 1980. At that time, the table indicates, the value of the investment illustrated here was $2,380,187. Since then, it has more than quadrupled to $10,338,589. So over that period, the value of any investment in the Fund (regardless of its size) has more than quadrupled.

Year ended December 31	1934	1935	1936	1937	1938	1939	1940	1941	1942	1943	1944	1945	1946
YEAR-BY-YEAR SUMMARY OF RESULTS													
Dividends reinvested during the year	—	—	$ 398	1,006	181	536	891	1,262	1,186	1,101	1,242	1,191	1,775
Value of investment at year-end assuming dividends reinvested[2]	$11,822	21,643	31,560	19,424	24,776	24,986	24,384	22,590	26,376	35,019	43,193	59,091	57,692
Dividends taken in cash	—	—	$ 398	976	170	498	806	1,089	969	861	942	878	1,277
Value of investment at year-end assuming dividends taken in cash[3]	$11,822	21,643	31,042	18,339	23,174	22,860	21,460	18,816	20,893	26,861	32,130	42,948	40,686
ANNUAL PERCENTAGE RETURN assuming reinvestment of dividends													
Income Return	0.0%	0.0	1.8	3.2	0.9	2.2	3.6	5.2	5.3	4.2	3.6	2.8	3.0
Capital Return	21.0%	83.1	44.0	(41.6)	26.7	(1.4)	(6.0)	(12.6)	11.5	28.6	19.7	34.0	(5.4)
Total Return	21.0%	83.1	45.8	(38.4)	27.6	0.8	(2.4)	(7.4)	16.8	32.8	23.3	36.8	(2.4)
Fund Expenses[4]	0.94%	1.13	1.19	1.53	1.89	2.02	1.88	1.95	2.13	1.72	1.45	1.06	0.98

[1] Results reflect payment of sales charge of 5¾% on the $10,000 investment. Thus, the net amount invested was **$9,425**. As outlined in the prospectus, the sales charge is reduced for larger investments. There is no sales charge on dividends reinvested or capital gain distributions taken in shares. Results shown do not take into account income and capital gain taxes. The total "cost" of this investment ($10,000 plus $2,647,096 in reinvested dividends) was $2,657,096.

FIGURE 4–13 *continued*

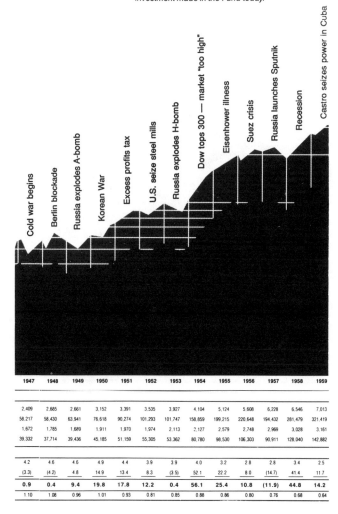

During the period illustrated, stock prices fluctuated and were higher at the end than at the beginning. These results should not be considered as a representation of the dividend income or capital gain or loss which may be realized from an investment made in the Fund today.

	1947	1948	1949	1950	1951	1952	1953	1954	1955	1956	1957	1958	1959
	2,409	2,685	2,661	3,152	3,391	3,535	3,927	4,104	5,124	5,608	6,228	6,546	7,013
	58,217	58,430	63,941	76,618	90,274	101,293	101,747	158,859	199,215	220,648	194,432	281,479	321,419
	1,672	1,785	1,689	1,911	1,970	1,974	2,113	2,127	2,579	2,748	2,969	3,028	3,161
	39,332	37,714	39,436	45,185	51,159	55,305	53,362	80,780	98,530	106,303	90,911	128,040	142,882
	4.2	4.6	4.6	4.9	4.4	3.9	3.9	4.0	3.2	2.8	2.8	3.4	2.5
	(3.3)	(4.2)	4.8	14.9	13.4	8.3	(3.5)	52.1	22.2	8.0	(14.7)	41.4	11.7
	0.9	**0.4**	**9.4**	**19.8**	**17.8**	**12.2**	**0.4**	**56.1**	**25.4**	**10.8**	**(11.9)**	**44.8**	**14.2**
	1.10	1.08	0.96	1.01	0.93	0.81	0.85	0.88	0.86	0.80	0.76	0.68	0.64

FIGURE 4-13 *continued*

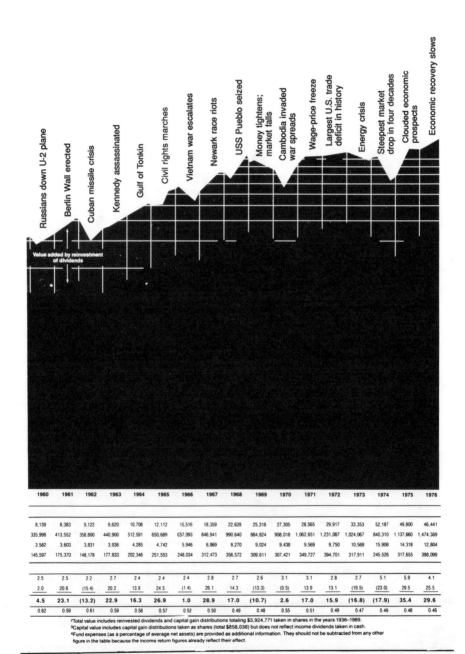

1960	1961	1962	1963	1964	1965	1966	1967	1968	1969	1970	1971	1972	1973	1974	1975	1976
8,139	8,383	9,122	9,620	10,708	12,112	15,516	18,359	22,628	25,318	27,305	28,565	29,917	33,353	52,187	49,800	46,441
335,998	413,552	358,800	440,900	512,591	650,689	657,093	846,941	990,640	884,824	908,018	1,062,651	1,231,087	1,024,067	840,310	1,137,660	1,474,369
3,582	3,603	3,831	3,936	4,285	4,742	5,946	6,869	8,270	9,024	9,438	9,569	9,750	10,569	15,908	14,318	12,804
145,597	175,370	148,178	177,833	202,346	251,553	248,034	312,473	356,572	309,611	307,421	349,727	394,701	317,911	245,526	317,655	398,099

2.5	2.5	2.2	2.7	2.4	2.4	2.4	2.8	2.7	2.6	3.1	3.1	2.8	2.7	5.1	5.9	4.1
2.0	20.6	(15.4)	20.2	13.9	24.5	(1.4)	26.1	14.3	(13.3)	(0.5)	13.9	13.1	(19.5)	(23.0)	29.5	25.5
4.5	**23.1**	**(13.2)**	**22.9**	**16.3**	**26.9**	**1.0**	**28.9**	**17.0**	**(10.7)**	**2.6**	**17.0**	**15.9**	**(16.8)**	**(17.9)**	**35.4**	**29.6**
0.62	0.59	0.61	0.59	0.58	0.57	0.52	0.50	0.49	0.48	0.55	0.51	0.49	0.47	0.49	0.48	0.46

2Total value includes reinvested dividends and capital gain distributions totaling $3,924,771 taken in shares in the years 1936–1989.
3Capital value includes capital gain distributions taken as shares (total $858,038) but does not reflect income dividends taken in cash.
4Fund expenses (as a percentage of average net assets) are provided as additional information. They should not be subtracted from any other
figure in the table because the income return figures already reflect their effect.

FIGURE 4–13 *continued*

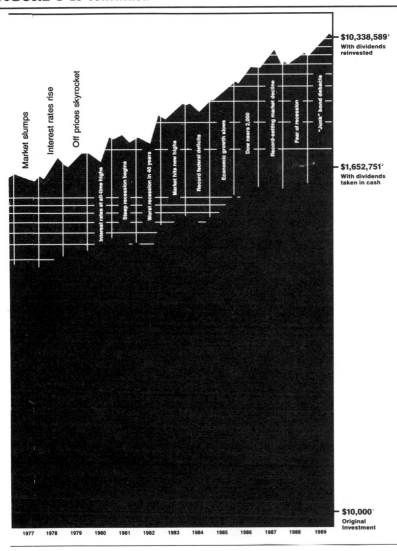

	1977	1978	1979	1980	1981	1982	1983	1984	1985	1986	1987	1988	1989	
	49,838	55,969	69,960	91,302	115,901	146,105	147,156	160,449	174,890	203,830	267,489	318,747	370,835	**Average annual compound rate of return for 56 years**
	1,436,402	1,647,483	1,963,310	2,380,187	2,401,091	3,211,997	3,859,712	4,117,187	5,491,890	6,685,657	7,049,178	7,989,285	10,338,589	
	13,279	14,386	17,347	21,746	26,420	31,589	30,264	31,680	33,152	37,328	47,452	54,382	60,741	
	374,307	414,421	475,669	552,242	530,864	670,590	774,518	791,971	1,017,904	1,200,518	1,220,928	1,327,375	1,652,751	
	3.4	3.9	4.3	4.6	4.9	6.1	4.6	4.2	4.2	3.7	4.0	4.5	4.6	**3.41%**
	(6.0)	10.8	14.9	16.6	(4.0)	27.7	15.6	2.5	29.2	18.0	1.4	8.8	24.8	**9.79%**
	(2.6)	14.7	19.2	21.2	0.9	33.8	20.2	6.7	33.4	21.7	5.4	13.3	29.4	**13.20%**
	0.49	0.49	0.47	0.46	0.45	0.46	0.44	0.47	0.43	0.41	0.42	0.48	0.52	

FIGURE 4–14   Real World Example Fund Number Two: A History

If you're interested in a retirement plan, here's how a couple laid a solid foundation by accumulating shares through 15 years of monthly investing. . .

Many shareholders who reinvest all of their income dividends and capital gain distributions while they are accumulating shares find it helpful to begin taking these dividends and distributions in cash when they retire.

Such was the case with John and Martha Thomas, who began an accumulation program by investing $250 on January 1, 1955. They added $100 each month thereafter until John retired 15 years later at the end of 1969. By that time, the value of their investment (shown by the circled number below) had grown to $43,687.

Now John and Martha began to take all their dividends and capital gain distributions in cash. The right-hand table shows what they received each year and the fluctuations in the year-end value of their shares for the past 20 years. As you can see, over the past two decades they received $47,206 in dividends and $58,668 in capital gain distributions—a total of $105,874 in cash. And by the end of 1989 the value of their holdings has grown to $100,801.

15 Years of Building
Total Investments: $18,150

January 1-Dec. 31	Dividends Reinvested	Total Cost (including dividends)	Capital Gains Taken in Shares*	Ending Value of Shares
1934-1948	$ 8,972	$27,122	$11,188	$40,357
1935-1949	8,846	26,996	10,259	38,527
1936-1950	8,820	26,970	9,354	40,519
1937-1951	9,421	27,571	10,020	44,541
1938-1952	10,215	28,365	11,230	47,692
1939-1953	10,227	28,377	10,658	42,977
1940-1954	10,243	28,393	11,938	60,648
1941-1955	10,298	28,448	14,756	67,649
1942-1956	10,089	28,239	16,958	65,444
1943-1957	9,499	27,649	16,609	48,957
1944-1958	9,164	27,314	15,849	61,944
1945-1959	8,901	27,051	17,252	62,244
1946-1960	8,888	27,038	17,762	58,244
1947-1961	8,971	27,121	18,863	65,246
1948-1962	8,752	26,902	18,213	50,356
1949-1963	8,404	26,554	17,499	54,607
1950-1964	7,818	25,968	10,343	54,461
1951-1965	7,298	25,448	17,408	59,271
1952-1966	7,095	25,245	18,082	51,926
1953-1967	6,919	25,069	17,345	57,712
1954-1968	6,725	24,875	15,745	57,316
1955-1969	6,529	24,679	15,269	43,687
1956-1970	6,601	24,751	14,319	40,111
1957-1971	6,688	24,838	12,768	42,369
1958-1972	6,641	24,791	11,868	43,973
1959-1973	6,430	24,580	10,343	32,249
1960-1974	6,905	25,055	8,555	24,267
1961-1975	7,079	25,229	7,130	29,962
1962-1976	7,112	25,262	6,339	35,558
1963-1977	6,972	25,122	5,623	31,328
1964-1978	6,800	24,950	4,308	32,327
1965-1979	6,909	25,059	3,625	35,115
1966-1980	7,294	25,444	3,494	38,981
1967-1981	7,955	26,105	5,160	36,255
1968-1982	8,894	27,044	6,422	45,064
1969-1983	9,697	27,847	7,404	50,324
1970-1984	10,474	28,624	8,614	49,994
1971-1985	10,848	28,998	9,396	60,360
1972-1986	11,417	29,567	18,658	66,844
1973-1987	12,392	30,542	20,098	64,353
1974-1988	13,336	31,486	24,287	66,028
1975-1989	13,632	31,782	21,724	74,302

20 Years of Benefiting
$43,687—Net asset value of shares accumulated as of December 31, 1969†

Year Ended Dec. 31	Dividends in Cash	Capital Gains in Cash	Value at Year-End
1970	$ 1,291	$ 1,918	$ 41,438
1971	1,291	860	46,267
1972	1,291	1,554	50,632
1973	1,357	1,091	39,652
1974	1,985	0	30,624
1975	1,787	232	39,388
1976	1,588	761	48,582
1977	1,621	926	44,745
1978	1,720	0	49,541
1979	2,050	595	56,221
1980	2,513	1,323	63,827
1981	2,843	4,365	57,147
1982	3,174	3,638	67,399
1983	2,909	2,976	74,476
1984	2,912	3,373	72,757
1985	2,912	3,241	89,358
1986	2,912	16,205	87,242
1987	3,441	4,961	83,405
1988	3,705	5,027	85,588
1989	3,904	5,622	100,801
Totals:	**$47,206**	**$58,668**	

* The value of the shares acquired with these capital gain distributions is reflected in "Ending Value of Shares."

† If all shares had been purchased at offering price (which includes the sales commission as described in the prospectus) on December 31, 1969 instead of accumulated in the shareholder account, the cost would have been $46,366.

FIGURE 4-14 *continued*

If you're interested in investing monthly

Here's what would have happened if you had invested $250 and added $100 every month...

...for 10 Years

(Total investments: $12,150)

Here's how you would have done in every 10-year period in the Fund's history:

Jan. 1-Dec. 31	Dividends Reinvested	Total Cost (including dividends)	Capital Gains Taken in Shares*	Ending Value of Shares	Jan. 1-Dec. 31	Dividends Reinvested	Total Cost (including dividends)	Capital Gains Taken in Shares*	Ending Value of Shares
1934-1943	$2,894	$15,044	$2,176	$20,301	1958-1967	$2,203	$14,353	$5,693	$25,137
1935-1944	2,797	14,947	2,172	21,652	1959-1968	2,232	14,382	5,203	25,456
1936-1945	2,595	14,745	3,148	25,638	1960-1969	2,347	14,497	5,434	20,422
1937-1946	2,866	15,016	4,060	23,278	1961-1970	2,401	14,551	5,046	18,931
1938-1947	3,434	15,584	4,691	22,665	1962-1971	2,450	14,600	4,351	20,113
1939-1948	3,651	15,801	4,445	20,370	1963-1972	2,389	14,539	3,906	20,701
1940-1949	3,771	15,921	4,384	20,366	1964-1973	2,295	14,445	3,244	15,292
1941-1950	3,867	16,017	4,201	21,961	1965-1974	2,472	14,622	2,355	11,575
1942-1951	3,815	15,965	4,250	22,728	1966-1975	2,556	14,706	1,733	14,568
1943-1952	3,527	15,677	4,058	21,666	1967-1976	2,572	14,722	1,485	17,563
1944-1953	3,408	15,558	3,595	19,207	1968-1977	2,614	14,764	1,379	16,089
1945-1954	3,306	15,456	3,944	26,649	1969-1978	2,724	14,874	1,049	17,508
1946-1955	3,384	15,534	5,137	29,928	1970-1979	2,941	15,091	998	19,770
1947-1956	3,535	15,685	6,459	30,247	1971-1980	3,159	15,309	1,157	21,935
1948-1957	3,538	15,688	6,721	23,668	1972-1981	3,545	15,695	2,228	20,434
1949-1958	3,457	15,607	6,468	30,248	1973-1982	4,074	16,224	3,016	25,498
1950-1959	3,215	15,365	6,888	29,341	1974-1983	4,411	16,561	3,527	27,938
1951-1960	3,009	15,159	6,656	26,123	1975-1984	4,442	16,592	3,899	26,153
1952-1961	2,831	14,981	6,560	27,678	1976-1985	4,339	16,489	4,007	30,036
1953-1962	2,632	14,782	5,896	20,719	1977-1986	4,380	16,530	8,124	31,882
1954-1963	2,368	14,518	5,180	21,618	1978-1987	4,497	16,647	8,138	28,996
1955-1964	2,139	14,289	4,901	21,362	1979-1988	4,548	16,698	8,112	28,103
1956-1965	2,079	14,229	5,192	24,124	1980-1989	4,517	16,667	7,722	30,820
1957-1966	2,143	14,293	5,721	21,923					

...for 20 Years

(Total investments: $24,150)

Here's how you would have done in every 20-year period in the Fund's history:

Jan. 1-Dec. 31	Dividends Reinvested	Total Cost (including dividends)	Capital Gains Taken in Shares*	Ending Value of Shares	Jan. 1-Dec. 31	Dividends Reinvested	Total Cost (including dividends)	Capital Gains Taken in Shares*	Ending Value of Shares
1934-1953	$21,255	$45,405	$22,726	$ 77,838	1953-1972	$16,503	$40,653	$30,838	$ 91,422
1935-1954	20,467	44,617	23,711	105,858	1954-1973	15,573	39,723	26,724	65,252
1936-1955	20,120	44,270	27,734	115,985	1955-1974	15,597	39,747	21,590	46,402
1937-1956	21,085	45,235	33,430	118,827	1956-1975	15,806	39,956	18,485	56,532
1938-1957	22,612	46,762	37,106	98,976	1957-1976	15,783	39,933	16,695	66,457
1939-1958	22,440	46,590	36,648	127,811	1958-1977	15,605	39,755	15,192	58,510
1940-1959	22,379	46,529	40,768	131,141	1959-1978	15,149	39,299	12,367	59,626
1941-1960	22,158	46,308	41,933	121,966	1960-1979	15,451	39,601	10,998	64,794
1942-1961	21,321	45,471	42,515	131,329	1961-1980	16,061	40,211	10,480	71,221
1943-1962	19,814	43,964	39,356	97,105	1962-1981	17,170	41,320	13,161	65,593
1944-1963	18,877	43,027	37,576	104,348	1963-1982	18,337	42,487	14,717	79,189
1945-1964	18,215	42,365	38,165	107,033	1964-1983	18,904	43,054	15,373	85,094
1946-1965	17,956	42,106	40,399	121,593	1965-1984	19,611	43,761	16,546	82,214
1947-1966	18,424	42,574	44,269	111,726	1966-1985	20,320	44,470	17,557	99,746
1948-1967	18,518	42,668	44,262	127,791	1967-1986	21,318	45,468	32,868	110,982
1949-1968	18,700	42,850	42,607	131,565	1968-1987	23,032	47,182	35,370	107,389
1950-1969	18,281	42,431	35,231	100,929	1969-1988	25,157	49,307	44,369	112,433
1951-1970	17,717	41,867	38,664	89,242	1970-1989	27,384	51,534	41,496	134,166
1952-1971	17,225	41,375	33,981	90,980					

...for 25 Years

(Total investments: $30,150)

Here's how you would have done in every 25-year period in the Fund's history:

Jan. 1-Dec. 31	Dividends Reinvested	Total Cost (including dividends)	Capital Gains Taken in Shares*	Ending Value of Shares	Jan. 1-Dec. 31	Dividends Reinvested	Total Cost (including dividends)	Capital Gains Taken in Shares*	Ending Value of Shares
1934-1958	$42,934	$73,084	$68,854	$224,329	1950-1974	$38,440	$68,590	$49,420	$100,828
1935-1959	41,292	71,442	73,171	222,688	1951-1975	37,417	67,567	47,663	118,183
1936-1960	40,120	70,270	73,548	203,548	1952-1976	36,015	66,165	42,145	134,004
1937-1961	41,109	71,259	78,923	231,456	1953-1977	34,402	64,552	37,444	113,961
1938-1962	43,019	73,169	82,102	189,468	1954-1978	32,492	62,642	30,616	112,809
1939-1963	42,047	72,197	80,587	207,593	1955-1979	31,319	61,469	26,082	116,603
1940-1964	41,551	71,701	83,798	216,983	1956-1980	32,116	62,266	24,579	126,903
1941-1965	40,704	70,854	88,127	245,078	1957-1981	33,880	64,030	28,922	116,000
1942-1966	39,900	70,050	92,322	216,796	1958-1982	36,054	66,204	31,517	140,074
1943-1967	38,226	68,376	88,415	238,212	1959-1983	36,718	66,868	32,114	149,136
1944-1968	38,129	68,279	84,600	243,398	1960-1984	38,154	68,304	23,187	144,556
1945-1969	38,314	68,464	86,100	191,733	1961-1985	39,179	69,329	35,621	174,247
1946-1970	38,834	68,984	83,153	176,281	1962-1986	40,714	70,864	61,773	192,767
1947-1971	39,677	69,827	77,801	187,763	1963-1987	42,614	72,764	64,343	182,342
1948-1972	39,175	69,325	73,490	193,366	1964-1988	44,506	74,656	79,254	184,455
1949-1973	38,382	68,532	67,189	142,078	1965-1989	46,857	77,007	69,622	214,677

*The value of the shares acquired with these capital gain distributions is reflected in "Ending Value of Shares."

FIGURE 4–15

Meek's Elite Mutual Fund Indexes

Year	Growth Fund Index	(S&P 500)	Income Fund Index	(Inflation)
1973	−19.1%	−14.7%	−7.2%	8.8%
1974	−20.4	−26.5	−9.7	12.2
1975	41.7	37.2	24.6	7.0
1976	31.5	23.8	25.2	4.8
1977	14.0	−7.2	4.4	6.8
1978	17.5	6.6	5.0	9.0
1979	35.8	18.4	10.3	13.3
1980	32.0	32.4	6.1	12.4
1981	5.4	−4.9	5.6	8.9
1982	27.4	21.4	34.5	3.9
1983	28.2	22.5	13.6	3.8
1984	6.4	6.3	12.9	4.0
1985	28.1	32.2	23.5	3.8
1986	18.3	18.5	16.8	1.1
1987	10.9	5.2	4.5	4.1
1988	18.8	16.6	10.3	4.6
1989	24.2	31.6	12.7	4.6
1990	−5.7	−3.1	2.0	6.6
Total	1,111.2%	609.5%	470.9%	212.3%
Annual	14.9%	11.5%	10.2%	6.5%

This chapter is designed to show the reader historical returns on various types of investments. The past does not guarantee similar returns in the future. The application of various investment alternatives is what the rest of the book is about. Let's see now if we can begin to put it all together.

Endnotes

[1]Roger G. Ibbotson and Rex A. Sinquefield, *Stocks, Bonds, Bills and Inflation (SBBI), 1990 Yearbook*

[2]Roger G. Ibbotson and Gary P. Brinson (*Gaining the Performance Advantage, Investment Markets*) New York: McGraw-Hill, 1987.

5

Asset Allocation "The Boz" Of Your Financial LIfe

There has been a famous linebacker in professional football known as *the Boz*. My wife didn't like this particular image much, but I like to use a football analogy in looking at investing. To be a good investor, you've got to have both a good offense and a good defense. However, the defense is more important. You can score 20 or 30 points in a football game, but still lose a lot of games—as my favorite team, the Dallas Cowboys, have proved on too many Sunday afternoons in recent seasons. On the other hand, if you can hold your opponents to 7 points, you'll be in the Super Bowl in most years.

A great linebacker is bold and aggressive, but his job is not to score points. It is to get the ball back for the offense. A great investor does the same thing, in my opinion. You need to have a little of the Boz in your investment life.

A good football team must have a game plan—for every season, every game, every play. You need to use judgment about your opponents' strengths and weaknesses, and what plays they may run in various circumstances. But you need to be able to adjust as things change.

As the defensive captain, you need to line your guys up based on an analysis of all the facts at hand. Let's say, for example, that it is third and long, late in a close game. You decide to send only three rushers, with everybody else dropping back for a pass. But the offensive team fools you, and they run a draw play. Of course, you must be able to adjust in the middle of the play to stop them. Investing is really a lot like that. The economy is liable to run a draw play when you were expecting a pass. You need your team to be lined up in a flexible enough formation, so that no matter what happens, you can make the play.

There are many angles to understanding asset allocation. We have to understand several aspects of risk. We also have to make some judgment of probable returns. And, just as an athlete must learn to adapt to his or her own personal strengths and weaknesses, we have to appreciate many personal constraints. Here are some of the most important considerations of risk for which we need to be prepared:

Inflation Risk. If inflation averages 4 percent, the cost of living will double in 20 years. If inflation averages 6 percent, the cost of living will more than triple. In other words, if you anticipate needing $70,000 of retirement income in today's dollars, you will actually need between $140,000 and $220,000 in just 20 years! Carrying these projections out 30 to 50 years becomes so frightening that belaboring this point seems futile.

Reinvestment Risk. Many conservative investors think that investing in short-term money market instruments is the answer. Today, CD rates are about 8 percent. Some economists believe that interest rates could return to the levels of the 1950s and 1960s when interest rates were 4 percent. This is perhaps the greatest risk for many conservative retired investors. The possibility of having to reinvest at lower rates and the threat of their income falling in half is a huge risk; indeed far greater than the market risk of stocks, bonds, and real estate that they may dread.

Time Risk. As we learned in Chapter 3, there are long periods when every type of investment outperforms or underperforms the rest. For example, there are 10-year periods when stocks may produce 15 to 20 percent returns. In other 10-year periods, stocks have produced only 0 to 5 percent returns. Though we are highly confident of businesses, i.e. stocks, to produce superior returns over 20 to 50-year periods, we human beings tend to have finite lives! We have to have a strategy to deal with this dilemma.

Job Risk. Every job has its own set of risks. In a competitive society, and one with such technological change, our careers are continually threatened. It may not be wise to further increase these risks by making investments tied to your own company's stock or stocks in the same industry. Further, this risk dictates that a cash cushion should be kept at all times to hedge against job setbacks.

Location Risk.   Irrespective of all other risks, you are subject to the influences of your local economy. As a professional, your own business will likely be subject to the fortunes of your community. This risk is often magnified by the fixed obligation of your home and its accompanying mortgage. Obviously, having a disproportionately large portion of your assets in local real estate or regional bank stocks would magnify your exposure.

International Risk.   As our world gets smaller, we are greatly affected by international economic and political developments. Interest rates rising in Germany, free trade in the European common market, or a real estate decline in Japan, for example, may well have a significant impact on you. With two thirds of the world's investment alternatives outside the United States, you can no longer afford to isolate your investment dollars in America.

Life Expectancy Risk.   You just might live longer than you think! As life expectancies expand, the risk of outliving your capital is a very significant risk for many people. You need to plan for this possibility.

Ability Risk.   There are too many investment options for any one person to be an expert on. Being busy with your own business or profession will preclude you from spending the time it takes to adequately study many different investment options. You will need to call on outside sources to help you manage your money. You should have a plan to diversify your own ability but also to control the risk of using outside money managers.

Necessary Return Risk.   Depending on your age, earning power, and current assets, you may have a need to achieve a higher-than-normal investment return to achieve your goals. How will you confront this?

Emotional Risk.   How much volatility can you handle? The best long-term investments will have the highest volatility. If you cannot control your emotions of fear and greed, you will absolutely fail to achieve a good return in even the best investments. This risk may be in dire opposition to your necessary return profile. You need to have a firm handle on this.

Bias Risk.   All of us have biases. Sometimes well founded but often irrational, these biases are never easy to shed. This is certainly true in investing. If you cannot change unfounded biases, you will need to compensate in other ways.

Market Risk.   Last but not least is market risk. This is the one most people think about. In reality, it is just one element in the picture. If a painting has a dozen different colors in it, the one you will see first is red. But we need to appreciate the entire painting and all of its richness for the full impact.

The Investment Supermarket

Investing is somewhat like shopping in a grocery store. There are hundreds of items to choose from. But in this store there are only four aisles labeled:

- Nonmarket risk
- Extended income
- Equities
- Tangible assets

Nonmarket risk, as I define it, is any fixed income investment with a maturity of less than five years. This is primarily money market instruments including CDs, Treasury bills, money market funds, or bonds nearing maturity. It also includes other savings vehicles that you could access, such as annuities or life insurance cash value.

Extended income is primarily long-term bonds, that is fixed income investments with maturities over five years. It could also include certain high yielding stocks such as preferred stocks or public utility common stocks, many of which tend to act more like a bond than a stock. A preferred stock is a stock that pays a fixed dividend like a bond's fixed interest payment. Unlike a bond, a preferred stock has no maturity date and is, therefore, perpetual like a common stock. Preferred stocks are "junior" to bonds but are "senior" to common stocks. This means that bond interest must be paid before paying any preferred dividends, while preferred stock dividends are paid prior to common stock dividends.

Equities are businesses, primarily in the form of common stocks. Common stocks represent ownership of corporations. This category includes privately held businesses as well as publicly traded stocks.

Tangible assets include your home and other real estate, precious metals, collectibles, as well as the broad list of personal items that are part of your net worth.

Virtually every type of asset can be included in one of these four categories. For example, a mutual fund could fit into any of these four depending on what type of investments the fund concentrates on. For a balanced diet with good nutrition, one would certainly not shop in only one aisle. You will take items from all over the store, checking labels and analyzing freshness and food value relative to cost. And just as you would not fight a war with only tanks, you need to have every investment weapon at your disposal. The process of asset allocation is developing a game plan strategy of how much to invest in each of these four categories.

I recommend first deciding how much you want to have in nonmarket risk investments. The expected return matrix in Table 5–1 will help you do this. Basically this chart is a simple way to help you quantify risk versus reward. To construct the matrix, I took the information from historical returns from Chapter 3. Then, for risk I took the approximate number of years out of each 20 years that one could expect to lose money with various mixes of nonmarket risk and market risk investments. As we learned in Chapter 4, Treasury bills have returned about one half of 1 percent over inflation in the long term. In recent years, CDs have been yielding about 3 percent over the rate of inflation. This return is somewhat high from a long-term perspective, but it is reasonable to assume that we can get somewhere in between or about 2 percent over inflation on the most conservative investments. So in constructing the matrix, I used a 2 percent over inflation expected return for nonmarket risk investments. For market risk investments, I averaged the long-term returns for big stocks and small stocks along with today's yields on corporate bonds. This average turns out to be approximately 6 percent above inflation. As real estate has been, as best as we can tell, reasonably close with this return, we then can lump all market risk investments together to construct the matrix.

TABLE 5–1
Expected Return Matrix

Nonmarket Risk Investments	Market Risk Investments	Expected Annual Yield above Inflation	Expected Total Return above Inflation in 20 Years	Number of Years in Each 20 Expect to Lose Money
100%	0	2.0%	49%	0
90	10%	2.6	66	1
80	20	3.1	83	1
70	30	3.5	100	2
60	40	4.0	118	2
50	50	4.4	135	3
40	60	4.7	152	3
30	70	5.1	169	4
20	80	5.4	186	4
10	90	5.7	203	5
0	100	6.0	221	5

With the chart you can anticipate a risk/reward profile of your portfolio. For example, having 60 percent in nonmarket risk and 40 percent in market risk suggests annual returns of 4.0 percent better than inflation, growing to 118 percent over inflation in 20 years, with 2 losing years out of the 20 total years.

So how do we use this information? Let's say that your initial financial planning goals call for a desired return of about 5 percent above inflation. That implies a mix of about 70 percent in market risk investments. But let's say that your emotional risk tolerance tells you that you could handle only one year out of 20 in which your total return is negative. That implies having only 20 percent in market risk investments.

You then reach a compromise with yourself to split the difference and put 50 percent in market risk, including stocks, bonds, and real estate. Of course, you have to reconcile yourself to a few more down years in performance. And you have to go back and plug in a lower rate of return in your long range plan by lowering your goals (i.e., either stretching out your retirement date, lowering your expected standard of living, or increasing your savings).

Determining your emotional risk tolerance is not easy. The following little quiz may be of some help to you. I designed it to focus on the investor's emotional risk tolerance, but also included some broader questions of your financial risk tolerance. Some investors discover from this quiz that they are taking too much risk. Others may be surprised to discover that perhaps they are not accepting enough risk, and thus should shoot for a higher return.

Investor Risk Quiz

(Select the most appropriate answer)

Score

1. You are very competitive and are bothered by not achieving the excellent investment results of others.
   True (1 point)   False (0 points)   _____
2. Portfolio volatility (i.e., the total portfolio value bouncing up and down) doesn't bother you too much as long as it is essentially in phase with the general market. In other words, would you be willing to put up with a 10 percent or more down year in your portfolio occasionally in order to have a high probability of making 10 to 12 percent annually on average in the long run?
   True (1 point)   False (0 points)   _____
3. You are distressed if one individual security in your portfolio drops a great deal, even though the overall portfolio is doing OK.
   True (0 points)   False (1 point)   _____
4. You cannot afford a large drop in the income from your investments, as your lifestyle would be hindered.
   True (3 points)   False (1 point)   _____

(This one may deserve an explanation. Contrary to what you may think, if you have a modest net worth that is primarily in investments like CDs, you may actually have to take a higher risk on some of your investments. In other words, you really need to invest in long-term bonds and stocks to guard against a drop in interest rates.)

5. You have an investment that loses 15 percent of its value in a market correction a month after you buy it. Assuming that none of the fundamentals have changed, your gut reaction is to (select the one best answer only):

    (a) Sit tight and wait for it to journey back up. You recognize that even the best investments have their ups and downs, so why worry about it? (1 point)
    (b) Buy more—if it looked good at the original price, it looks even better now. I know that the only way to come out ahead is to take advantage of opportunities. (2 points)
    (c) Sell the turkey and rid yourself of further sleepless nights. (0 points)
    (d) Sell it, not because I'm worried about it, but because my experience tells me to sell my losers and hang onto my winners. (1 point)
    (e) You would sit tight for now, but determine to sell as soon as you get close to even. (0 points)
    (f) You would study the situation to determine why it dropped. Depending on whether the investment is still a good value or not, you might do any of the above. (2 points)
    (g) I wouldn't know what to do but would certainly worry about it. (0 points)   _____

6. You absolutely cannot handle any volatility in your investments and are very willing to accept a

much lower long-term return to eliminate portfolio volatility.

      True (0 points)   False (1 point)   —————

7. You are:
  (a) basically an optimist and a confident person. (3 points)
  (b) basically a pessimist and a worrier. (0 points)   —————

8. Your time horizon for good investment ideas to produce results is:
  (a) less than 2 years   (0 points)
  (b) 2 to 5 years   (1 point)
  (c) 5 to 10 years   (3 points)
  (d) over 10 years   (5 points)   —————

9. You understand how investments work and are comfortable with the concepts.

      True (1 point)   False (0 points)   —————
(After reading this book, you better say True!)

10. If inflation rises at just 4 percent a year, it will take twice as much income in 20 years to live on as it does today. If inflation rises at 6 percent a year, it will take 3 times as much income as today. This fact
  (a) Definitely bothers you and you feel the need to invest to beat inflation. (1 point)
  (b) You couldn't care less. (0 points)   —————

11. Your income and/or net worth are so high that it hardly matters what happens to your portfolio, you'll be fine.

      True (1 point)   False (0 point)   —————

12. Your thoughts on investment risk include:
  (a) It is possible to pretty much eliminate risk. (0 points)
  (b) There is risk in anything you do. The key is managing the risk. (1 point)   —————

13. When you get your monthly statement from your broker, if there has been a big change in the investments' values from the previous month, you

(a) have the strong urge to call him at home. (whether or not you actually call) (0 points)

(b) study the report in detail to see if any changes are necessary in your portfolio. (1 point)   _____

14. If you were to own stocks, and the Financial News Network has an interview with someone who warns of an impending recession,
    (a) your stomach tightens up. (0 points)
    (b) you react logically and unemotionally. (1 point)   _____

15. "The best time to invest is often during periods of disappointment and bad news. Also, sometimes the correct course of action is the least obvious one." You
    (a) disagree with this concept. (0 points)
    (b) agree with this concept. (1 point)   _____

16. If all your friends have been making big money in a particular type of investment, you
    (a) tend to jump in. (0 points)
    (b) are basically skeptical and can resist the temptation to go along with the crowd. (1 point)   _____

17. You are willing to risk the following percentage of your net worth on a single highly speculative investment?
    (a) less than 1%   (0 points)
    (b) 5–20%   (1 point)
    (c) over 50%   (0 points   _____
    (Answer (c) may also look strange at first glance. If you are willing to risk 50 percent of your net worth on a single investment, you might be too big of a gambler to do well, and should actually take less risk than you might want.)

18. Selling a stock at a loss is, for you,
    (a) not hard to do if logic fully supports a further decline. (1 point)

    (b) is an absolutely gut wrenching experience. (0
          points)   _____
19. You can't sleep nights if you
     (a) have too much in the market. (0 points)
     (b) have too little in the market. (1 point)   _____
     (Think about this for a second before you answer!)
20. You have an investment advisor/financial consul-
     tant in whom you are very confident.
               True (1 point)   False (0 points)   _____
21. Consistency of returns is important to you and
     you would give up a little higher long term return
     to get a little more consistent year-to-year results.
               True (0 points)   False (1 point)   _____

                                        Total Score: _____

                            (Maximum score: 30)

                         Scoring:
                  Score Between   *Risk Quotient*
                        0–10   Conservative
                        11–20   Moderate
                        21–30   Aggressive

Another important consideration is your age. At various stages in your life, you have different needs for income versus growth. In this analysis (Table 5–2) we take the first two asset allocation categories—nonmarket risk and extended income—and combine them. We then compare this combined income category to a growth category that is a combination of the equities and tangible assets groups.

During the first 15 years, investments for children can be growth oriented. There is enough time before needing the money for college that the ups and downs will even out. However, by age 15 or so, one needs to become more conservative because the need for income for college costs beginning at age 18 is, for most people, fairly certain. After college, there is usually not much income, so even until the mid-20s income producing investments are necessary.

From the mid-20s until the early to mid-50s, most of one's investments should be in growth. Although during the 50s one needs

TABLE 5–2
Investment Life Cycle Chart

Age	Growth (%)	Income (%)
0–15	70%	30%
15–25	30	70
25–50	80	20
50–60	60	40
60–70	40	60
70–100	30	70

to become more conservative to plan for retirement, one should still have a significant portion of assets in growth—40 percent or so. Life expectancies are too long and inflation too much of a problem not to invest for growth as well as income. Only after age 70 do I suggest possibly cutting back to only 30 percent growth. Even then, it is important to have growth in your portfolio, not only because of inflation, but also because you should be thinking about your heirs' or favorite charities' financial health after your death. I believe you should try to be the very best possible steward of your assets throughout your life. Now we can get into the really fun part of your asset allocation strategy.

Table 5–3 entitled "Asset Allocation Worksheet" will be the mechanism to get your own plan in writing. It is a simple, one-page strategy sheet that you can complete now and then at least once each year.

TABLE 5-3 Asset Allocation Worksheet For _____ Date: _____

Asset Class	Net Value (After Debts)	% of Net Worth	Recommended Current Weighting	Desired Long-Term Goal
Income: Nonmarket risk (maturities under 5 years, annuities, etc.)	$_____	_____%	$_____ (_____%)	$_____ (_____%)
Income: Extended income (bonds, misc. income)	$_____	_____%	$_____ (_____%)	$_____ (_____%)
Growth: Equities (stocks/total return)	$_____	_____%	$_____ (_____%)	$_____ (_____%)
Growth: Tangible Assets (real estate, precious metals, etc.)	$_____	_____%	$_____ (_____%)	$_____ (_____%)
Net Worth	$_____	100 %	$_____ (100 %)	$_____ (100 %)

Life insurance death benefit   + $_____

Desired Risk Profile   Low _____   Moderate _____   High _____
Desired Return Profile   Low _____   Moderate _____   High _____

Estate Value $_____

Approx. Taxable Income $_____   Marginal Tax Bracket _____%

Comments & recommendations:

First, on the left side of the sheet list an approximate value of all your assets. For each of the four asset allocation categories, put in the total dollar value and its percent of your net worth under the heading "Net Value". For assets on which you have indebtedness, I suggest you show the value after indebtedness. That way, when each of the four categories are added together, the result will be your net worth.

Then fill in the column on the right "Desired Long-Term Goal." You may complete the dollar amounts, but just filling in the percent is enough for this purpose. These percentages are your target asset allocation strategy. This is where you really want to be.

Sometimes you will have an intermediate step, either because you have some illiquid investments that will take time to change, or because your current outlook for various markets dictates a somewhat higher or lower weighting for awhile. If so, fill in the "Recommended Current Weighting" column. Otherwise, immediately reallocate your investments to the desired level.

Here's where we get back to the football analogy. A crucial concept in this asset allocation approach is that you are at all times flexible enough to "move with the play." In our strategy we will use all four asset allocation categories. As a defensive back, we want to be able to shift our strategy depending on which way the play goes.

I hope you grasp the dynamics of this! First of all, we have here a mechanism to help us get out of overvalued assets into undervalued assets. If one category gets out of whack with our strategy, that is a signal to action. For example, let's say we have targeted 40 percent to stocks (equities). Because of a bear market, the percent drops to 35 percent. That would be a signal to take some assets from other categories to buy enough stock to bring us back to 40 percent! In the same way, rebalancing periodically will force you to sell assets that may be too high.

As reported in a September 1987 syndicated column of Jane Bryant Quinn, this asset allocation approach can help protect you in difficult times. She used a simplified example from Marshall Blume, professor of finance at the Wharton School in Philadelphia and a principal in Prudent Management Associates.

According to Blume, if an investor had put $10 into stocks in August 1929, just before the Great Crash, it would not have been until 1945 that he recouped his losses. However, if he had put $5 into stocks and $5 into bonds, and rebalanced his investments monthly to keep a 50–50 split, he would have recouped his losses by October 1935.

To illustrate this another way, take two theoretical investments: one that gains 100 percent in the first year and falls 50 percent in the second year, and a second investment that drops 50 percent in the first year while rebounding 100 percent the second year. The final result put the portfolio back to even. However, if the two investments were structured in a 50–50 mix and rebalanced yearly to bring the weighting back to 50–50, the return would be 25 percent per year, or 56 percent cumulative over the 2 years! It works because the system forces you to buy some of the cheap assets and sell the expensive ones at the end of the first year.

Within each of the four categories, we will select the very best investments we can. We expect each individual investment to make a good return. But there will be volatility and unexpected movements in value. And we want to be prepared to take advantage of them.

Another aspect to this is to reduce the overall volatility of our net worth. While part of our portfolio may be declining in value because of economic cycles, another part will be going up. Many people miss this notion.

Remember the Hunt brothers from Dallas? They got involved in silver in a big way. They may have thought to themselves that "if the silver deal doesn't work out, at least we'll have our real estate and oil investments to fall back on." Where did they go wrong? They had different investments, yes, but they were all in the Tangible Asset category! If they had only had a simple asset allocation plan like the one in this chapter, they would still be in the game. Bonds and stocks in turn zoomed while tangible assets fell in the 1980s.

Mathematicians have proved the relationships that I've been attempting to explain in simple common sense terms in this chapter. Without getting into Ph.D. stuff too far, let me show you a neat little graph that illustrates the risk/reward trade-off between stocks and bonds. See Figure 5–1.

This chart shows a measure of risk called "Standard Deviation" on the horizontal axis. (We'll get more into statistics in Chapter 9.) It shows investment return on the vertical axis. As you can see on the chart, if you had 100 percent of a portfolio in bonds during the period

Figure 5-1   Return/Risk Trade-Off: Stocks and Bonds

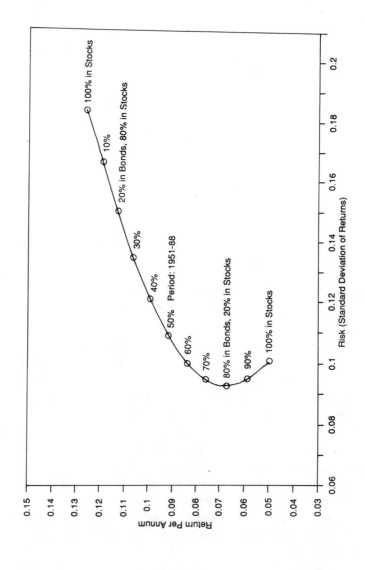

between 1951 and 1988, you would have the lowest possible return at a very low risk. If you had 100 percent in stocks, you would have the highest return but with a very high risk. Now if you had 80 percent in bonds and 20 percent in stocks you would have the lowest possible risk profile, but with a higher return than bonds alone!

Also notice the slope of the curve as you go from 40 percent bonds (60 percent stocks) to 0 percent bonds (100 percent stocks). In this range you get a relatively small pick-up in return compared to a relatively high pick-up in risk. So the best risk/reward point is somewhere in the middle.

The concept is that it is the *relationship* between asset classes within a single portfolio that becomes important. In Chapter 9 you'll see a similar chart that compares U.S. bonds to foreign bonds (Figure 9–2).

Stock and bond prices tend to move in the opposite direction about half the time. With four asset allocation classes there will be even more opportunity to reduce portfolio volatility with offsetting movements.

At first blush, you might have this thought about asset allocation: "Doesn't having my assets spread over so many different types of investments just have the gains and losses cancel each other out, thereby keeping my returns too low?" The answer is no. All of the investments you make should be carefully selected to make a good profit. Hopefully all four asset classes will appreciate in value over time. And within each of the four categories you want to select the best of all possible alternative investments. The key to asset allocation is to control risk. If you successfully control risk, the return will take care of itself.

Here's an approach you might consider for bonds. I've developed a bond market timing model to manage bond portfolios. Its purpose is to help us get in or out of bonds at appropriate times.

The concept is that interest rates cannot be predicted. Even top economists have not been able to do so consistently. However, major trends develop in interest rates and prices which can be identified. The basis of the program is to identify and act on these trends in bond prices as they unfold.

In order to recognize a trend change early enough to take advantage of it, I use several indicators. The primary technique is what is known as a stochastics method of technical analysis.

Stochastics is a computerized analysis of price trends which graphically illustrates whether a stock or bond is high or low compared to its
recent past. It also shows the trend in its price. Note the chart in Figure
5–2 Dow Jones Bond Average. It shows the Dow Jones Bond Average
of corporate bond prices with a stochastics chart under it. The
interpretation is that a buy signal is given whenever the stochastics
line first turns up. A sell signal is given when the stochastics line first
·turns down. (There are various sources of stochastics data. The one I
use is from Telescan, Inc., of Houston, Tx.)

I also use other methods to confirm or to back up the stochastics
method. One of these is a "Two Point Reversal" method of identifying
trends. This method simply takes the weekly closing price of a 30-year
Treasury bond, and when the price reverses 2 points from the level in
the opposite direction of the existing trend, a buy or sell is given. For
example, let's say the bond you are following, after a period of decline, ·
closes at a price of 90 at week's end (that is, a price of $900 for a $1000
bond.) Then a few days later, it closes the day at a price of 92 ($920).
That constitutes a buy signal.

Another method is the "Industrial Materials Prices" correlation.
Trends in industrial materials prices (a measure of inflation) has
historically correlated to trends in interest rates. Note the accompanying chart (Figure 5–3) and the correlation to interest rates on Treasury
bond yields.

I did a study of a hypothetical bond trading program covering the
period 1983 to 1990 using a combination of the Two Point Reversal
method and the Industrial Materials Prices method. Using these two
methods in tandem would have produced very positive results in the
bond market. One would have increased his principal by approximately 55% (plus interest) after estimated transaction costs, compared
to only 20% (plus interest) that one would have earned on a
buy-and-hold strategy. I assumed that one would have been in either
the 30-year Treasury bond or a money market fund during the period.

Keep in mind that this is a trend following model. We generally do
not try to predict interest rates or bond prices. Thus we will seldom be
successful in picking the exact top or bottom of a price trend change.
Rather, our approach is to wait until a change is underway and
identified by our indicators before acting fully on it.

This may also mean that we must be willing to sell out even at a loss

Figure 5-2   Dow Jones Bond Average

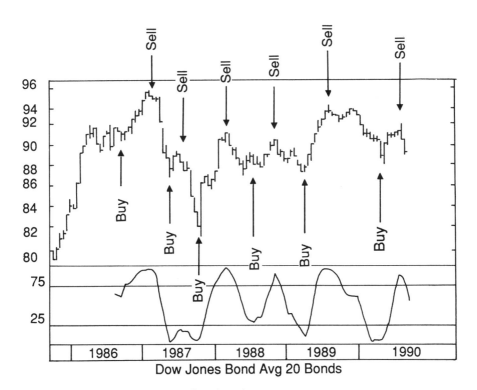

Dow Jones Bond Avg 20 Bonds

Stochastic
Length= 20 WKS
Stochastic
Moving
Average=10 WKS

SOURCE: Reprinted with permission from Telescan, Inc. Houston, Texas.

Figure 5–3   Yield on 10 Year Treasury Bond / Industrial Materials Prices / Initial Unemployment Claims

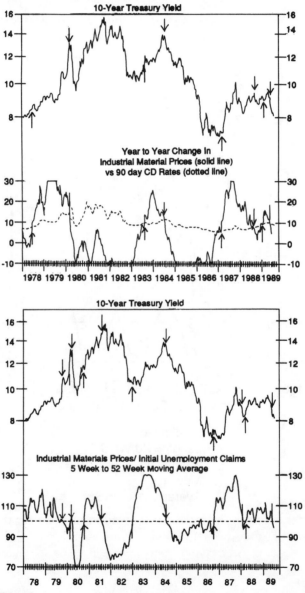

SOURCE: Merrill Lynch

if the trend turns down. For this approach to work, we need to be prepared for an occasional losing trade. This may be necessary in order to preserve our capital. You never know how far a trend will carry once started. Investors in bonds in the early 1980's who doggedly hung in there when interest rates were skyrocketing got slaughtered.

What bond should be used with this strategy? Normally the 30-year Treasury bond is best. Treasuries offer a very liquid market. Long term bonds are best because they offer the most capital gains potential. Though bonds are often bought for their high income, substantial price appreciation is also possible with bonds. Like the far end of a teeter-totter, the longer the bond maturity, the greater the swings in price. Capital gains are an objective of this program, therefore long term bonds are the best vehicle to capture price moves.

Of course, long bonds have a higher risk as well. However, with this program we have a game plan to limit risk. We will sell out if the market (bond prices) appears to have started down, thus protecting our principal.

Even though the 30–year Treasury bond is excellent for this program, municipal bonds, corporate bonds, or mortgage backed bonds such as Ginnie Maes may also be used. In this regard, the tax bracket of the investor is a consideration, as we discussed in the financial planning section of the book. (Only municipal bonds are tax exempt.)

The relative "yield spreads" of various fixed income markets are also important in identifying the best values in the bond market. For example, note Figure 5–4, which shows the Ratio of Municipal Bond Yields to 30 Year U.S. Treasury Bond Yields. In 1986, for example, interest rates on municipal bonds were the same as (100% of) Treasury bonds. But these relationships are cyclical. The astute investor bought municipals in 1986 because their risk/reward characteristics were better than Treasuries. After 1986 as yield relationships returned to normal, municipal bond prices performed much better than Treasuries. Remember, the opportunities in bonds develop when a market has declining interest rates. This is true on a relative basis as well as on an absolute basis.

Should this timing model be the only strategy for your bond portfolio? No, not at all! Diversification is always appropriate. I

Figure 5-4   Ratio of Municipal Bond Yields to 30-year U.S. Treasury Bond Yields

SOURCE: *The Bond Buyer*.

recommend using some of one's bond assets to buy and hold intermediate and/or long term bonds, or perhaps bond funds.

Going back to the overall asset allocation process, precise allocation will never be possible. Not only can one not consistently predict the future, but each individual has his or her own unique set of circumstances. Indeed, we make the assumption with our asset allocation model that we need not predict the markets and, further, don't really have to try.

There are two ways to use the model however. One is to have an absolute fixed ratio. Another way is to have a range of allocation percentages based on your outlook for the various markets.

You might, for example, set an asset allocation range on extended income of from 20 to 30 percent of total net worth. When the model points to lower interest rates, thus higher bond prices, move to 30 percent allocation. When you get a sell signal, cut back to 20 percent in bonds. As you move in or out of the extended income (bond) segment, you would simultaneously rebalance the nonmarket risk (cash) sector in the opposite direction. Because nobody can accurately predict the direction of any market all of the time, I believe you should have a least 10 percent or so of your assets in each category at all times.

What about real estate and other tangible assets? Harry J. Stone, Jr., president of Professional Investment Counsel, Inc., of El Paso, Texas, suggests that the rate of inflation has an important bearing on the performance of various assets. As demonstrated by Figure 5–5, he makes a distinction between whether we have inflation or deflation, whether the rate of inflation or deflation is accelerating or decelerating. For example, when inflation is over 5 percent and climbing (accelerating), real assets (real estate and precious metals) are the place to be. If the rate of inflation is over 5 percent but declining (decelerating), stocks and bonds on a roughly equivalent basis are the place to be positioned.

Because real estate is so regional, it is difficult to be very precise about general trends. What is happening in Michigan real estate may be totally different than in Florida. And precious metals prices are affected by a variety of worldwide influences in addition to our domestic inflation. But it does make intuitive sense to pay attention to the broad trends in national inflation and how it affects tangible

FIGURE 5–5 Areas of Investment

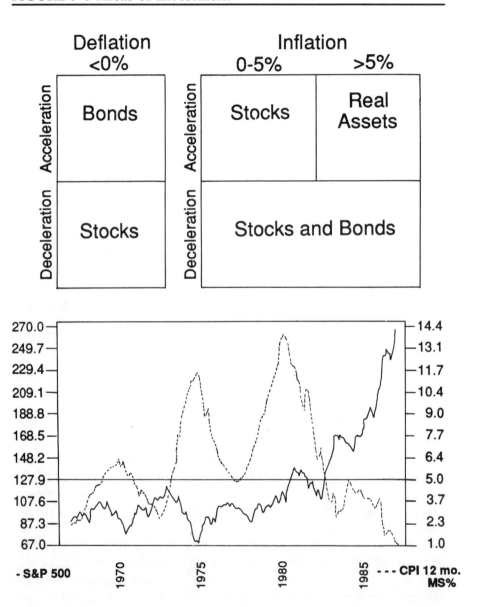

SOURCE: Harry J. Stone, Jr./Professional Investment Counsel, Inc. (El Paso).

assets. Thus, when inflation is over 5 percent and accelerating—for example, moving from 5 to 6 to 7 percent, etc.,—increasing the tangible asset part of your portfolio would be appropriate. However, when inflation begins to decelerate—from 10, to 9, to 8 percent, etc.—that is a signal to cut back somewhat on the tangible asset category. You can follow inflation by watching the consumer price index (CPI) in *Barron's* magazine.

Some people find themselves frightened to put a significant part of their assets into an area with which they aren't familiar. If you are not experienced in stocks, for example, having say 25 percent of your assets in them could be scary. But think about it this way: If you have 25 percent in one sector and that sector declines 10 percent in value, that represents only 2.5 percent of your net worth. Right? That would be an insignificant risk to your entire investment picture!

You may ask: "Doesn't all this switching increase your transaction costs?" It does not need to. Many people merely use new incoming cash flow with which to do the rebalancing. You can also use a mutual fund family, allowing you to switch from a stock fund, to a bond fund, to a money market fund. Within mutual funds from the same organization (family) you can switch without a fee.

If by now you're feeling a bit bewildered, here are three possible ways to allocate, depending on whether you are a conservative, moderate, or aggressive investor. You may simply select the one you are comfortable with and stick with it, rebalancing periodically to keep the same percentages.

	Conservative	Moderate	Aggressive
Nonmarket risk	40%	20%	10%
Extended income	30	20	10
Equities	20	40	60
Tangible assets	10	20	20
	100%	100%	100%

I think you'll find this process a lot of fun. You don't need to spend much time at it. Annual or semiannual rebalancing is adequate.

However, a good time to at least review your allocation is monthly when you get your monthly statements. I suggest keeping a log or at least making yourself a few notes on strategy each month. You will soon be in control of your finances—the "Boz" of your assets, Super Bowl ring in hand.

6

Stocks For Everyone: How to Manage Your Own Portfolio

If you are both mentally athletic and emotionally stable, you might want to try developing and managing your own stock portfolio. As we've seen, the stock market is a fantastic place to invest, having provided the highest returns of any investment medium. However, in my experience, a majority of investors who try the market have a bad experience with it and ultimately fail!

There are several reasons for their lack of success. They include:

1. *Inadequate diversification.* Most investors start out timidly with one or two or three stocks. Sooner or later one of the issues will take a large drop. A small portfolio just can't handle a large drop in one of its stocks, so the portfolio goes nowhere.

2. *Inadequate research.* You need to have access on an ongoing basis to good information. Many investors, for example, select stocks on the basis of an article in a magazine or newspaper. The article might be correct, but the problem comes later with a lack of follow up information. Things may be turning sour for the company a year later. Since you obviously aren't in touch with whoever wrote the article you are not getting the information you need to make decisions.

3. *Emotionalism.* This is probably the worst factor. Most investors get excited into buying or frightened into selling at just the wrong times.

137

4. *Lack of time spent.* It doesn't require a huge time commitment to be successful in stocks. But it does require *some* effort. Most folks are just too busy to do it justice.

5. *Lack of discipline.* You need to consistently apply a *rational* process to managing a portfolio. You need to have a *game plan* on what you will buy and when you will sell. You will be competing against too many pros out there to do this thing on a haphazard basis.

In the next few pages I'll outline a complete approach that you can use to eliminate the above problems, and find peace and happiness in the stock market. Well, that's probably an overstatement, but here goes.

First of all, let's set a diversification rule. We'll put no more than 5 percent of our portfolio in any one stock initially. However, we reserve the right to increase that to 8 percent to 10 percent of the portfolio at a later date. Normally that would happen if a stock we already own drops to a point that we consider an especially good buying point.

This, by the way, very often happens. I don't think I ever bought a stock right at its bottom. (It has been said that only fools and liars do that.) By using this approach, we gain a couple of advantages. First, we are able to *take advantage* of market fluctuations that inevitably occur, rather than having them take advantage of us. Second, we gain a subtle psychological advantage. It may give us enough courage to go ahead and establish a position in a good stock even though it may appear to be a bit high at the moment. The courage comes from the knowledge that if the stock does drop after we buy it, we have a game plan. At the same time that we first buy the stock, we set a specific price to buy more if we are fortunate enough the get a pull-back in the share price. If the pull-back doesn't come, we own enough of it to be meaningful as the stock advances. A typical situation would be if we have, let's say, $100,000 invested in the program. We initially invest $5,000 in a certain stock. It drops to our predetermined "buy more" price. We then buy another $2500 worth. If it drops still further to a new predetermined price we pick up $2500 more. At that point we are maxed out and our program doesn't allow any further pur-chases. Through this discipline, we will have a maximum of 20 stocks in our portfolio and generally a minimum of 10.

Let's talk about stock selection. In screening for stocks we are going to set a rule that all stocks we buy must have a *minimum potential of a 25 percent annual rate of return over a two to five-year period.* By setting a high hurdle rate, we eliminate a lot of stocks that are already fully priced. It also gives us a margin of error. You may ask: "Doesn't this high return criterion lead to buying speculative stocks?" To some degree this is true. However, the stocks selected are not necessarily speculative stocks, but may be blue chips that happen to be priced right. Your program will control risk through diversification, careful selection, the discipline built into the program, and the asset allocation aspects of how this stock program fits into your overall investment strategy. I think, though, that unless you are willing to take some "businessman's risk," you are better off in mutual funds.

Here are the tools you will need to start:

1. *The Value Line Investment Survey.* This is usually available in your local library, at your financial consultants office, or you may subscribe from:
Value Line, Inc.
711 Third Avenue
New York, NY 10017

2. The *SRC Blue Book of 5-Trend Cycli-Graphs* published quarterly by:
Securities Research Company
208 Newbury Street
Boston, MA 02116

3. Contact with an investment firm that has a research division.

4. A good computer screen such as:
The Zweig Performance Ratings Report
P.O. Box 360
Bellmore, NY 11710
or
Techno-Fundamental Ranks
c/o Ned Davis Research, Inc.
P.O. Box 1287
Nokomis, FL 34274–1287
1–800–241–0621

There are several ways to apply our 25 percent rate of return rule. The fundamental method is to analyze the expected growth rate of a company's earnings per share compared to its price-earnings ratio. Earnings per share are the company's total earnings after tax divided by the number of shares of stock outstanding. The price-earnings ratio (P/E) is a measure of how high the stock is relative to its earnings and is simply the share price divided by the earnings per share. Your investment firm should be able to give you an estimate of their research analyst's expected earnings per share growth rate of various companies over the next few years. (Be sure you're getting an estimate of future growth, not past growth.) If a company's earnings are growing at 25 percent per year, and the stock keeps up with the underlying earnings growth, you've got your 25 percent rate of return. This means that as long as you don't pay too high a price, i.e., too high a P/E, which would risk not being able to sell it at a later date at the same P/E ratio, the earnings growth takes care of your total return.

Now, if you want to buy a company that has a growth rate in its earnings of less than 25 percent per year and still get a 25 percent rate of return on the stock, you must be able to buy it at a low enough price to get an *increase* in the price-earnings ratio to make up the difference. This is referred to as a *multiple expansion,* meaning an expansion in the P/E multiple. I've constructed a table (Table 6–1) to help you make this relationship. The first column shows the expected earnings growth rate. The third column shows a price-earnings ratio that my own experience shows has been fully valued for stocks with that earnings growth rate. The second column gives the P/E ratio that you would have to pay to achieve a 25 percent rate of return, assuming that you were able to sell at the fully valued P/E price four years later.

A few comments: It is *very* hard for a company to achieve an earnings growth rate in excess of 25 percent over any sustained period of years. My general rule is to assume that any estimates over that are inflated, and I would be unwilling to pay more than 25 times earnings (P/E over 25) on *any* stock. This chart also shows how hard it is to make a superior return on a slow growing company. You really have to buy a slow grower mighty cheaply (under 7 times earnings, and sell it in a strong market at over 14 times earnings) to make the hurdle rate of return. By the way, I pretty much ignore dividends with this analysis. Remember that dividends are part of total earnings, and total earnings

TABLE 6-1
Estimate of Maximum P/E to Pay to Achieve a Return of 25 Percent
Per Annum over Four Years

Earnings per Share Growth Rate	Buy Point P/E	Fully Valued P/E
25%	25.0	25
22%	20.0	22
20%	17.0	20
18%	14.5	18
15%	11.5	16
12%	10.0	15
10% or below	7.0	14

are factored in through our analysis of the P/E ratio.

Another detail is to use only *trailing* earnings in the denominator of the P/E ratio; that is, earnings over the preceding 12 months. Some people talk about P/Es based on future estimated earnings, which doesn't work with our analysis.

There are certainly shortcomings with this type of analysis. Obviously, your estimated earnings growth is crucial. And some industry groups tend to sell consistently above or below my fully valued P/E levels. You may, therefore, want to make some compensating adjustments to these mechanical rules. However, I think *all superior money managers use some variation of this system to determine overvalued and undervalued stocks.* My suggestion is to stick with this basic profile unless some overriding reason based on rational thought dictates a prudent exception in a specific instance.

In determining when to sell, we may be a little more flexible. An old investment rule is to "cut your losses short and let your profits run." Applying this to our formula, you may wait until the P/E ratio reaches 10–15 percent over the fully valued level. For example, the fully valued P/E for a 20 percent grower is 20 times earnings. You might hold the stock until it gets to 22 times earnings before selling. I also like to "scale out" of a stock. Just as we sometimes buy more of a stock on dips, we can sell portions gradually. For example, determine in advance to sell half of your position at 20 times earnings but keep half to see if it can't make it to 23 to 25 times earnings. Stocks have a way of going down farther than you think in bear markets and going higher than you think in bull markets. As you get close to your sell targets, I recommend placing an open order to sell, so that if it touches your price even momentarily, you'll be out.

What about stop-loss orders? A stop-loss order is an order designed to protect you if the stock starts to drop. For example, for a stock that is now at 40, you might enter such an order, which becomes a market order to sell if it ever touches 35. My feeling is that a stop order is usually an excuse for poor analysis. I generally don't encourage stop orders. However, I do believe in reevaluation *points.* In this illustration, if the stock drops to 35, or if it begins to significantly underperform most other stocks, restudy the stock. If it still looks good, *buy more* at that point. However, if the fundamental outlook appears to be possibly deteriorating, by all means sell it. For example, the expected growth rate may have been lowered by the research analyst you are following. Don't be afraid to sell a stock at a loss! He who takes his money and runs away, lives to play another day.

We have discussed at length in previous chapters the empirical evidence of various investment techniques that have beaten the stock market. We're now ready to put all this information together. There are many viable approaches to selecting stocks. We can take the above basic formula and branch out. I suggest broad categories of places to look for specific stock ideas:

Growth Stocks.   These could be established, famous growth companies. They could also be small emerging growth companies. In either case, we merely apply the above rules. Notice the chart of Abbott Laboratories in Figure 6–1. This chart, from Securities Research Company, has a lot of information on it. The heavy dotted line shows the earnings per share. For example, at the end of the third quarter of 1989 the trailing earnings were approximately $3.70 per share, with the stock selling at $70 per share. The P/E ratio was thus $70 divided by $3.70, or 18.9. (These charts are arranged so that when the price is touching the earnings line, the P/E is 15.)

FIGURE 6-1 Abbott Laboratories

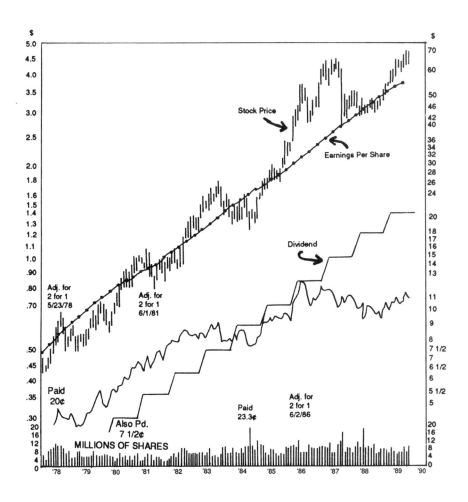

SOURCE: Chart courtesy of Securities Research Company, a Division of Babson-United Investment Advisors, Inc., Babson-United Building, 101 Prescott St., Wellesley Hills, MA. 02181–3319.

Securities Research provides an overlay to help you determine the growth rate in the earnings or in the stock price itself. You could also figure it out yourself by taking two separate points and looking up the change in the compound interest table (Table 2–2.) It turns out that the earnings growth is consistently about 18 percent per annum. There have been several times when we could have bought the stock at our 14.5 P/E point (criteria for an 18 percent grower) such as in 1979, 1980, 1981, 1984, and 1988. We could have sold at our fully valued 18 P/E point in 1983, 1986, and 1989. (Securities Research's chart overlay also will help you determine the P/E.) Our formula's value is well illustrated on this company, where we take an 18 percent growth rate stock and turn it into at 25 percent rate of return. It's been 2,000 years since anybody turned water into wine, but lots of folks turn 18 percent into 25 percent in the stock market.

Companies with Exciting New Products.   Sometimes these companies will also be recognized growth stocks from the previous category. Other times they may be slow growers that have a newly defined future because of a new product. They may also be very young companies that have no earnings at all. In this latter case, it will be impossible to use the basic P/E formula. (There will be no P/E ratio since there are no earnings.) This is a difficult situation for anyone to analyze, let alone the average at-home investor. If you are really into this stuff, you could become your own analyst by making some guesstimate as to future sales and earnings and applying a P/E ratio to it. A more reasonable solution is to ask your financial consultant to have his or her firm's research analyst estimate what price the stock could sell for in the future and when it might get there.

You can then use the compound growth table (Table 2–2) in the Chapter 2 to see if it will earn 25 percent based on the future price target. Or, here's a simplified table (Table 6–2). The "future value multiple" gives a minimum future value target. As an example, let's say the stock is now at $20 per share. The analyst thinks that it can reach $40 in three years. That's 2.0 times today's price. Bingo. It exceeds the 1.95 factor in the table.

TABLE 6–2
Appreciation Factor to Achieve a 25% per Annum Return

Years	Future Value Multiple
1	1.25
2	1.56
3	1.95
4	2.44
5	3.05

Important Investment Theme. Some investors are successful in identifying major themes. For example, here are several I think will be important in years to come:

- *Death of communism theme.* This may be the single most exciting investment opportunity in the next 25 years. Find companies that will benefit. The first companies that will benefit are European companies.

- *Aging population theme.* The average age of our populace is extending. Look for companies that provide products and services to the elderly.

- *Infrastructure theme.* Our bridges, roads, sewer systems, and dams are wearing out. There will be tremendous expenditures in this segment of the economy over the next several years. Look for the companies that will do the work.

- *Pollution control theme.* We've spent the last 50 years growing at the expense of our environment. Every aspect of business will be involved in the clean-up and prevention of pollution. Tremendous investment opportunities are at hand. Just apply our standard valuation criteria before investing.

Out-of-Favor Stocks. This is an entire discipline in itself. Some of the most successful money managers use this method alone. Here you may find companies that are depressed in price due to some industry or operating problem. An example of this was General Public Utilities, which was the company that suffered the Three Mile Island nuclear disaster in 1979. After the disaster, you could have bought all the stock you could handle under $5 per share. Common sense suggested that as a public utility, the company would not be allowed to go out of business. Subsequently, the stock rose to $46. (see Figure 6–2.)

You normally have plenty of time to buy a stock such as this. Don't get in too big of a hurry. As you can see, waiting two or three years after the break until the stock stabilized still gave you plenty of opportunity to buy it.

An astute securities analyst may apply several basic value tests to a stock that is out of favor. He might look for companies selling well below book value, or companies that have an unusually high dividend or be low relative to future earning power. The initial clues for the investor are that these stocks may not only be depressed in price but are surrounded by bad news or at least apathy. Ask yourself this question: *Is there compelling underlying value in this stock at the current price?* In the case of General Public Utilities, you could simply have reasoned that the stock could at least return to its previous level of 15 within five or so years, thereby meeting our minimum appreciation factor.

A man by the name of Benjamin Graham is considered the father of security analysis. He authored or co-authored several books on the subject, and is reported to have made a fortune in stocks using his methods of selecting out-of-favor issues.

Graham's basic formula was using a set of 5 "value criteria" and 5 "safety criteria." He said to find stocks that had at least one of the below value criteria and one of the below safety criteria. The below data can be unearthed from the *Value Line Investment Survey*.

Value Criteria

1. The earnings yield should be at least twice the AAA bond yield. (The earnings yield is the inverse of the price/earnings ratio, i.e., the earnings per share divided by the price per share.)

2. The stock's price/earnings ratio should be less than 40% of its highest price/earnings ratio of the previous 5 years.

3.   The stock's dividend yield should be at least two-thirds of the AAA bond yield.

4.   The stock's price should be no more than two-thirds of the company's tangible book value per share. (Tangible book value is the accounting cost of assets after subtracting out all liabilities and any good will. Goodwill is an intangible asset which may appear on a balance sheet as a result of buying another company out above its own book value.)

5.   The company's stock price should be no more than two-thirds of its net current assets. (A company's current assets are items that could be converted to cash in one year, including cash itself, inventories, and receivables. Current liabilities are debts due in one year. Net current assets are current assets minus current liabilities.)

Safety Criteria

1.   A company's total debt should not exceed book value.

2.   Current assets should be at least twice current liabilities.

3.   Total debt should be less than twice net current assets.

4.   Earnings growth should have been at least 7% per annum compounded over the previous decade.

5.   There should have been no more than 2 annual earnings declines of 5% or more during the previous decade.
     The Ben Graham formula is only useful when studying a potential out-of-favor stock. True growth stocks can never be bought at the prices Ben Graham insisted on. This points out that there is never only one approach to investing. In fact, even some of the Ben Graham followers actually use different formulas or statistics than these listed. We'll throw out a couple more as we go along.

FIGURE 6–2 General Public Utilities

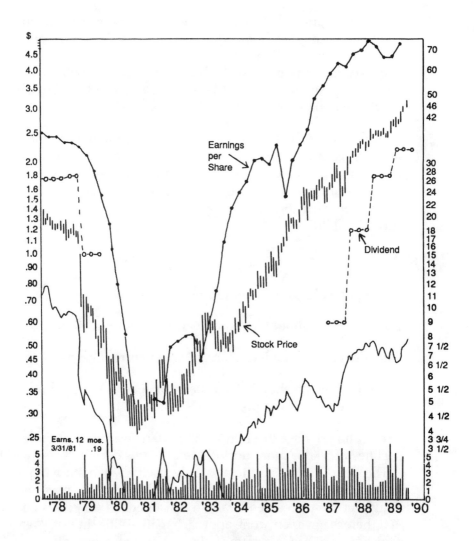

SOURCE: Chart Courtesy of Securities Research Company, A Division of Babson-United Investment Advisors, Inc., Babson-United Building, 101 Prescott St., Wellesley Hills, MA 02181–3319.

Using Technical Analysis. Proponents of this type of analysis concentrate on the trend in the price of a stock, generally ignoring the fundamentals of earnings, book value, and so forth. I suggest looking at just two concepts out of the dozens that "technicians" talk about: (1) break-out from a long base and (2) relative strength. Refer to Figure 6–3, the chart of Angelica, an apparel rental firm.

Notice that by 1980, the stock had been backing and filling for years. It was "building a base." Then it "broke out" above its previous tops at $5½. This can often be a sign that a change has occurred and it is a buy signal. When this happens, it suggests the stock could go up for years. The technicians even go so far as to say that the extent of the upward move is directly related to the time and distance it has been in the base pattern. If you merely measure the horizontal distance on the chart (in inches) while in the base, then measure that same distance vertically from the price break out point, you've got at least a rough upside price target. Obviously, this is crude, because it depends on the scale of the chart used. But it does give you an idea of the potential. In this case, that price was 26. It made the target in 1983.

Another concept is relative strength, shown in the chart by the thin line under the stock price. This is a measure of how the stock is doing compared to the Dow Jones Industrial Average. When it is going up, the stock is outperforming the Dow, and vice versa. I like to see the relative strength in a distinct uptrend.

There are 2 ways to define a chart trend. An uptrend can be defined as each increase being higher than the previous high point. Alternatively, a trend changes from down to up when the line connecting a series of descending tops is broken to the upside. A downtrend is the opposite of these.

In fact, I like to see good relative strength on all six stock selection categories. On Angelica, the stock's relative strength line broke out above its previous high points at about the same time that the stock itself emerged. Another source for relative strength is *Investor's Daily* newspaper. They rank stocks' relative strength from 1 to 100. A reading between 70 and 100 is considered good.

FIGURE 6–3 Angelica

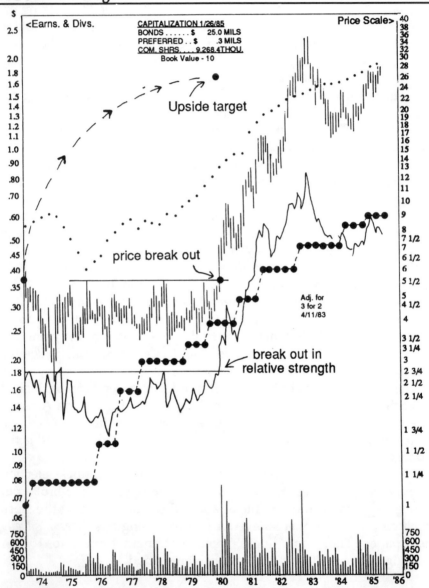

SOURCE: Chart courtesy of Securities Research Company, A Division of Babson-United Investment Advisors, Inc., Babson-United Building, 101 Prescott St., Wellesley Hills, MA 02181–3319. (Hand written notations are those of the author, not Securities Research Co.)

FIGURE 6–4 Uptrend and Downtrend Definitions

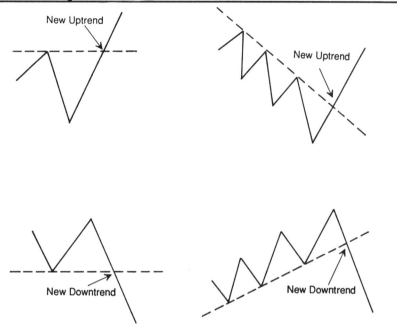

Special Situations.   Most great investment ideas will fit neatly in one (or more) of the previous five categories. In fact, my experience is that if a stock does not seem to fit one of the above, it is probably just an another stock and not likely to provide above average appreciation potential. However, there are situations that pop up from time to time that we can take advantage of that don't fit the preceding categories. These situations might be take-over candidates, short sale opportunities, cyclical companies about to have an earnings spurt, or whatever.

In our previous categories, we emphasized that it may take two to five years for our investments to work out. However, in our special situations group, these opportunities are more likely fairly short term in duration—perhaps one to two years.

We still apply the same standard of a 25 percent potential annual rate of return. If you cannot, by some power of rational thought, justify a potential annual return of 25 percent, the risk-reward ratio is not good enough to play, in my opinion.

Let's talk a little about selling short. Selling short is selling a stock before buying it in hopes that it will drop. Technically, you borrow the stock from your broker, then replace it whenever you've bought the stock back, that is, "covered" your short position. Your profit is the difference, just as if you had bought it first. Shorting can be a great profit mechanism. Stocks drop faster than they rise. We as investors should use this technique more often than we do.

I suggest concentrating your initial search for short sale candidates in the SRC Blue Book. Also, the Zweig screen, is helpful in picking up ideas. Look for companies that have deteriorating fundamentals and/or stocks that are selling at prices 25 to 50 percent over their fully valued P/E. Even good companies can get temporarily very overvalued. Look again at the chart on Abbott Labs in Figure 6–1. In the summer of 1987, before the Crash, Abbott was selling at 26 times earnings, or 44 percent over our fully valued P/E of 18. Further, the relative strength line had broken down below a previous low point, suggesting a down trend. While you may buy stocks to own for several years, normally your short selling trades will be closed out in a few months. Stocks do have a long term upward bias, so you don't want to overstay your market.

In general, use the same concepts for selling short as you do for buying—but in reverse. By the way, I think having a short or two in your portfolio will make you a more objective investor. It will help you think more clearly. It is an excellent way to improve your investment *discipline.* I strongly recommend including stocks from all six categories in your portfolio. The more balanced your portfolio is in this regard, the more you reduce risk and the higher the chance of achieving a fair return.

An invaluable source of information is the Value Line Investment Survey. You can subject your candidates to several financial tests with this resource. Referring to the sheet on Unisys (Figure 6–5), let's look at some useful statistics. I looked at Unisys in the summer of 1989 as a possible investment. At that time the stock was at 24, down from a high of 48. It appeared to be a possible out-of-favor candidate. Let's look at several pieces of information:

Relative Strength.   Value Line is another source for this in addition to the SRC Blue Book. As you can see, the relative strength line (under the stock price chart) was in a distinct down trend. That was a negative.

FIGURE 6-5 Unisys Corp.

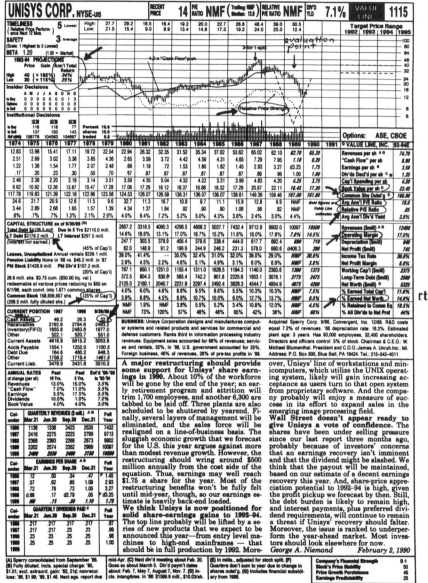

SOURCE: Chart courtesy Value Line, Inc. 711 Third Avenue New York, NY 10017. Hand written notations are those of the author, not Value Line.

Three to five Year Total Return Projections.   Note the section near the upper left hand corner marked "1992–94 Projections." Value Line projects a potential annual return of between 25 to 34 percent. However, at the time of the evaluation, their projection was lower than shown. (This projection can be another way to justify our 25 percent minimum return hurdle.)

Relative P/E ratio.   This figure shows the P/E of the stock dividend by the P/E of the market as a whole. For example, a 1.50 relative P/E shows that a stock is selling at a 50 percent higher P/E than the stock market as a whole. You can see the trend of a stock over time. A lower ratio than in the past is a good sign. In this example, Value Line shows "NMF" here because Unisys is losing money, thus no P/E can be calculated.

Cash Assets versus Long Term Debt.   A company that has less cash than long term debt could be in an unhealthy financial position. Unisys shows cash of only $32.6 million compared to long term debt of $3.178 billion!

Trend in Cash Assets.   Further, Unisys is showing declining cash, down from $46.2 million in 1987. Another negative.

Trend in Shares Outstanding (Float). A company with a decreasing number of shares outstanding could be a good sign, as the company might be buying its own stock. On the other hand, an increasing float is negative. This was the situation for Unisys which showed float steadily increasing to 161 million shares outstanding.

Price/Book.   If you can buy a company below book value, you may have something. The book value in 1989 was $16.45 per share. But the price at the time of review was 24, somewhat over book value. No great bargain.

Operating Margin.   This is the pretax earnings as a percentage of sales. Ten to 12 percent is a high figure for most industries. But, it's also comforting to see the ratio in an improving trend. In 1989, Unisys' margins were on the decline.

Percent Earned on Net Worth.   A highly profitable company will earn over 20 percent on its net worth. Unisys's best year was 12.7 percent in 1987, and it subsequently began declining.

Common Stock percent of Total Capital.   This shows how leveraged, i.e. how heavily in debt, a company is. There is no real rule here, but its nice to have a sense of how leveraged, thus how risky, the company is financed. Unisys has only 35 percent of its capital in stock, the rest of it being indebtedness. If things don't go right, the debt will drag the company down. All things being equal, I prefer to see a company with little debt, for example, common stock at least 75 percent of total capital.

You are never going to have everything in place for a given company. But it is advisable to check these few items before buying. Because of the poor relative strength, poor trend in cash, and the poor trend in float, I passed on this stock. As you can see, it subsequently dropped to nearly $12 per share, then later to $4 per share.

Another excellent source of assistance is to use a good "screen." The best one I know of is the *Zweig Performance Ratings Report*. Zweig puts a battery of variables in his computer that have historically correlated closely to stock performance. His record is very impressive.

One important variable in such a computer screen is what is called *earnings momentum*. You'll recall we discussed this concept in Chapter 3. The idea is to spot companies that have accelerating earnings growth trends. This has been a proven technique to pick stocks, but you need a computer to help you.

I recommend checking your possible buy candidates against such a screen. You should be aware that these screens look only at past and present data. To make estimates of *future growth*, etc., you'll still need to read brokerage reports. A good broker's help is important.

Putting It All Together

I know. I know. It's beginning to look overwhelming. There are only so many hours in a year! Let's keep it as simple as possible. Here's a simple three-step process:

1. Check your broker's projected earnings growth rate versus the P/E ratio. If it passes that test or another 25 percent rate of return criterion hurdle, based on rational and objective thought, go on the second step.

2. Check the Zweig rating. If it is either 1, 2, or 3 (on his 1 to 9 scale), go to Value Line. At this point you've probably eliminated 90 percent of all stocks. If it doesn't get this far, forget it, unless you've got some overriding reason.

3. Use the information in Value Line and the SRC Blue Book to do a quick check-off using the "Equities Worksheet" shown in Figure 6–6. *Use the worksheet to discipline your thinking.* Set a rule for yourself that you will never, ever, buy a stock without filling out this worksheet. It is amazing how putting your thoughts in writing will help you. Remember, you'll never find any stock that looks perfect, but the worksheet will help you confirm good ideas from steps one and two.

Word of warning: You're going to have to stay after all of this. Don't start the program, then ignore your stocks. If you have a broker/ financial consultant that will help you on a regular basis with this program, you can probably get by with an hour or less a week. The most important thing is the *discipline.* Follow the guidelines very strictly. That's the key.

Here's a bit more on when to sell:

1. Sell if the stock's objective is reached.

2. Remember, you have a maximum of 20 stocks in your portfolio. Sell a stock if you find another one to replace it that has significantly better risk/reward picture.

3. Sell if the overall market picture is cloudy based on your Meek Market Model work. (see upcoming chapter.)

4. Sell if the reason you bought the stock has changed such that the potential is no longer there to achieve its objective. Deteriorating relative strength may be a warning. Be realistic. Don't rely on hope.

Your overall goal for the program should be to achieve an overall return *at least equal to one* of the following *over a complete market cycle* (usually four to five years).

1. 10 to 15 percent per annum. This is somewhat better, than the stock market as a whole has achieved over the long run. Note that even though the goal for individual stocks is 25 percent, they won't all work out.

FIGURE 6-6 Equities Worksheet

1. Company name:_____ Price:_____ Date:_____

2. Rational for 25% annual return:

3. Type of situation: (Circle one)

   High   New   Investment Out of Technical Special
   growth Product Theme   Favor   Analysis   situation

4. Expected growth rate E.P.S.:_____

5. Current P/E (on trailing earnings):_____

6. Brokerage firm ranking:_____   7. Zweig rating:_____

8. Relative strength (From SRC Blue Book chart or Value Line):

   Positive   Neutral   Negative

9. Stock owned by these top money managers:_____

10. Earnings and balance sheet data (from Value Line):

    a. 3-5 year annual total return
        projections: Low____% High____%

    b. Relative P/E ratio: Historical: Low____   High____
        Current____

    c. Cash/Long-term debt_____ f. Price per share ÷
    d. Trend in cash assets   Book value per
        Positive (increasing cash)   share
        Neutral
        Negative (decreasing cash)   g. % earned on net
    e. Trend in shares outstanding   worth
        Positive (decreasing float)   _____%
        Neutral   h. Operating margin
        Negative (increasing float)   _____%
                                         Trend: UP DOWN
                                     i. Common stock % of
                                         capital_____%

    j. Comments on earnings and balance sheet data:_____

11. Other thoughts on this company:_____

2.   8 percent better than inflation.

3.   The Value Line Index (geometric) of 1700 Stocks. This index has, in my experience, been the best indicator of the individual investor's experience in the stock market.

If you follow the outline, you'll make it to the NFL Playoffs, if not to the Superbowl!

Rising Dividends Program

Some investors in stocks like to receive dividends from their investments. The approach outlined so far in this chapter is one designed to achieve maximum capital gains, with dividends really incidental. I've developed an alternative strategy that reverses the focus—dividends as the main goal with capital appreciation as a secondary consideration.

The goals of this strategy are threefold:

1.   To provide dividend income at least 25 percent better than the Standard and Poor's 500 Stock Index;

2.   To provide for an increasing stream of dividend income over time;

3.   Provide for modest appreciation in capital value over time.

I use a multi-faceted strategy to accomplish these goals, as listed below:

1.   Stocks selected should generally have a minimum dividend yield of 5 percent at the time of purchase. This is somewhat higher than the goal of 25 percent over the S&P 500, which was just under 4 percent at the time of this writing.

2.   A point system is used which combines the current dividend rate plus the expected growth rate in the dividend, as estimated by the Securities Research Division of my own investment firm. The sum of these 2 statistics should generally be near 11 percent or higher. For example, assume a stock has a current dividend of 7 percent and the actual dollar amount of the

dividend is expected to increase at 4 percent per annum over the next few years. The point total is 7 percent plus 4 percent thus a total of 11 percent.

3. An alternative method for stock selection may be used. Stocks may be selected that have unusually high dividend yields because their share price is depressed due to current operating or industry problems. Such situations may offer investment potential by purchasing the shares when the price is depressed (i.e., when the dividend rate is high) and selling them after conditions have normalized and the price has appreciated (i.e., when the dividend rate is lower).

    This method is the primary reason why a strategy referred to in Chapter 4 of this book of keeping one's portfolio in the 10 highest yielding Dow Jones Industrial stocks has worked so well. Table 6–3 details the success of this strategy, using the 10 highest yielding Dow stocks alone.

4. A stock may be sold if:

    a. It can be replaced with another one with a significantly better dividend or total return potential after transaction costs.

    b. The dividend rate drops to 4% based on the stock's market value.

    c. The price trend falters.

    d. It is deemed prudent to hold cash due to anticipated market conditions.

5. The stochastics method of technical analysis will be used to aid in timing buy/sell points. Stochastics is a computerized analysis of price trends which attempts to graphically illustrate whether a stock is high or low compared to its recent past. It is useful in identifying trends and turning points in cycles of a stock's price. We discussed stochastics earlier in the book relative to bond prices. It is also helpful with high dividend stocks. It is not too useful with low dividend stocks, I have found. Notice the stochastics chart in Figure 6–7, which shows its correlation to Houston Industries, a utility company. The

interpretation is slightly different for a stock than for bonds. For a stock, a sell signal is given when the stochastics line crosses above the overbought 75% line, and then falls below that line. A buy signal is given when the stock reaches an oversold mark of 25%, then crosses back above it.

6. When fully invested, you should have 10 to 20 securities representing several industries groups.

7. In addition to common stocks, other securities may be used such as convertible bonds, convertible preferred stocks, and zero coupon convertibles. (Convertible securities are ones which may be exchanged for the common stock of the company.)

8. Writing of covered call options or index options may be used as a conservative technique to increase the income or to hedge against possible market declines. (A covered call option is the right to buy a stock at a given price for a given time period. An investor may "write" or sell a call option on a stock you own, taking in an immediate cash "premium" but obligating yourself to potentially sell the stock at a later date at the election of the option purchaser. An index call option is similar, but is based on a stock index such as the S&P 500. As an investor, you would not own or be able to deliver the entire index if called on you, but rather you could deliver cash or buy the option back at a profit or loss later.) The call option writing strategy would normally be used after a bull market has increased prices of the Dow Jones Industrial Average (or other indexes) 60% or more. Call option writing would be de-emphasized after a bear market drop of 20% in the Dow.

9. In order to reduce risk, cash (money market funds) may be used when stock market risk appears high. The techniques in the Meek Market Model chapter should be used.

The Rising Dividends Program approach is a good approach for the investor desiring income from their stocks. It is somewhat more conservative than the more detailed approach outlined in the first part of this chapter, because most of the companies used will be mature ones. Though it may not offer as high a return potential, it should be considered as part of your strategy.

Table 6–3 below presents numerical results from January 1972 through December 1988, assuming that total return proceeds are reinvested in a top 10 yielding portfolio at the beginning of each calendar year. "Total Return" is defined as the "Capital Return", i.e. the gain or loss derived from changes in stock prices, plus the return from dividends received. Results do not include transaction costs.

TABLE 6–3

Porfolio of Ten Highest Yielding Dow Stocks VS Dow Jones Industrial Average

| | HIGH YIELD DOW STOCKS | | ALL DOW STOCKS | |
	Total Return	Capital Return	Total Return	Capital Return
1972	23.8%	18.1%	18.5%	14.6%
1973	−6.2	−11.5	−13.3	−16.6
1974	−2.9	−9.9	−23.8	−27.6
1975	58.2	49.1	45.0	38.3
1976	35.5	27.8	23.0	17.9
1977	−3.9	−10.0	−12.9	−17.3
1978	−3.1	−9.9	2.7	−3.1
1979	14.4	6.0	10.7	4.2
1980	24.8	15.6	22.2	14.9
1981	−4.5	−11.8	−3.6	−9.2
1982	25.0	15.4	27.2	19.6
1983	30.7	22.2	26.1	20.3
1984	6.0	−1.5	1.2	−3.7
1985	32.4	24.7	34.1	27.7
1986	27.9	21.3	27.4	22.6
1987	5.5	0.9	5.5	2.3
1988	24.4	18.3	16.2	11.8
Compound Annual Return	15.6%	8.4%	10.6%	5.4%

FIGURE 6–7 Houston Industries

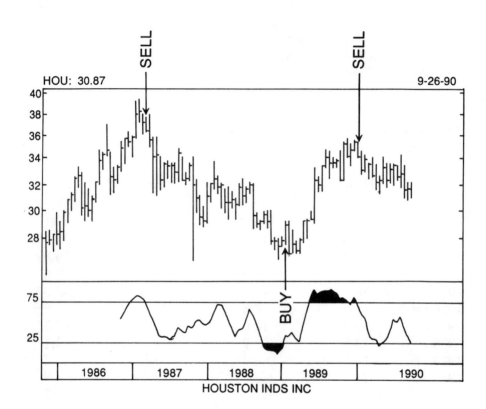

HOUSTON INDS INC

STOCHASTIC
LENGTH= 20 WKS
STOCHASTIC
MOVING
AVERAGE = 10 WKS

7

The Meek Market Model: Dealing With Stock Market Cycles

In New York State, Section 899 of the Code of Criminal Procedure provides that persons "pretending to forecast the future" shall be considered disorderly under Subdivision 3, Section 901 of the code and liable to a fine of $250 and/or six months in prison.

Since recorded history, man has practiced economic forecasting. In the Bible (Genesis 41: 29,30), Joseph, from a dream, correctly predicted that "There will come seven years of great plenty throughout all the land of Egypt, but after them there will arise seven years of famine." From this Biblical boom-bust cycle until today, economic cycles have been a reality. Indeed, cycles are not limited to economics but are common to all of nature. There are cycles in physics, cycles in weather, even cycles in the reindeer population in Alaska.[1]

But let's take a look at economic history to see if we can glean any wisdom that can help the modern investor. Figure 7–1, entitled "American Business Activity from 1790 to Today," is an interesting display of the history of modern economic cycles.

Analysts have studied the ups and downs of the economy and identified many different cycles—some long, some short term in

FIGURE 7-1 American Business Activity From 1790 to Today

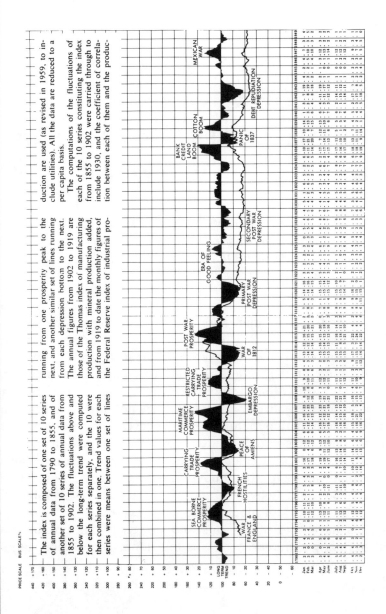

The index is composed of one set of 10 series of annual data from 1790 to 1855, and of another set of 10 series of annual data from 1855 to 1902. The fluctuations above and below the long-term trend were computed for each series separately, and the 10 were then combined in one. Trend values for each series were means between one set of lines running from one prosperity peak to the next, and another similar set of lines running from each depression bottom to the next. The annual figures from 1902 to 1919 are those of the Thomas index of manufacturing production with mineral production added, and from 1919 to date the monthly figures of the Federal Reserve index of industrial production are used (as revised in 1959, to include utilities). All the data are reduced to a per capita basis.

The computations of the fluctuations of each of the 10 series constituting the index from 1855 to 1902 were carried through to include 1930, and the coefficient of correlation between each of them and the produc-

FIGURE 7-1 (continued)

tion series running from 1902 through 1930 was computed. Their deviations were then multiplied through by constants so as to equate their amplitudes of cyclical fluctuation. Each of the 10 series was then given a weight based on its degree of correlation with the production series, and with these weightings they were combined into a single index.

In a similar way the computations of the fluctuations of each of the 10 series constituting the index from 1790 to 1855 were carried through to include 1882, and the coefficient of correlation between each of them and the first 28 years of the index running from 1855 to 1902 was computed. Their deviations were then multiplied through by

The 10 series with these weights are pig iron consumption 15, railroad freight ton miles 15, cotton consumption 14, canal freight (New York and Sault Ste. Marie) 12, coal production 12, construction of miles of new railroads 12, blast furnace activity 10, rail production 6, locomotive production 2, and ship construction 2. The 10 series combined

constants so as to equate their amplitudes of cyclical fluctuation. Each of the 10 series was then given a weight based on its degree of correlation with the first 28 years of the index from 1855 to 1902, and with these weightings they were combined into a single index. The 10 series with these weights are commodity prices 20, imports 18, imports

gave results closely similar to those of the production series for the overlap period from 1902 through 1930. The heights of prosperities, and the depths of depressions, were closely alike in the two series. The coefficient of correlation for the period was .95. Their average deviations for the period were equal.

retained for consumption 16, government receipts 14, ship construction 12, government expenditures 6, coal production 6, exports 5, iron exports 2, and tons of registered shipping in service 1. The 10 series combined give results closely similar to those of the other index for the overlap period from 1855 through 1882. The heights of prosperities,

FIGURE 7-1 (continued)

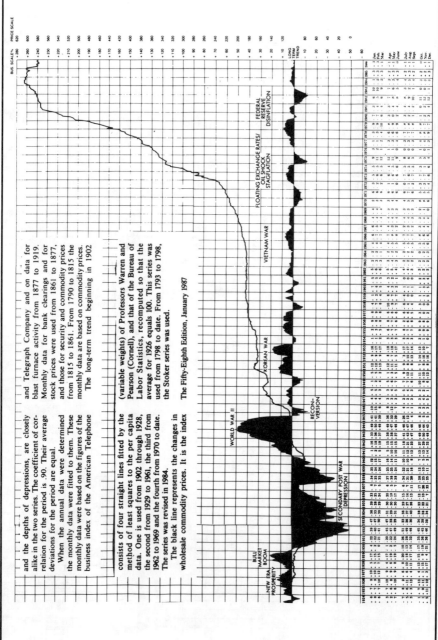

duration. One of the more interesting long term cycles was identified by the Russian Nikolai D. Kondratieff in the 1920s. Figure 7.2 shows the so-called Kondratieff Wave from the late 1700s to 1976. This intriguing theory shows cycles of 50 to 60 years in inflation and interest rates. This report appeared in 1976, and the theory correctly predicted the run-up of inflation and interest rates from 1978 to 1981—and the subsequent drop into the late 1980s.

Here's an interesting quotation:

> *It is a gloomy moment in the history of our country. Not in the lifetime of most men has there been so much grave and deep apprehension, never has the future seemed so incalculable as at this time. The domestic economic situation is in chaos. Our dollar is weak throughout the world. Prices are too high as to be utterly impossible. The political cauldron seethes and bubbles with uncertainty. Russia hangs, as usual, like a cloud, dark and silent, upon the horizon. It is a solemn moment. Of our troubles no man can see the end.*

This quotation appeared in Harper's Weekly magazine in October 1857. It could just as easily have been written in the 1970s or 80s. Yes, the more things change, the more things seem the same.

With regard to investment market prices, cyclical fluctuations have long been recognized. The concept of rising (bull) and declining (bear) markets is evident in the literature going back hundreds of years. Charles Mackay in his book *Extraordinary Popular Delusions and the Madness of Crowds* (London: Bentley, 1841), refers to numerous boom-bust cycles of past eras. Among the more famous to which Mackay referred were the wild tulip bulb speculation in Europe in 1634 and the South Sea "bubbles" of the early 1700s in which numerous "joint-stock" companies were formed to ride the unbelievable crest of speculation (and subsequent crash) of world trade ventures. Edwin Lefevre, in his book *Reminiscences of a Stock Operator* (Larchmont, New York: American Research Council, 1923), details many exciting stories of the famous speculator Jesse Livermore. The accounts dramatize the rising markets and subsequent crashes of the late 1800s and early 1900s in America. Bernard Baruch, in his autobiography *My Own Story*, Volume 1, (New York: Holt, 1957), recalls numerous cycles of exciting market advances and ensuing panics of the early 1900s.

An interesting aspect to these stories is that crowd psychology

FIGURE 7-2 The Economic Key to Your Investment Survival

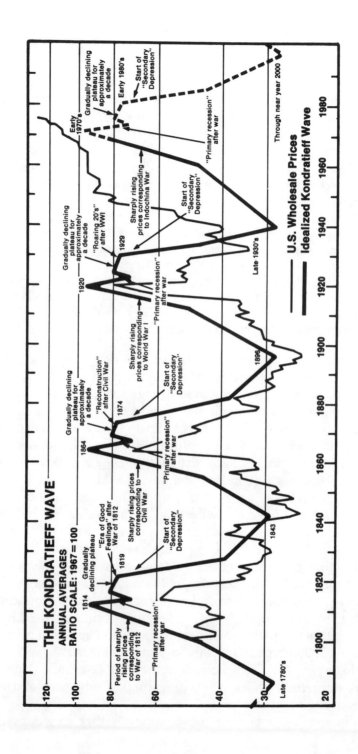

SOURCE: International Moneyline. © 1976 International Moneyline.

played a role at least as great as that of the economic fundamentals. skyrocketed in the late 1970s. Silver, for example, went from five dollars to fifty dollars an ounce in a flurry of hype and worldwide attention on the Hunt brothers trying to corner the market (See Figure 7–3).

- American high technology companies soared to tremendous heights in the early 1980s, reaching price-earnings ratios of 60 or more by 1983. Everyone was enamored with "high tech." Subsequently prices collapsed, with some shares dropping within 18 months to a mere 10 to 20 percent of their high prices!

- The entire Japanese stock market, as of mid-1990, had increased to tremendous levels, with the average price-earnings level near 60. Will history repeat and send Japanese prices south? History suggests so.

  [Reviewing this text in November 1990 just prior to publication, I should add that the Japanese stock market is down 40 percent from its peak. This has been a profitable event for my clients, as we bought put options on Japan and realized a 550% increase on them in less than a year. A put option is the right to sell the underlying instrument at a given price. It's a way to make money in a declining market.]

Notice how the chart of the Japanese stock market (Figure 7–4) compares to the silver market between 1973 and 1979. There was a period of gradually rising prices leading to an acceleration phase. This is a very typical pattern that investment markets often portray prior to a big drop.

Let's take a look at the U.S. stock market. Figure 7–5 shows the Dow Jones Industrial Average for most of this century. There are several observations to be made. The long term is up, but one of the most interesting things is that there have been long periods of stagnation in the market, followed by upward surges in prices. The stagnation or trading range periods, shown by dotted line boxes, have been characterized by war and inflation. The upward surges are often referred to as *secular* bull markets. There have been three secular bull markets in this century:

FIGURE 7-3   Silver and Gold Prices, 1969 to 1984

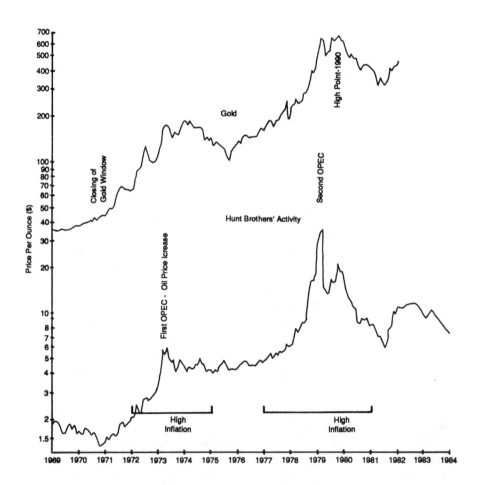

SOURCE: Roger G. Ibbotson and Gary P. Brimson, *Gaining the Performance Advantage, Invest-ment Markets* (New York: McGraw-Hill, 1987).

**FIGURE 7-4   Nikkei 225 versus Dow Jones versus S & P 500,
January 1969 to December 1989**

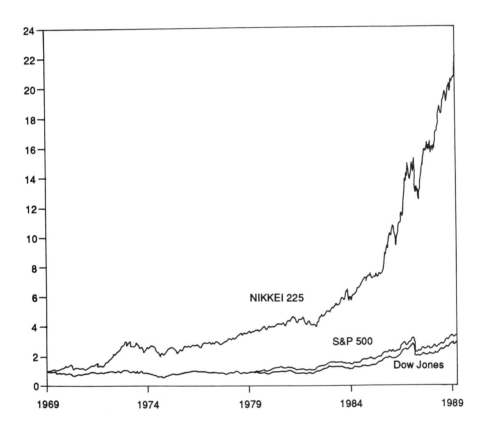

FIGURE 7-5   Dow Jones Industrial Average and Consumer Price Index in the 20th Century

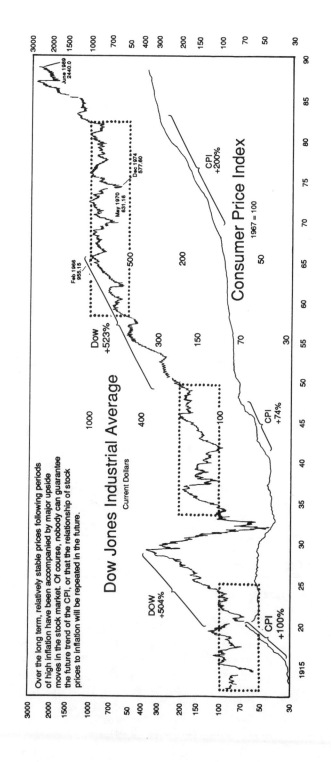

SOURCE: Courtesy Media General Financial Services, Richmond, Virginia.

1.   1921 to 1929 (break-out point in 1924).

2.   1941 to 1966 (break-out point in 1950).

3.   1974 to 1987 (break-out point in 1982).

The so-called break-out points were the places where prices emerged for good from the trading range. Each of the three stagnation periods showed trading ranges equal to approximately 100 percent:

1.   Dow Jones 50 to Dow Jones 100 equals 100 percent.

2.   Dow Jones 100 to Dow Jones 200 equals 100 percent.

3.   Dow Jones 500 to Dow Jones 1,000 equals 100 percent.

The extent of the upswings from just prior to the break-out points has been roughly 500 percent. Applying this relationship to the present bull market, the Dow Jones Industrials, when counting from the 800 Dow level, which prevailed just prior to the break-out point in 1982, could reach to between 3,500 and 4,000 before the end of this secular bull market.

Again, notice that bull markets often begin from long periods of inactivity. As they emerge, they gradually build up steam and eventually enter the acceleration phase. Prices usually go much farther than anticipated. They then peak out in a dramatic "blow-off." But a cautionary note to today's investor: These cycles should not be expected to be precise. The Dow peak of 3000 reached in 1990 is close enough to the predicted goal that the latest secular bull market might be over.

Now, breaking down the very long secular trends into shorter-term trends, we note rather distinct swings averaging about three to four years. These cycles are referred to as *cyclical* trends. On average, the bear market portion of these cycles has been about one year, while the bull portion has averaged a little over two years. Thus the market has been in bear markets one-third of the time, and in bull markets two-thirds of the time. Some cycles are longer or shorter than average and may range from two to six years, including both the bull and bear phases.

Looking at bear markets alone, Figure 7–6 arbitrarily illustrates only market declines that lasted 10 months or more. As you can see, the general pattern is for bear markets to show drops of 20 to 40 percent as measured from their high point. This chart is particularly interesting as it gives one some perspective on the 1987 Crash relative to other bear markets. As you can see, with its 40 percent or so drop, it was within the norm of most bear markets in history.

My own inclination is to include in the definition of a bear market all drops that are near 15 percent on the Dow Jones Industrial Average (or 20 percent on broader indexes such as the Value Line Index of 1700 stocks) if they fit into the normal three to four year cycle pattern. With this broad definition of a bear market, drops such as 1953 and 1984 would qualify as minibears.

Cyclical bull markets not only last twice as long as bear markets but produce percentage gains more than double the drops of bear markets. As measured from the bottom of the bear market lows, some of the shorter bull markets were 1966 to 1968 and 1978 to 1981, both

FIGURE 7-6 Bear Market Declines: How Bad Were They?

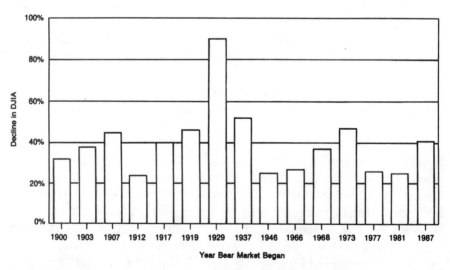

SOURCE: P.R. Chandy and George Christy, "A History of Bear Markets: How Bad Were They?" *AAII Journal*, October 1989. American Association of Individual Investors, P.O. Box 11092, Chicago, IL 60611-9737.

of which increased about 40 percent. Many bull markets show gains of 80 to 100 percent, for example 1942 to 1946 and 1974 to 1976. And once in awhile, you have one come along much greater than average such as 1984 to 1987, which was up 150 percent.

Some cycles are so extreme and occur so seldom that we can eliminate them from practical planning considerations. The 1929 era is the noticeable anomaly in this regard, both in terms of how far that market went up *and* down. Further, the precise beginning or ending point is fuzzy for some cycles. The Dow Jones Average may show one thing, while another index may show another. However, we can allow for these differences to construct a range of "normalized" cycles. Accordingly, the history of market cycles is summarized in Table 7–1.

TABLE 7–1

Stock Market Cycles (Normalized)

	Duration		
	Minimum	Average	Maximum
Bear Phase	6 mo.	13 mo.	25 mo.
Bull Phase	14 mo.	26 mo.	50 mo.
	Extent		
	Minimum	Average	Maximum
Bear Phase	15%	30%	50%
Bull Phase	40%	70%	150%

In addition to the cyclical trends, there are many smaller trends. The next smaller trends are 3 to 18 month moves that interrupt the cyclical trend. As a practical matter, these intermediate trends are too small to worry much about. We'll refer to them later in the chapter.

The concept of repetitive market cycles is not new. In my newspaper column in 1977 I wrote an article (Figure 7–7) that compared the 1920s market with the 1970s market. The gist of the comparison was that the modern market had the potential to leap ahead, just as it did

FIGURE 7-7 Seventies, Twenties Compared

Seventies, twenties compared

By CHARLES MEEK

Does history repeat itself?

According to followers of Nikolai Kondratieff, a 1920's Russian economist, the market is now unfolding a crucial historical cycle. The report, entitled "The Economic Key to Your Investment Survival" comes from International Moneyline.

The reasoning holds that for hundreds of years we have gone through long economic waves of about 54 years average length. Each wave peak is marked by fantastic highs in inflation and interest rates.

The last peak, 1974, is comparable to the peak in 1920. Each peak has been associated with a major recession, followed in 8 to 10 years by yet another major "secondary depression."

That recession would come around 1982, as it did in 1929. But the interim period until 1982, as in the mid to late 1920's, will be of relative equilibrium.

According to cycle theorists, this interim plateau period should witness signifi-

market savvy

cant easing of inflation and interest rates. The Dow should boom to 1500 or even higher.

Many comparisons can be made between the early 1970's and the early 1920's. For instance, in 1919-1920 there was also an energy shortage, and various experts were warning within a few years the world would run out of oil.

We also had the Teapot Dome scandal as a counterpart to Watergate.

Notice the chart which compares the 1970's Dow with that of the 1920's. Such comparisons never continue precisely, and in fact many believe that a mild recession in 1978 may delay the expected advance.

But it certainly isn't hard to visualize much higher stock prices. All that is needed is a return to more normal price-earnings ratios.

Throughout history, man has been faced with the rise and fall of business cycles. These ups and downs "are merely stages in a repetitious pattern, which must be understood in order to maximize chances for profits and/or survival."

Like the tides and seasons, history does repeat itself.

Questions, comments, suggestions may be directed to Charles Meek in care of The Austin American-Statesman or by calling 474-5811.)

ON THE KONDRATIEFF TRACK

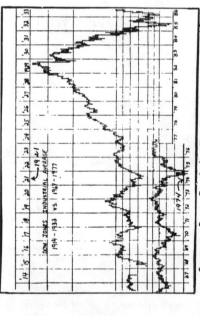

Source: Burns Fry Ltd., Toronto, Canada

SOURCE: *The Austin American-Statesman,* July 3, 1977, p. C14.

during the 1920s. Though the timing was imperfect, the general course of subsequent events has been playing out as expected. Intriguing, isn't it?

Will the next big down move be as devastating as the one from 1929 to 1932? It seems unlikely. Though cycles repeat, each cycle has its differences. The difference today compared to 1929 is that there are many safeguards built into our economy. These include guarantees for bank and brokerage deposits, social security, unemployment insurance, and better control of the supply of money by the Federal Reserve. However, we'll never repeal the law of supply and demand nor alter the emotions of human fear and greed. So cycles of some form will always be with us.

My approach is to concentrate on the cyclical trends. Dwelling on these trends, the question becomes: Is it worth taking advantage of these cycles? As part of an independent study for my MBA degree, I studied this question.[2] I looked at the period from 1949 to 1976 as an example, which essentially included one entire secular bull market with the ensuing period of stagnation. Ignoring dividends received and commissions paid, if one had invested $10,000 in the Dow Jones Industrial Average at the June 1949 bottom (Dow 161.60) and held his position until March of 1976 (Dow 1009.21), his portfolio would have grown to $62,451. However, there were eight cyclical swings during this period. If one had bought within 10 percent of each cyclical low point, and sold within 10 percent of each cyclical peak, his $10,000 would have grown to $111,965.36.

This approach would have *doubled* the total return over the period. This does not appear to be an unreasonable goal. Remember that with the Dow near 2000, for example, missing important turns by 10 percent would be the equivalent of 200 points, a fairly large margin of error. And note that one would have had two chances at each turning point—going into the turn and then again coming out of it.

Refining the possibilities a bit more, if one could have bought and sold within five percent of the absolute bottoms and tops, the $10,000 would have grown to $251,004. Or, instead of merely keeping cash during the bear markets, if one had sold short within 5 percent of the tops and covered his short positions and bought to a fully invested long position at 5 percent from the low points, his $10,000 would have grown to $787,923.

A study by *World Investment News,* April 1987, conducted on the New York Exchange noted the following:

1. 50 to 60 percent of a stock's appreciation is attributable to the general economy and general market movements.

2. 20 to 30 percent is attributable to the performance of its industry.

3. Only 10 to 30 percent is attributable to firm-specific influences like management, research and development, and marketing.

Overall market trends are very important to the movement of a particular stock. The astute investor is not oblivious to the general market and its cycles.

To be perfectly fair, I must point out that there are those who say market timing is folly. They point out various facts such as this one: The 1982 to 1987 bull market produced annual gains of 26%. However, if you missed the best 40 days during that period, your return dropped to only 4% per annum. Thus, they say, the chance of missing the good times by being out of the market if you guess wrong, outweighs the risk of buying and holding through possible bad times. My response to that is to let the reader of this chapter make up his or her own mind about whether to be a market timer or not. Let's look further at how you can put knowledge about market cycles to work for you.

The long term trend of the stock market has always been up. The reason is that companies, i.e., people, continually create new value by developing new products, ideas, services, and markets. But within the long term uptrend, the existence of market cycles is clearly evident. It is doubtful that any investor is ever able to consistently demonstrate anywhere near perfect market timing. However, the more that an investor can develop an awareness of this phenomenon of cycles, the more he should be able to improve the performance of his portfolio.

Most investors are aware of the cyclical nature of the stock market

FIGURE 7–8

ratio of Public Shorts to Total Shorts, probably our most reliable indicator, gave a cluster of 9 straight SELL signals

MONETARY INDICATORS

Elsewhere, facts about the economy sparked action--some appropriate, some riot--in the stock market.

ACCORDING TO MANY CHARTISTS, whether or not a move by the Dow-Jones industrials is confirmed by the transportations is highly significant.

Negative Volume Index,

OUR FLOW-OF-FUNDS ANALYSIS INDICATES THE NEXT MAJOR MARKET MOVE WILL BE DOWN . . .

We sense that a growing number of advisers are becoming more bearish, and that, of course is bullish.

"In fact, there was a lot of disappointment in Mr. Carter's remarks, particularly about his anti-inflation program, which might take several weeks more for him to unveil," said Charles Jensen, chief technical analyst at Merkin & Co.

RETAIL SALES rose 2.4%

30-Week Weighted
Moving Average

"It seems the market will have to rebound from its own internal strength, without any help from the President," commented Harry W. Laubscher, first vice president at Blyth Eastman Dillon & Co. Robert Mintz, vice president at Philips, Appel & Walden Inc., believes the market will remain "listless until President Carter unveils his energy program." Its implications to "Americans as to expected changes in life style is far-reaching and has forced investors into a defensive position," Mr. Mintz asserted.

INSIDER BAIL OUT

Today the Real M2 indicator is in a pronounced upward trend and is graded bullish

JANUARY BAROMETER SPEAKS

Pressure yesterday on blue chips and glamours reflected the swithching of stocks by money managers preparatory to dressing up their portfolios for the end of the first quarter, analysts said.

BEAR-MARKET RALLY

Short Interest Ratio

Margin debt — money borrowed from brokers by stock traders--has become one of the more baffling indicators followed by market analysts.

The budget deficit grew to $6.55 billion last month from January's $2.66 billion, but officials said the U.S. is still spending less than it should.

Double-digit inflation may be a clear danger

THIRD-QUARTER GNP FIGURES SUGGEST THAT ECONOMIC ACTIVITIES HAVE PEAKED

If any single investment concept has run like a thread through the stock market during the past two years it is the emphasis on high dividend yield.

LEADING INDICATOR TROUBLES

BUT DON'T EXPECT THE U.S. ECONOMY TO FOLLOW STOCK PRICES:

Most Prices Increase In Delayed Response To Money-Supply Fall

ADVANCE-DECLINE RATIO

BIG BLOCK INDEX   Odd Lot Short Sales

THE DIRECTION OF THE MARKET'S NEXT MAJOR MOVE WILL PROBABLY REFLECT ECONOMIC DISAPPOINTMENTS

On the other hand, the lack of volume on both dips and rallies, coupled with the huge air pockets that seem to be developing under a variety of issues, suggest that the Dow is still flailing around in search of a bottom.

THE "NEW" TWO-TIER MARKET

price trends.

DEBT/COLLATERAL RATIO

Speculation Index

EXPECTATIONAL INDICATORS

The market is benefiting from an "improved technical picture," said Newton D. Zinder, vice president at E. F. Hutton & Co.

FED INDICATOR

optimism and complacency still reign

and, further, that there are numerous factors affecting share prices. Portfolio strategy is thus a continuous effort to weigh and evaluate the various determinants of market fluctuations.

A real problem for most investors, however, is often not the availability of investment information, but rather the ability to wade through the swamp of data already at hand and to translate it into a realistic portfolio posture. Figure 7–8 is a sample of the type of data that an investor faces daily. This blizzard of data can be bewildering to the investor. The financial press, government statisticians, market writers and analysts, as well as the emotions and concerns of the individual investor himself all join in the barrage.

Let me ask you this: How do you feel when you come home from work, turn on the TV, and see on the evening news that the Dow Jones was up 50 points? Do you feel excited that things are happening and you need to get in? Or do you feel a rush of nervousness because the market must be too high? The correct answer is that you should not feel either. You should be able to approach investing with a cold rationality rather than emotional judgments.

What's the poor investor to do? How can one make sense out of all this? How often have you, as an investor, regretted making an emotional decision, ignoring good common sense? Or "whipsawed" yourself by weighing some factors heavily at one time, then overlooking the same factors another time? Or become too flustered to take a stance that you could sleep with, worrying about the what-ifs?

What really would help many investors is a decision framework or model to guide them, without losing the necessary flexibility for intelligent input. For those investors who are interested in the concept of market cycles and timing, I have developed a simple but balanced model. I believe this approach can help investors effectively evaluate market cycles and, simultaneously, improve their portfolio strategy for more consistent profits.

There are essentially four basic ingredients, or cycle components to the market. The first is *economic*, that is, what are the economy and corporate profits doing? The second is *monetary*, i.e., what are interest rates doing? The third is *psychology*, which is essentially the supply/demand trends for stock prices. The fourth is *momentum*, which is the study of the trend of the market and tendencies of extremes of cycle movements themselves. Virtually any determinant of market trends fits into these four components. Note that the economic and monetary indicators are defined as fundamental in nature, while the psychology and momentum indicators are termed technical in nature. Thus fundamental analysis and technical analysis are given an equal weighting.

Each of the four cycle categories is assigned a rating—either a plus, neutral, or negative. A plus is given if, on balance, the factors are bullish for the market. You would assign a negative if your interpretation suggests a bearish outlook. Do not let your feelings about one cycle category affect your decision on the others. And put it in writing. Adding the four ratings together gives you a maximum bullish reading of plus four and a maximum bearish reading of minus four. This summation is the model composite.

Judgments must be made when assigning ratings. Most serious investors already make at least intuitive judgments about these four factors. They often simply do not know how to use them collectively to make a realistic decision. This model offers a systematic approach to portfolio posture decisions.

The model is primarily designed to capture the cyclical market movements. Generally, these movements demonstrate 15 percent or more swings. However, indicators of intermediate moves—generally 8 to 15 percent—may also be factored in so that the model is also helpful in identifying these trends as well. Later in the chapter we will discuss how to use the system to adjust your real world portfolio. But first, let's examine each of the four cycle categories to learn to make a reasonable judgment of bullish, bearish or neutral.

A word of warning. Some of the stuff in the rest of this chapter may seem to get a little hairy. If you've not had any experience so far in market cycle analysis, you may think the author went off the deep end. If the details start bogging you down, just skim through it to get the feel for the concepts. Then come back to this chapter some other time if you decide you want to really get into this! Frankly, this is for the real market buffs only. Here goes . . .

I. The Economy

Perhaps the best demonstration of the cyclical nature of the economy is real GNP. Gross national product (GNP) is the value of all goods and services produced in our economy. "Real" GNP eliminates inflation. For example, 7 percent GNP growth minus 4 percent inflation would leave 3 percent real GNP growth. Figure 7–9 shows a one year moving average of the percentage changes in real GNP. At each point on the graph, real GNP has grown at the corresponding rate over the last one year.

Noted on the chart by arrows are points at which cyclical turns in the market have occurred. The down arrows note the beginning of bear markets. The up arrows note the beginning of cyclical bull markets.

Without hypothesizing why such cycles occur, we merely note that our economy is structurally unable to sustain growth rates greater than about 7 to 8 percent. The ball inevitably rolls down hill. Stock prices anticipate this and begin to fall at the peak rate of growth. When real GNP growth reaches about 5 to 6 percent, a market top is usually near.

Note that since business news is still excellent at this point, most investors are caught completely unaware. Note also that in fact it is not necessary to have a recession for a bear market to ensue. A recession, loosely defined, is when growth drops below zero. It is necessary only to have a slowing in the growth rate for the market to decline. Notice on the chart that growth never got below zero in 1962 and 1966, yet sharp bear markets occurred.

I should point out that this chart is configured to show the growth *rate* of GNP. It does not show the *absolute* growth. A chart of the absolute change in GNP would show a generally upward graph ending much higher than it begins. Obviously, GNP was much higher in 1988 than it was in 1949. The most enlightening way to view most economic statistics is to look at the rate of change. Most investors make the mistake of looking at the absolute levels of change.

Business cycle troughs do not reach as consistent levels as do peaks. It is relatively easy to know how strong the economy can get on the upside, but difficult to tell how far down economic activity can go before natural forces arrest the slide. Since World War II, most declines have taken real GNP (one-year moving average) to around minus 1 to minus 3 percent. The associated bear market in stock prices has ended anywhere from three to twelve months prior to the bottom of this

FIGURE 7-9 Real GNP

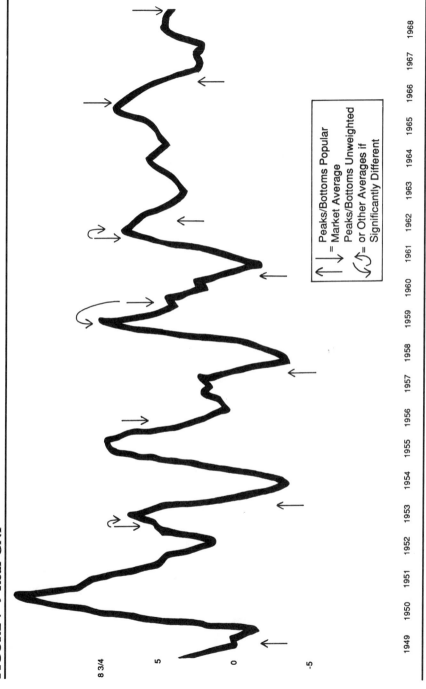

Peaks/Bottoms Popular
↑↓ = Market Average
Peaks/Bottoms Unweighted
↩↪ = or Other Averages if
Significantly Different

FIGURE 7-9 (*concluded*)

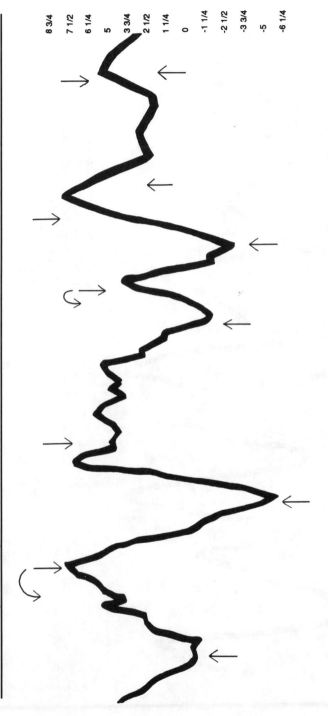

indicator, usually as the indicator reaches the zero mark. Significant is the fact that bear markets usually end before or near the gloomiest days of the recession—when business news is worsening. Only the more farsighted investors are thinking of the business recovery that inevitably will come, when economic news is bad and real growth has been declining for some time. It is then that we should begin to anticipate a cyclical recovery. GNP statistics can be obtained from the Federal Reserve Bank of St. Louis, P.O. Box 442, St. Louis, MO 63166, in their publication *National Economic Trends.*

Another set of basic economic statistics that can be helpful are the government's monthly report of "leading, coincident, and lagging" economic indicators. A source for this data is the monthly *Survey of Current Business* available from the Superintendent of Documents, Government Printing Office, Washington, D.C. 20402–9371. The government calculates what is called diffusion indexes for the three series, which show the percentage of the components that are expanding within each of the three series.

Gray Emerson Cardiff, editor of *Sound Advice* newsletter (191 North Hartz Avenue, Danville, CA 94526) suggests taking certain components of these indexes to assist with one's stock market timing. Historically, the leading indicators have been good at predicting stock market bottoms, while the lagging indicators have helped signal market tops.

Here's how his method works. Even though there are actually 11 leading indicators, Cardiff says to track these six:

Key Leading Indicators To Identify Market Bottoms

5. Average weekly claims for unemployment insurance, state programs.

8. Manufacturer's new orders in 1982 dollars, consumer bonds and materials industries.

29. New private housing units authorized by local building permits.

32. Vendor performance—slower deliveries diffusion index.

92. Change in manufacturers' unfilled orders in 1982 dollars, durable goods industries.

99. Change in sensitive materials prices, smooth.

The concept is that when the economic statistics show maximum weakness, the market is near a bottom.

Just watch these statistics as reported in the *Survey of Current Business*, and when all six are weaker than their level of six months earlier, that's a buy signal. (Because number 5 deals with unemployment rather than employment, this one is interpreted inversely and must be above its six-month earlier level.)

To spot market tops, watch the lagging indicators. Though there are actually seven of these in the government report, the following six are used by Cardiff:

Key Lagging Indicators to Identify Market Tops

62. Change in index of labor cost per unit of output, manufacturing.

77. Ratio, manufacturing and trade inventories to sales in 1982 dollars.

91. Average duration of unemployment in weeks.

101. Commercial and industrial loans outstanding in 1982 dollars.

109. Average prime rate charged by banks.

120. Change in consumer price index for services.

When all six lagging indicators are above their level of six months earlier, that's a sell signal. (Like number 5 in the leading group, number 91 in the lagging group deals with unemployment rather than employment, so it must be below its six-month earlier level to trigger the signal.) The idea is that at this point the economy is overheated and due for a setback along with the stock market.

As you can see from Figure 7–10, the leading-lagging indicator system has a terrific record. However, no one's approach is perfect. In actuality, the sell signals in 1984 and 1987 were received a bit too late to be really helpful. Cardiff factors in certain monetary triggers that, when used with the leading-lagging indicators, improved the sell signals in 1984 and 1987. His book *Panic-Proof Investing* details his entire system.

In terms of our model, we can use the GNP indicator, the leading-lagging indicator, or other indicators you may learn about to assign a rating for the economic component. You should be able to get a consensus weight-of-the-evidence opinion on scoring. For example, if real GNP is near 6 percent and/or the lagging indicators are near the maximum, a minus score is warranted.

On the other hand, if real GNP has crossed below zero percent growth over the last one year, and/or if all the leading indicators are below their six-month earlier level—bingo. Assign a plus score. Generally, stay with a rating until you near an extreme in the opposite

FIGURE 7-10 Cardiff Diffusion Index Indicator

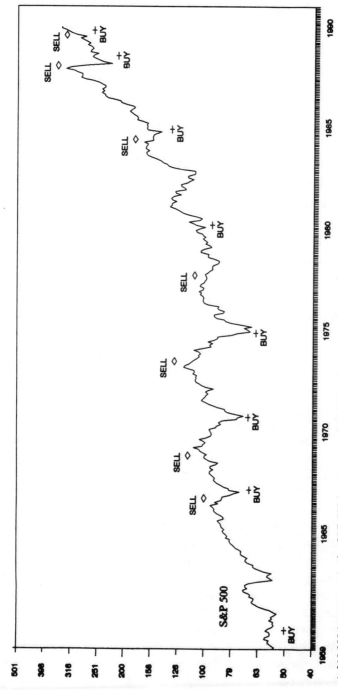

A $10,000 investment in the S&P 500 has grown to $51,619 since November 1959 (including dividends). However, that same investment has grown to $325,207 by following the signals of the Diffusion Indexes (shown above). Thus, these signals have allowed investors to outperform the market by close to 7 times.

SOURCE: Sound Advice, 191 North Hartz, Suite 6, Danville, CA 94526, (415) 838-8100

direction. The general rule is that you assume a trend to remain in force until proven otherwise. However, a neutral rating is appropriate if the indicators are conflicting.

Remember this: We live in an imprecise world. No forecasting method is absolute. The purpose of this model is to give you a sound but flexible framework to make decisions for the future. You will have to make judgments even though all of those judgments will not be perfect. But I think you can see as we continue to lay out the evidence that you will shortly have all the basic tools to make decisions with confidence.

There are other indicators of economic cycles. The beauty of this model is that it is not static. You can use other data that your own study or reading uncovers. The key is to have sufficient historical data to correlate with market movements.

II. Monetary

Other books have been written on the relationship between interest rates and stock prices. The concept is simple. Rising interests rates are bad for the market because it hurts business and diverts money away from stocks to interest bearing deposits. Falling interest rates are likewise good for stocks. There are several ways to analyze these trends:

- Level of interest rates.

- Direction of interest rates.

- Dividend yields and P/E ratios on stock themselves.

Level of Interest Rates.   There are dozens of ways analysts quantify whether interest rates are too high or too low. I'll just highlight a couple that anyone can easily follow.

The Treasury Bill/Discount Rate Indicator.   Treasury bills are short term securities issued by the U.S. Treasury. The discount rate is the rate charged by the Federal Reserve Board to member commercial banks for borrowing money. The concept is that when the T-bill rate trades in the open market above the artificially set discount rate, the Fed (Federal Reserve Board) is forced to tighten credit. This is negative for stocks. Likewise, when T-bill rates are below the discount rate, that's a good sign for stocks. Figure 7–11 shows how this indicator worked in the past. The downward arrows marked sell points, and the upward arrows marked buy points on this indicator. If confirmed by other monetary indicators, the sell points imply a minus score for the model. The buy points imply a plus score for the model.

A good place to get this information is in *The Wall Street Journal* or *Barron's*. By the way, T-bill rates are quoted in two ways. They are traded at a percentage discount to face value and are thus often quoted by their discount amount (not to be confused by the Fed's discount rate). The effective yield to the buyer is higher than the discount percentage (since the effective yield is based on investing an amount that is less than face value.) So they may be stated as yield-to-maturity instead of discount percentage. For this indicator, we use the discount rather than the effective yield-to-maturity.

FIGURE 7–11 Three Month Treasury Bill & Discount Rate

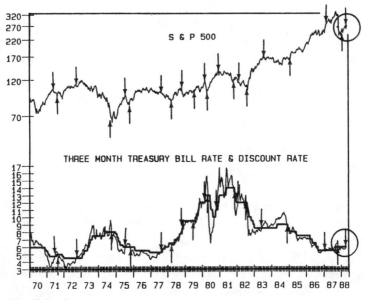

SOURCE: Merrill Lynch.

The Treasury bill/S&P 500 dividend yield indicator. This time the yield-to-maturity rather than the discount is arbitrarily used. This indicator compares T-bill yields to dividend rates on the Standard & Poors Index. As you can see in Figure 7–12, when rates on T-bills are 2.0 percent higher than dividend yields, trouble is brewing. When T-bill yields have dropped to less than 1.6 percent over stock yields, buy signals are given. *Barron's* is again a good source for ongoing data on this indicator.

Direction of Interest Rates. In addition to the level of rates, the direction is also important. You can watch any of several interest rate indicators, but the easiest to follow is the prime rate. The prime rate is the rate banks charge their best customers. It is well publicized, and its direction is obvious since it is changed in distinct steps.

Historically, stock prices have taken an upward direction with the first drop in the prime. However, it may take several increases to break the back of a roaring bull market. This is true because in the latter stages of an economic advance, usually the second or third year of a bull market, the market is going up with the economy. Interest rates are also going up because of strong demand for credit. As far as the market is concerned, the accelerating economy is a more powerful influence than increasing interest rates. But sooner or later the increasing rates will catch up with the market.

Here's the basic formula for the prime rate indicator: This indicator

FIGURE 7–12 Ratio T-Bill Yields/S&P 500 Dividend Yields

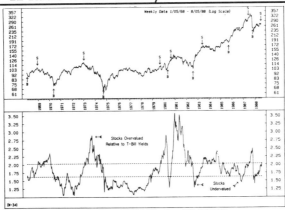

SOURCE: Ned Davis Research, P.O. Box 2087, Venice, FL 33595.

is in *plus* territory whenever the most recent change in the prime was downward. This indicator is in *minus* territory after the prime has increased at least one full percentage point within one year.

Historical studies have shown that using this indicator alone, or slight variations of it, have produced results 2 to 7 percent better annual returns than the stock market as a whole, depending on the exact method and time period studied.[3]

This indicator has "made" some terrific calls over the years. For example, October 4, 1974 was the day the prime rate was first lowered after months of increase. It was also the very day that the most devastating bear market since the Great Depression ended! And in early September 1987, just a month before the now infamous Black Monday, the prime rate was raised to 8¾ percent, which was 1 percent higher than earlier in the same year, triggering a sell signal. What a timely indicator!

Dividend Yields and P/E Ratios.   Dividend yields are the cash dividends paid to investors as a percentage of the market value. The price/earnings ratio (P/E ratio) is the market value of the stock(s) divided by the earnings per share. This is a standard measurement of how high a stock is selling compared to its earnings. According to Value Line, at the secular peak in 1968 P/E ratios were a high 19.0 and dividend yields were a low 2.7 percent for the approximately 1700 companies in their survey. At the 1974 secular low point in the market, P/E ratios were an incredibly low 4.8 and dividend yields were a very high 7.8 percent. Though these ratios give us a general feel for extremes in market valuations, they are difficult to use in our model because turning points are not consistent. For example, high P/E ratios were evident during the entire bull market of the 1960s, as shown in Figure 7–13.

However, most investors are familiar with these ratios. Extremes in them are warning signs for trend changes in the market. (P/E ratios are a form of inverted interest rates, thus they should be considered as a monetary indicator.) High P/Es and low dividend yields lend support to a negative model rating, and vice versa. It is helpful to

FIGURE 7–13 Standard & Poors Composite Index

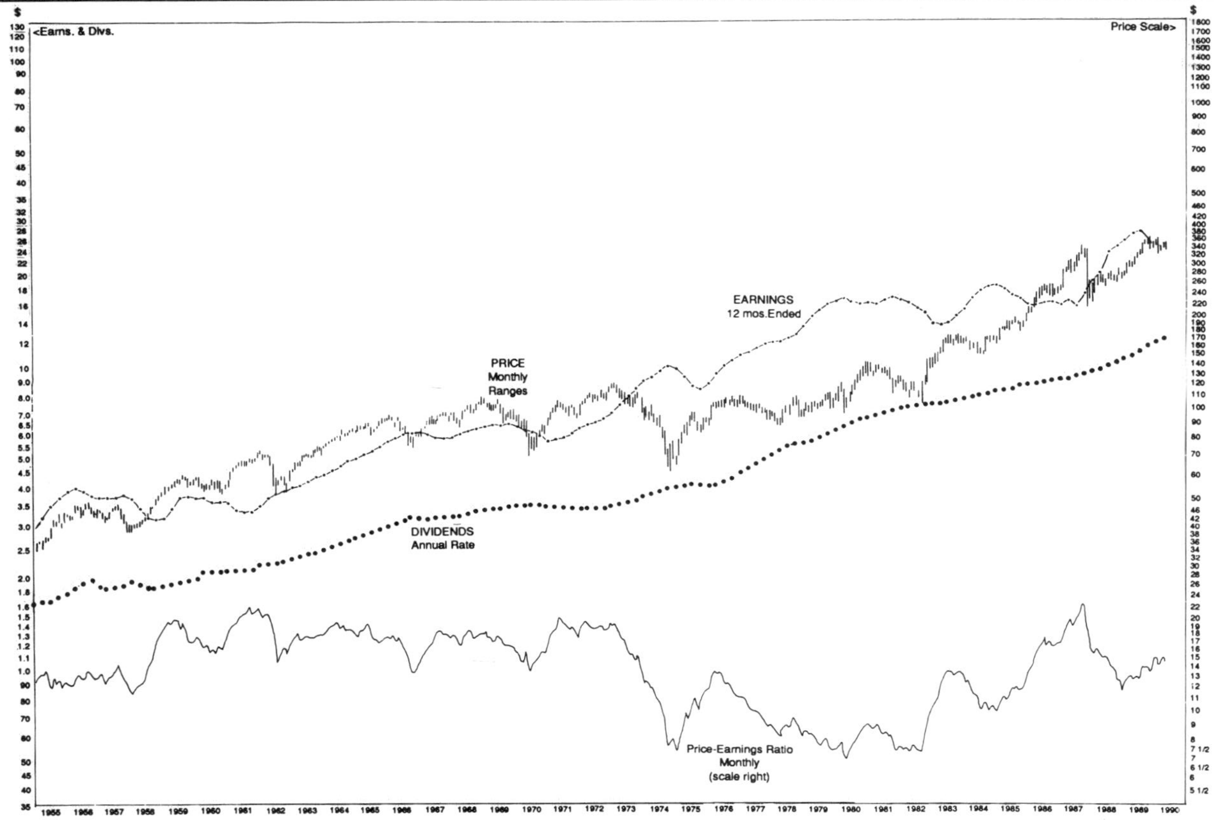

observe the trend in the P/E ratio, especially in identifying market peaks. Note that a drop in the P/E ratio has preceded or coincided with cyclical tops.

Interest rates are perhaps the favorite topic of discussion among investors (next to politics!). Available data confirms the importance of interest rates as an indicator of stock market trends. Rising rates are bad for the market, declining rates are healthy. Interest rate trends should be obvious to any observer. The message is: Heed what you see!

The model forces you to gather the data and formulate a decision on how monetary indicators are affecting the market. You can use simple interest rate indicators, or get very involved with fancy monetary models if that's your bag. You can add other monetary indicators you read about. I actually track over 20 of them myself, but that's not necessary. Tracking even two or three will help you evaluate the monetary component. Hopefully the explanation in this section gives you the ability to formulate a "weight-of-the-evidence" opinion based on your analysis of each indicator and assign a plus, neutral, or negative into the model.

III. Psychology

Anyone who has dabbled in the stock market is undoubtedly aware that there seem to be other factors involved in market fluctuations that cannot be explained fully by fundamental analysis. Oftentimes, for example, trends are carried to extremes that seem to have little relationship to underlying fundamentals. Here is where an understanding of crowd psychology begins to play an essential part in the understanding of cycles.

The important concept is that investor sentiment tends to be most negative at market bottoms and most optimistic at market tops. This is a very important concept, although it is, perhaps, just the opposite of what one might expect. Actually, it is not too hard to understand.

In a bull market, for example, more and more investors come into the market. At each stage of advance, investors gain more confidence in their recent successes and are inclined to commit progressively more capital. The success of these participants encourages bystanders, who then begin to get into the market. The optimism builds to a crescendo, at which point a majority of investors are fully invested. Obviously, if one is fully invested, he is maximally optimistic! But if everyone is fully invested, there is no buying power left. And alas! Prices are then the most vulnerable to any selling pressure.

As the inevitable downward cycle begins, the selling gets progressively greater. At the bottom of the market a relatively large number of investors are selling (which of course is the reason that stock prices are going down). Gloom and doom pervade the investment community.

This concept is age old. Charles E. Merrill, founder of Merrill Lynch, wrote these words in 1911 in a piece entitled "Making Money—Why Follow the Crowd":

> *Nearly every man who makes an investment violates the principals he applies to his own business. Relying on merely a superficial knowledge of all that is involved, he undertakes to manage the entire job himself; whether investor or speculator, he begins by buying at the tops and ends by selling at the bottom. The various articles he reads in the newspapers about prosperity, bumper crops, shortage in freight cars, heavy foreign trade balances, factories running overtime inspire him with confidence. His own business is booming, collections are good and the tight-fisted bankers are using his dollars to make more dollars to their personal profit.*
>
> *Even the snug sum in the savings bank, drawing from three to four percent interest, points an accusing finger. "Put me to work," says Mr. Bank Balance. "Give me a chance to prove my mettle. I, too, can grow like Jack's beanstalk. Don't you know that Mr. Nextdoor Neighbor made ————." But Mr. Average Investor has heard enough. He buys something—anything. He follows the crowd and buys when everyone is buying. When the inevitable reaction comes and the pendulum swings the other way, when "demagogues stand on the graves of great, dead industries and boast to the multitude of the unemployed of their bloody deeds," and prices crumble daily, the odds are fearful that Mr. Average Investor again follows the crowd and sells when everyone else is selling. He begins with a light heart and heavy pocketbook and ends with a heavy heart and a light pocketbook.*
>
> *What has he gained? Experience. What is his conclusion? That the investment of money requires specific knowledge and experience, in the same degree that the management of his own business requires specific knowledge and experience; that the time to invest, either for income or profit, is when good securities are selling near the average low prices and "to be thankful if they go lower, that he may buy more at a cheaper price."*

Now, as then, when investor psychology becomes very one-sided, the astute investor can usually assume that the correct thing to do is the opposite of general expectations. To put it another way, to outperform the investing masses, you must buy before the crowd buys, and sell before the crowd begins selling. This approach is sometimes referred to as the "Theory of Contrary Opinion."

How does one accomplish this? Well, old timers on Wall Street advise developing a cynical attitude toward everything that is around you. Much of what comes out of the media is oriented to the immediate past and should be taken with a grain of salt. Investors become complacent and conditioned to a trend and are unable to adjust to a trend change. This is particularly true with secular trends. As we have discussed, secular trends last 10 to 20 years—long enough for people to become conditioned. The secular bull market peaks in 1929 and 1968 were similar in two respects:

1.   It was generally felt that recessions had become obsolete.

2.   The vast majority of the people in our nation were invested in stocks.

Daniel Cashman and James Farrell, Jr., successful contrary opinion money managers, in a timely report before the 1987 market crash, called attention to the following statements made in 1929:[4]

- Eugene Stevens, president of the Continental Illinois Bank, said, "There is nothing in the business situation to justify any nervousness."

- Irving Fisher, widely quoted economist from Yale University, said, "Stock prices have reached a permanently high plateau. I expect to see the stock market a good deal higher than it is today within a few months."

- *The Wall Street Journal* (July 8, 1929) said, "Some traders are so bullish they have stopped naming tops for certain stocks, and they say they will never stop going up."

- *The Wall Street Journal* (July 9, 1929) said, "We will continue in a major bull market indefinitely."

- *The Wall Street Journal* (September 5, 1929, just two days after the top) said, " . . .There is still an absence of abnormal trading volume and feverish turnover that usually precedes a change in the wind."

- *The Wall Street Journal* (September 28, 1929) said, "The market has suffered a very severe break, but the decline has been orderly . . . the street terms it the type of healthy reaction from which there is always a substantial recovery."

The problem is that at the time of important tops, the rationale for high prices seems perfectly sound. Cashman and Farrell say it this way:

> . . . *No matter where or when important tops were made, the vast majority of investors, the brightest or the dumbest, were unable to recognize the change that was about to visit them. Having been seduced by the illusory myth of the day they became incapable of rational thought. Illusion is too strong a narcotic.*[5]

The attitude that prevails at important turning points is "this time it's different." Rationale is presented to try to make old concepts obsolete. David Dreman, another successful contrary opinion money manager, reported this thinking by a strategist in Forbes magazine, in 1969, in the early stages of a devastating decline:

> *I would therefore like to propose the thesis that as a result of all that has been happening in the economy, the world, and the market during the last decade, we are in a different—if not new era—and traditional thinking, the standard approach to the market, is no longer in synchronization with the real world.*[6]

The early stages of bull markets are characterized by people missing the rise because they are afraid of recession or are waiting for the market pullback that doesn't come. A rising market has further to increase if many investors are waiting for a correction to buy but never seem to have that setback. A declining market has further to drop if the prevailing mood is that investors are waiting for a rally to sell, but can't seem to get the rally they want. A clue to an impending top is when a flurry of forecasts predict higher prices. A clue to a bottom is when a flurry of public forecasts mention a downside target below existing prices. Cyclical lows and highs are often marked by glamorous news stories in the media. In the fall of 1974, the Dow Jones Industrial Average was under 600 and the Value Line Index was under 50. The bottom of the long 1969 to 1974 bear market was at hand. But you would never have recognized that by the news stories:

"Bearish" Articles Near 1974 Low.
Value Line Stock Index . . . 50

> "Questions and Answers on the Prospects for a World Depression."—*Barron's*, September 1974.

> "World faces unprecedented economic, political, military crises, Kissinger says."—*The Wall Street Journal*, September 24, 1974.
> "Economic catastrophe at hand, oil prices rise—and depression looms."—*New York Times*, September 30, 1974.

Of course, the market soon rallied with great force in the face of this awful sounding news.

The summer of 1979 was similarly marked by several articles of gloom. The Value Line Index of 1700 stocks was trading near the 123 level when the articles appeared.

"Bearish" Articles During the Summer of 1979
Value Line stock index . . . 123

> *Wall Street Journal* headline July 9, 1979 "Some on Wall Street See Stocks Vulnerable to Recession's Impact"
> *Business Week* cover and feature story Aug 13, 1979 "The Death of

Equities How Inflation Is Destroying the Stock Market"
Wall Street Journal headline Aug 15, 1979 "Some People Expect An
Economic Disaster, Act Now to Be Ready
Heeding Warnings of Seers Like Howard Ruff, They Stock Food,
Tools, Guns
Memories of 1930's Linger On"

Again, the market exploded upward. Not quite four years later,
Business Week ran another feature story, this time a bullish one. This
article appeared in May 1983, shortly before the June high in the Value
Line Index of 208—69 percent higher than when the previous articles
appeared. If you had let those bearish articles in 1979 affect you, you
would have missed the tremendous advance into 1983!

"Bullish" Article after market advance.
Value Line Index . . . 208

Business Week headline and feature story May 9, 1983 "The
Rebirth of Equities
The Rally Launches A New Age for Stocks"

If you had fallen for the bullish press in 1983, guess what would
have happened to you? Between June 1983 and July 1984, the broad
market got hit with a 20 percent decline as the Value Line Index
dropped to 165, and many small company growth stocks and technology companies dropped to mere fractions of their 1983 highs! The
NASDAQ Index of over the counter stocks lost nearly 40 percent of its
value during this period. In the market place, fear creates value, while
greed creates risk. Clues to the level of fear and greed are often found
in the mass media.

Kiril Sokoloff, author of the newsletter *Street Smart Investing* (P.O.
Box 173, Katonah, NY 10536) points out that best selling books can be
an intriguing contrary indicator of psychology. Though authors may
be expressing a valid concept as it's being written, often by the time
the book becomes popular, watch out! Here's what he says:

*The easiest and simplest measure of employing contrary thinking is a close
study of best-selling business and investment books. The fifty-year record of*

these books as a contrary indicator is as close to infallible as you can find. For example, in 1924, Edgar Lawrence Smith wrote a book entitled Common Stocks as Long-Term Investments, which came to the then revolutionary conclusion that stocks were excellent long-term investments. Ironically, the book only became a best seller in the summer of 1929, just months before the crash. Between 1932 and 1968, the country had the greatest bull market in stock market history, but it was not until 1968 that an investment book made the best seller list. Ironically, The Money Game by Adam Smith became the number one best seller on July 7, 1968, exactly five months before the market topped out. While the drop in stock prices between 1968 and 1974 wasn't as severe as the 1929–32 crash, many stocks lost 70%–80 percent of their value. The next important sell signal in a market came in April 1974, when Harry Browne's You Can Profit from a Monetary Crisis became the number one national best seller. In that book, Browne recommended gold and silver as well as foreign currencies. Gold made a double top that year at just under $200 an ounce in March and again in December, but gold shares hit their peak in April. By mid-1976, gold had fallen to $103 an ounce, and an index of South African gold shares had lost 85% of its value.

The peak of inflation and the forthcoming shake-out in inflation hedges were forecast by a myriad of popular 'inflation forever' books in 1979–81. For instance, the popularity of Howard Ruff's How to Prosper During the Coming Bad Years, a 1979 best seller, suggested to contrarians that gold and silver prices had peaked in January 1980. Crisis Investing—Opportunities and Profits in the Coming Great Depression by Douglas Casey was the best-selling book of 1980, attaining the number one position in the week of September 21, 1980. The book recommended such classic inflation hedges as gold, silver, and natural resource stocks. Oil stocks peaked two months later, at the end of November, and gold and silver hit their post-1980 recession peaks of around $725 and $22 an ounce, respectively, in the last week of September. The Coming Currency Collapse by Jerome Smith, which was about the total destruction of the U.S. dollar, became a best seller in late-1980, just as the dollar began a remarkable three-year bull market. The 1981 peak in interest rates was suggested to contrarians by William E. Donoghue's Complete Money Market Guide, which became a best seller in March 1981, only five months before interest rates peaked. More recently, the demise of the high-technology stocks was indicated by the popularity of John Naisbitt's Megatrends, which became the number one best seller on March 29, 1983. Megatrends, among other things, predicted that the industrial age was dead and that we would now enter a new technology or *information age. Since their peak on June 24, 1989 many high technology issues have fallen 50% or more. What's more, the current widespread belief that the industrial age is over indicates that some of the best investment opportunities lie in the out-of-favor heavy industrial companies. Interestingly, since this summer, these stocks have been acting better than the rest of the market.*

If these contrary "forecasts" work out, you won't need to make another prediction until a stock market book reaches the best seller list, at which time it will be time to sell.

The typical cycle shows the following changes in investor psychology. As the market begins its ascent, most investors are scared. They have seen how damaging a bear market can be. Economic news is lousy. During the early stages of the bull market most investors are selling into strength as prices recover to a point that they can "get out even." Shares are passing from weak hands to strong hands.

During the middle stages of the bull market, most investors are still skeptical. They may have some money in the market, but not too much. They may have a trading mentality, taking small profits because of a timid attitude. Every small downturn in the market brings back memories of the previous bear market, and fear jumps back up. This attitude keeps cash levels and buying power high. A poll of investors will show a majority confused or skeptical about the economy and the market.

During the latter stages of a bull market investors gain confidence. There will be lots of predictions in the media of substantially higher share prices. Proponents will extol the benefits of stock investing and demonstrate this by presenting the high returns of mutual funds and stocks over the last few years. Hot young money managers will look like geniuses. Investors will become convinced that trading is for the birds—buy and hold is the way to wealth.

Down she goes. As the market starts down, the first drop looks like a great buying opportunity. Anyone who wasn't in before takes the opportunity to get a bargain. This is understandable since the economic news is good. As the market proceeds down, the economic news gets worse and worse and "recession" starts appearing in the newspaper. Near the bottom absolute fear and panic set in. Predictions of even lower prices are evident. Large numbers of investors bail out and promise to never return. "I can't compete with the institutions" and other rationalizations are muttered in the streets.

The only way to take advantage of low prices after a price collapse is to buy (more). But I will assure you this: Those times will be filled with great doubt and uncertainty, fear, panic, horror, and disgust. If you already own stocks, you'll be sick at your stomach. Your reaction will be to try to ignore the situation. When you used to delight in watching your stocks, you'll skip over the financial pages in the paper. It'll take a gut-wrenching courage to go after them when they're truly cheap. The psychology is the same at every cycle low. As money manager John Templeton says: "To buy when others are despondently selling and to sell when others are greedily buying requires the greatest fortitude and pays the greatest reward. In the stock market, the only way to get a bargain is to buy what most investors are selling."

The job of the market analyst is to try to statistically quantify psychology. This is done by analyzing the investment patterns of various investor groups such as mutual funds, insiders, foreigners, investment advisory services, specialists, put and call traders, margin account speculators, odd-lotters, cash account investors, and pension funds. Each has different investment patterns. Let's look at mutual funds, as an example, as the first of 3 easy-to-follow indicators.

1.   Mutual Fund Cash Indicator

Each month the Investment Company Institute (1600 M Street, NW, Washington, DC 20036) reports various statistics for mutual funds. These statistics, which are also reported in *Barron's,* include the cash that mutual funds have as a percentage of their total assets. I adjust the raw figures to reflect distortions created by the level of short term interest rates. During periods of high rates, investors are encouraged to keep cash (i.e., money market instruments). During periods of low rates, there is a disincentive to hold cash. The adjustment is very simple. I multiply the raw data by a factor that is determined by the discount yield level of three-month T-bills, as follows:

T-Bills	Factor
less than 4%	1.4
4–5%	1.1
5–7%	1.0
7–10%	.9
10–13%	.8
over 13%	.7

As you can see from Figure 7–14, adjusted cash levels tend to fluctuate between 5 and 10 percent. High levels of cash represent excessive pessimism and high potential demand for stocks, and have been seen near market lows.

Low levels of cash represent excessive optimism and low potential demand for stocks, which is typical near market tops. A plus model rating is indicated when adjusted cash reaches 9 percent, and a negative rating is warranted when adjusted cash dips below about 6½ percent.

You might think that mutual fund managers would be smarter than other investors. Of course some are. But when taken as a whole, mutual funds are a good indicator of the emotional tone of investors in general.

2. AAII Sentiment Indicator

Another interesting indicator is the AAII Individual Investor Sentiment Survey. It appears in each issue of the AAII Journal (P.O. Box 11092, Chicago, IL 60611–9737), and also in *Barron's*. The AAII (American Association of Individual Investors) regularly polls its members as to whether they are currently bullish on the stock market.

As you can see in Figure 7–15, this is a good contrary indicator. When the percentage bullish is over 50 percent, such as in mid-1987 or mid-1989, the market is near a peak. Thus, with readings over 50 percent, a minus rating for our model is implied. When readings of fewer than 22 percent bullish are reached, such as happened several times in 1988 and 1989, a plus rating is implied. Of course, use this indicator along with others in the psychology category to arrive at a consensus score—either plus, neutral, or minus.

FIGURE 7-14 Meek's Adjusted Mutual Fund Cash/Assets Ratio

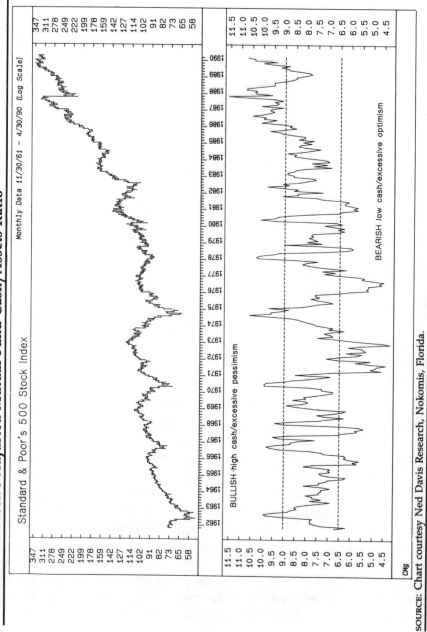

SOURCE: Chart courtesy Ned Davis Research, Nokomis, Florida.

3. Services Bearish Indicator

A third worthwhile psychology indicator is the percentage of investment advisory services expressing a bearish opinion. Again, the information is in *Barron's* each week. The theory is the same. A lot of bears out there suggests higher prices to come. A low number of bears . . . look out below. Having studied this indicator for several years, I suggest interpreting the data slightly differently than other analysts. This indicator tends to fluctuate from about 10 percent bearish to 70 percent bearish at extremes. Here's the rule:

1.   Market peaks are at hand when the Services Bearish Indicator reaches 30 percent or below and fails to make a new low point for five months. For example, let's say it reached 25 percent, but stayed above 25 percent for five months, you've got the makings for a stock market top and a minus rating. If within that five months, the level dropped below 25 percent, you start

FIGURE 7-15   AAII Individual Investor Sentiment Survey

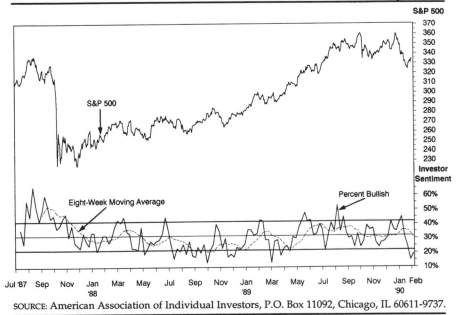

SOURCE: American Association of Individual Investors, P.O. Box 11092, Chicago, IL 60611-9737.

counting months from the new low point. The sell signal and thus the minus rating remain in effect until the buy signal hits.

2.   Market bottoms are near when the percent bearish increases 25 points from a low point. For example, if the indicator reaches a low point of 20 percent bearish, then increases 25 points to 45 percent bearish, that's a buy signal. Though this buy signal is sometimes a couple of months early, that is your trigger point. Here is the evidence to consider a plus in the model, if your other indicators agree.

A key aspect to the Psychology indicators is that unanimity of opinion is usually wrong. The point is this, as Warren Buffett said: "The investor pays a very high price for a cheery consensus!" By taking the contrary view, one can apply an appropriate rating to the model. With the Psychology component, I look at these 3 indicators along with several others to make a judgment on whether to assign a Plus, Neutral, or Minus rating for the Model. I also find it fun to make a subjective judgment of investor sentiment based on newspaper articles, discussions with investors, etc. You might find this mental exercise valuable and challenging as well.

4.   Momentum

The fourth factor in our analysis of stock market cycles is what we call *momentum*. Perhaps a more realistic term would be *periodicity*, as the primary emphasis, as we will develop it, is on the natural rhythm of market prices themselves. The psychology indicators are essentially analyses of the stock market versus other forms of assets. The momentum indicators can be seen as analyses of the market versus itself in different time periods. This factor is something of a catch-all category. It can include such things as election-year cycles. It can include many of the tools of the traditional technical analyst such as trend lines, volume analysis, support and resistance levels, and so forth. These terms are used by investors, brokers, and the news media. They are part of the language of investing and the stock-in-trade of the hard core technical analyst (technician). I am, frankly, skeptical of most of this. I have found little evidence to document the usefulness of most of these concepts.

However, one basic concept is applicable and useful: the concept of *overbought* and *oversold*. This concept merely attempts to recognize statistically the idea that when the market moves too far too fast, natural forces emerge to change or to slow the market's direction. If prices have had a measurably significant advance over time, investors will be tempted to take profits. On the downside, after a sharp decline, investors will come in to buy to take advantage of the relatively low prices.

Markets can be compared to phenomena in nature. Think about hilly or mountainous terrain. If you are driving your car on flat ground approaching a hill, you first begin the ascent on a gradual slope. As you continue, your rate of ascent, i.e., the steepness of the mountain, increases. Then, as you approach the top, you notice that the steepness decreases. During this stage you are still going up, but the rate of ascent is declining. This is the concept of momentum.

In applying this notion to stocks, there are many ways to statistically quantify this analysis. I will highlight a couple of methods.

Rate of Change Indicator.   This analysis indicates the percentage by which the market (S&P 500) is above or below its level of a year earlier. Figure 7–16, developed by Robert Farrell of Merrill Lynch, shows the rate of change of the Standard & Poors 500 Index. As can be seen, the market for over 100 years has fairly consistently reached a rate of advance in most bull markets of 20 to 30 percent or more before falling off. If other momentum indicators are confirming, a minus rating is warranted when the trend reaches 20 percent and then falls back below the 20 percent level.

You'll notice that some bull markets have two crossings above then below the 20 percent level. A sell (minus) signal is temporarily cancelled if the indicator goes back above 20 percent. But a second drop below 20 percent is an especially powerful signal.

Declines have usually reached between zero and minus 30 percent in the annual rate of descent after crossing below zero, but then only when the indicator has moved back up 10 percent from a low point. For example, if it reaches −15 percent then rallies to −5 percent, your buy (plus) signal is on! The long term history available for this indicator dramatically demonstrates the market's rhythm over time. (Data for this indicator is in *Barron's*.)

Moving Average Analysis.   A moving average is a simple calcula-

FIGURE 7-16 Rate of Change Indicator

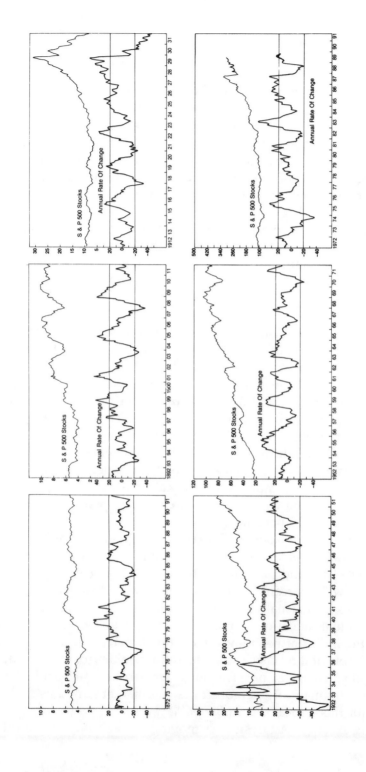

tion of taking an average value of an index over a certain number of days. Then, as you add a new day, you drop the oldest day from the average. Figure 7–17 shows the Dow Jones and Standard & Poor's stock averages along with a 10 week and a 30 week moving average. There are several ways to use this information.

1. Ignore the short term moving average (10-week) and focus on the 30-week average. Whenever the Dow or S&P has gotten at least 15 percent over the moving average, you are at an overbought point. This happened in March, then again in August of 1987. These points are sell points, especially if the NYSE Advance-Decline Line has not confirmed the new peak in the index itself. The Advance-Decline (A–D) line shows the number of stocks that are advancing in price compared to the number declining.

Notice that the NYSE Advance-Decline Line in March of 1989 was making new highs along with the Dow and the S&P. However, in the August peak, the Advance-Decline Line failed to exceed the level it reached in March! This is what is referred to as a nonconfirmation, and it occurs frequently at major market peaks.

This analysis suggests that one need not be too concerned about run-ups as long as most stocks are participating, as evidenced by the Advance-Decline Line also making new highs. However, when you have a big run-up in the market, with the A–D not confirming, as in August 1987, look out, hombre! This is an ideal time to factor in a minus weighting in your model.

2. When the Dow or S&P drops below the 30-week moving average, this is confirming evidence that the trend has changed. You can see how this would have gotten you out of stocks in early October 1987, before Black Monday.

The difficulty is that this method can "whip-saw" you. Notice that in 1988, the Dow and S&P crossed above and below the 30-week moving average several times, giving false signals. But that is why I advocate using more than just one indicator to help you decide when to assign a plus, neutral, or minus rating into the model. No single indicator is perfect.

A buy (plus) rating is simply given when the Dow or S&P is 10 percent under the moving average, indicating an oversold market. (It rarely gets as oversold as it did in October 1987.) Then when it gets

FIGURE 7-17 Trendline Daily Action Stock Charts

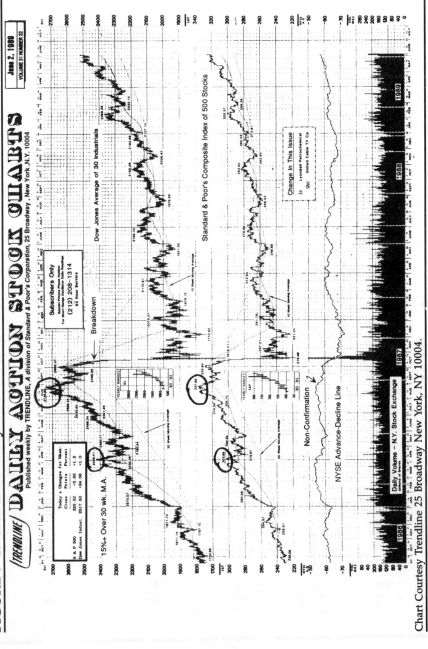

Chart Courtesy Trendline 25 Broadway New York, NY 10004.

back above the moving average, an uptrend is confirmed.

You can track the moving average information by subscribing to *Trendline* (25 Broadway, New York 10004), or most libraries and brokerage offices have *Trendline* available. You also can easily calculate your own moving average. Just take the closing price each week of the Dow Jones Industrial Average for 30 weeks, adding a new figure each week and dropping the oldest figure. Then calculate the percentage amount that the Dow is over or under the moving average. It just takes a minute.

Moving average analysis has become more well known in recent years because of Dick Fabian's *Telephone Switch Newsletter* (P.O. Box 2538, Huntington Beach, CA 92647). Fabian uses a slightly different moving average calculation than the one I described, but he claims that a $10,000 investment in this approach in 1926 would have grown to over $1,500,000 by 1989 compared to growing only to $160,000 in a buy-and-hold approach in the Dow Jones Industrial Average. Moving average analysis does have long term investment merit.

3. Bull-Bear Distance Approach. As we studied early in this chapter, bull and bear markets are historically definable moves. Using this information, I suggest factoring in a bit more data. When a bull market has been around for at least two years or has increased at least 50 percent from the bottom, begin getting increasingly picky about interpreting the indicators. Start looking for a top. Likewise, when a bear market has been around for at least 10 or so months, and prices are down over 20 percent, start looking for a bottom. This can help you analyze the data. For example, in 1988 when the Dow flirted above and below the moving average, you might not have put too much weight on this, since the Dow had not fulfilled the 50 percent/two-year up test yet.

Every major brokerage firm has a research department that uses a variety of statistical data to construct a variety of momentum indicators. You might find others you like for the purposes of our model. Assign a plus rating when the market is statistically oversold and/or begins to regain momentum—a minus when the market is overbought and/or begins to lose momentum. As before, assume a signal is still in force until proven otherwise.

You may, as in the other cycle categories, get as immersed in it as you desire. You can adapt the various sources you have available to your own working of the model.

Putting It Together

I suggest two alternative approaches on putting the model into practice, depending on how much energy you want to put into it.

Simplified Method.

By adding up the four category ratings, you get a composite ranking. The maximum is thus plus four, the minimum is minus four. Cyclical trend changes or important intermediate moves are usually signalled by readings of plus two or minus two. These I refer to as *major trend* signals. Using this model as a basis for decisions over the years tells me that this is the point at which trends change. A plus two *major trend buy* signal suggests being substantially invested in stocks, up to a maximum percentage of your portfolio consistent with your goals and risk tolerance, i.e., asset allocation guidelines as we discussed in Chapter 5. A minus two *major trend sell* signal implies being substantially out of stocks. A plus or minus two in the opposite direction of the existing *major trend* cancels the *major trend signal* and gives a new *major trend* signal (in the reverse direction).

The model composite often hovers at or near neutral zero, because there are almost always conflicting indicators and cross-currents in the market. The approach to the model assumes a trend remains in force until the composite is thrown far enough in the opposite direction to reverse strategy.

If this is beginning to sound mystical, well what can I say? It really is not. It is just a method to help you organize your own thinking about the market.

What is different about my approach from other books you may read is that there is not a single cut-and-dried method that promises you sure wealth. What we're offering you is a framework to apply all the information you may have. It therefore becomes your model, not mine. You can use it to your own use and modify it as you see fit. With this simplified approach to the model, you merely need to have one or two indicators to use within each of the component categories. Then assign a plus, neutral, or minus rating to each component, depending on which way the indicators as a group are leaning.

Advanced Method.

Especially if you are using five or more indicators in each component category, you can assign a percentage weighting. Let's say you have five indicators, three are bullish, one is neutral, and one is negative. Ignore the one that is neutral. The one that is negative offsets one of the three positive indicators. Thus, you have two net positives. The two represent 40 percent of the total five you follow. If there are on-balance negatives, the percentage would be a minus number.

$$\frac{3 \text{ positives} - 1 \text{ negative}}{5 \text{ total indicators}} = 40\% \text{ net positive}$$

Next, add the percentages together from each component category. For example:

Economic	+40%
Monetary	−80%
Psychology	0
Momentum	+90%
Composite:	+50%

The maximum composite possible would thus be plus or minus 400 percent. Here's what to do next. Use the scale below to interpret how you should be invested:

Buy signal 100% invested	+150%
Level I sell signal 75% invested	−150%
Level II sell signal 50% invested	−200%
Level III sell signal 25% invested	−250%
Level IV sell signal 0 invested	−300%

This is really sounding like hocus-pocus now, eh? This formula is merely what not only makes sense but has worked for me in the past.

Using the scoring, a score of +150 percent cancels all sell signals, dictating a fully invested position. The percentage invested applies to that portion of your net worth that you would normally have in stocks. For example, if you normally would have $100,000 invested in stocks, a 75 percent weighting implies having only $75,000 invested. The other $25,000 would be in either money market instruments or bonds. Sell signals at each successive level remain in force until a stronger sell signal or a +150 percent buy signal is given. A buy signal remains in force until a sell signal is given. This weighting reflects the long term upward bias of stocks. It is easier to get into stocks than out of them by this system. There has to be a strong case to sell. In other words, this reflects the fact that it has been a bigger error to miss a bull market than to sit out a bear market, since stocks always come back.

The goal of the model is to offer a basic approach for the serious investor. If nothing else, it is a road map to organize your thinking. It is a tool to help you eliminate the emotion in your investment decision process, while encouraging intelligent judgment. The time horizons mentioned in this chapter are representations. But the basic concepts presented are immune to changes in time. Likewise, the value of specific indicators will change. But the model allows one the flexibility to add, subtract, and refine indicators within the model itself. Throughout all history the marketplace has been subject to cycles, and the same forces of change always will be an integral part of its understanding.

> *"In the stock market, the individual pits his reason, his knowledge, his vision and his guts against a variety of forces: his own human impulses, the large and varied uncertainties of the future, and the collective wisdom and irrationality of other investors."*
> C.J. Rolo

Endnotes

[1]For some interesting general information on all kinds of cycles, read *Cycles: The Mysterious Forces that Trigger Events*, by Edward R. Dewey, with Og Mandino, New York: Hawthorn Books, 1971. Also, Foundation for the Study of Cycles, 124 South Highland Ave., Pittsburgh, PA 15206.

[2]Charles S. Meek, "A Practical Model for Dealing with Stock Market Cycles," Independent study prepared for the degree of Master of Business Administration, St. Edwards University, February 1977.

[3]See the book by Martin E. Zweig, *Martin Zweig's Winning on Wall Street*, New York: Warner Books, or the article by William A. Remaley. "A Synthesis: Priming the 200-Day Moving Average" in the *AAII Journal*, July 1989.

[4]David Cashman and James Farrell, Jr., "The Wheel Turns," August 16, 1987, from Cashman, Farrell & Associates, 1235 Westlakes Drive, Berwyn, PA 19312.

[5]Ibid.

[6]David Dreman, *The New Contrarian Investment Strategy: The Psychology of Stock Market Success* (New York: Random House, 1983).

8

Horror Stories: Mistakes People Make

*"The successful speculator must be content at times to ig-
nore probably two out of every three apparent opportunities to make money."*
Charles Dow

Anybody who has been in the investment business for any length of
time can relate stories of successes and failures. Basically, Americans
are optimistic people. We tend to dwell on the success stories. But
from an instructional point of view, we can often learn more from our
failures.

Other books you may have read conveniently leave out the bad
stuff. Investment people (as well as authors) are especially prone to
the optimistic side (otherwise they would be accountants!). Have you
ever read, for example, an investment advisory newsletter that
admitted a mistake? They usually spend half the time patting themselves on the back and the other half of the time making flamboyant
statements of omniscience.

In this chapter we'll take a glimpse at several folks who goofed.
Maybe we can learn from their mistakes. The names and precise
details have been changed to protect the guilty. But they are based on
real people or real circumstances.

Junk Bond Janie

A "junk" bond is a bond that has a rating below the top four categories. Moody's Investor Service and Standard & Poors Corporation rate bonds. Their ratings appear below. As you might suspect, junk bonds have higher yields than investment grade debt. But as they say, you don't get something for nothing. (Or alternately, there ain't no free lunch—to be candidly trite!)

Janie stumbled on to the junk bond market in the early 1980s. She found two juicy morsels—Global Marine and LTV. She bought $50,000 face amount of the Global Marine 16 percent bonds due in 2001. She paid a price of 101½, that is 101.5 percent of face value, for a total cost of $50,750. She also bought $50,000 face amount of LTV 14 percent bonds due in 2004. But she got a bargain on these, as she paid a price of only 91, making her total cost $45,500.

Investment Grade		Junk Bonds	
Moody's	*S & P*	*Moody's*	*S & P*
Aaa	AAA	Ba	B
Aa	AA	B	CCC
A	A	Caa	CC
Baa	BBB	Ca	D
		C	

At the time of these purchases, investment grade bonds were available with yields of around 12 percent. So she was able to significantly increase her return by investing in lower-rated bonds. And of course, these two companies were big, well-known companies with substantial assets and sales. Surely they would be able to pay these bonds. What a deal!

Oh, yes. And one more thing. . . . She bought the bonds on margin. Junk bond junkies love to buy on margin. It never takes them long to figure out that they can get a higher interest rate on the bond than they have to pay on the margin loan.

Within three years, the oil industry was deteriorating severely, and the operating condition of Global Marine, an offshore driller, was waning. And the American steel industry worsened, taking LTV into a "Chapter 11" bankruptcy, which surprised even many excellent Wall Street analysts. And Janie was getting "maintenance" calls. She threw in the towel and sold the Global Marines at 23 and her LTVs at 42½. The total hickey?—A loss of $63,500 (not counting interest earned after margin costs)! Ouch.

Moral: The real problem here is one of diversification.

Various studies show that junk bonds do in fact provide a better return than investment grade issues, with a fairly low default rate. For example, Edward Altman, professor of finance at New York University, calculates that from March 1978 to March 1984, a portfolio of high-yield bonds would have yielded 490 basis points (4.90 percent) more in annual compounded rates of return than a portfolio of long term government bonds. (*Financial World*, January 20, 1987.) This seems to be confirmed by the excellent performance of some well-managed junk bond mutual funds. Some such funds have performed even better than many common stock funds in recent years. In spite of the Drexel junk bond hullaballo, these bonds are a viable investment medium.

But junk bonds are for the pros. And diversification is a must. Ideally, don't invest in junk bonds except in a diversified, professionally managed mutual fund.

This brings up a point. Sometimes an event is so startling or so obvious that a contrary investment idea jumps out at you. I call this a "flag job", as if someone was waving a flag to tell you to take notice. Here are recent examples:

1. When Japanese business got so cocky that they advertised an automobile without ever showing it (the Nisson Infinity) in early 1990, that was a signal that the party was over for their stock market.

2. When a painting (Irises, I think it was called) sold for $50 million with great fanfare in the worldwide press, that *had* to be the top of the art market.

3. And when junk bond king Michael Milken got a 10-year prison sentence, that was a flag job that the bottom of the junk bond market was imminent!

Penny Stock Paul

Penny stocks are stocks selling under three dollars per share; however, the definition can be expanded to stocks selling under ten dollars per share. Paul's rule of investing is to never buy anything over ten bucks a share. Here are some of Paul's picks:

Company	Reason for Purchase	Cost per Share	Recent Price
A Canadian soft drink distributor	Getting in on ground floor of new company	7	Out of business
An oil stock	Good reserves in the ground	5⅛	Out of business
A computer company	Management had great record with former company	9	1

Moral: The value of a company is not related to the price per share. The price is only significant to the earning power of the company's assets. Similar to Junk Bond Janie's experience, Paul would have been better off investing in two or three mutual funds that specialize in small stocks. As illustrated by the long-run superior performance of small companies (see Chapter 4), there is nothing wrong with investing in emerging companies. However, diversification and serious research are the keys to success.

Hot Tip Henry

If you hang around a stock brokerage office, or if you associate with anyone who does, stand by for the once-a-year tip. Oh yes, once a year without fail, the once-in-a-lifetime tip shows up.

My friend Henry buys them all. The latest one was Western Company of North America. Western has been a highly successful oil well service company, which dropped from a high of 52 just a few years ago, to 7. The rumor was that Schlumberger (or was it DuPont?) was going to offer 12 on a buy out. Note: All good hot tips always relay who the buyer is, lending great credence to the story. Henry bought 5,000 shares at 7, expecting a quick ride to 12. At the time of this writing, Henry still owns the 5,000 shares—now priced at 1½. Henry's source mysteriously forgot to tell him when to get out.

Moral: Stand aside. My experience suggests that selling the rumors short would make you more money than buying into them.

Lookin' Back Linda

Linda, bless her heart, is always living in the past. But then that's easy to do. We are all conditioned by our past. Linda's father lost money in stocks in the early 1930s and swore he'd never do that again. He missed one of the greatest bull markets in history in the 1950s and 1960s because he was still living in the 1930s.

Linda got involved in mutual funds in 1968 because all her friends were making a bundle and the experts were saying that we would never have another Depression (or even a recession). Then came the bear market of 1969–1974. When she finally got back even in 1975, she sold out and swore never to try that again. Of course Linda, still on the sidelines, missed the entire bull market of the 1980s. She blames her misfortune on the "institutions." ("The small investor just doesn't have a chance against the big institutions.")

Moral: It is usually wise to assume that in investing, things will be different in the future rather than the same, when compared to the recent past. Making absolute judgments about past experiences often leads to an inflexible attitude about the future.

Venture Capital Vick

We've all heard stories about buying into start-up companies, where a small investment became a fortune. Venture capital is investing in newly formed private companies before they are large enough to go public. Vick wanted to get in on the action. His theory was to invest

$10,000 in each of several venture deals. All it would take is for one of them to be a home run, and easy street would be on its way.

Here's what Vick bought:

- A start-up computer company run by a former successful vice president of Control Data Corp. The guy had a record of taking over small divisions at this big company and turning them into very successful operations, and he had now started his own company. It looked like a pretty good bet that he could do it again!

- A company that invented a way to transport natural gas safely by truck. There appeared to be a real need for this, as pipelines were too expensive for small gas fields.

- A new restaurant franchise that invented a delicious new sandwich with a unique bread.

- A high tech company that developed products through a government funded program for the Navy. Since the Navy was behind the research, this one looked like a great opportunity.

All told, Vick put $40,000 in the four deals. Vick lost all $40,000.

Moral: Venture capital is a tough business. Successful venture capitalists review hundreds of proposals for every one they invest in. They hire consultants to evaluate the technology and the market potential. They diversify over dozens of investments. This is another one of those games for the pros.

If you are going to play this game, here's my advice: Let time be your ally. For most investors, you'd be lucky to stumble across one truly good venture opportunity in a lifetime. Put some money aside just in case that opportunity actually does present itself someday. Don't invest in every deal that comes along. If you do, you'll be out of cash when opportunity comes knocking. But be ready to act if and when the chance of a lifetime arrives.

Greedy Gary

Gary had his own business. He built up a reputation in the community as the best in his field. He developed a proprietary product, and with good common sense business management, made his company grow. In time, Gary accepted a merger offer and received a million dollars' worth of stock of a New York Stock Exchange listed company.

When the stock's value increased to $3½ million, Gary thought about selling. But he decided not to sell because the "taxes would kill him." Well, bad times came on the company. The stock dropped. Gary still owns the stock, but could barely get enough out of it now to pay off the mortgage on his house. Had he sold when he had the chance, Gary would be on the French Riviera today. Instead, Gary is punching a time clock.

Moral: Don't be greedy. Sell at least part of a successful investment. Don't let your future ride too long on only one big holding. And don't let tax considerations keep you from making good investment decisions.

Mortgage Mary

My home town, Austin, Texas, experienced a great real estate boom from 1980 to 1984. Mary saw many of her friends making big bucks in the real estate market, and she decided to attend one of the "no money down" seminars. She learned all the ways you can buy real estate with little or no cash.

Mary had some initial success. The appraised value on her properties rose substantially. Her banker friends were falling all over themselves to lend Mary and her partners even more money, based on the property appraisals. It didn't seem important at the time that most properties had negative cash flows, that is, were bringing in less rental income than mortgage and other expenses. Property was "turning" easily, so Mary was able to sell a property any time to meet debt repayment schedules.

The warning to Mary should have been that it was too easy. It seemed like everybody who was anybody had made a fortune in real estate in Austin, Texas. Having developed a national reputation as a center for high tech industry, investors poured in from everywhere. Office buildings, apartments, and high-dollar homes were springing up. Land prices tripled and more.

Ah, but reality set in. There just weren't enough people in Texas to fill all the buildings! The situation reached more than just "overbuilt."

It reached mania proportions—the old "greater fool theory." It was okay to pay exorbitant prices for something, because someone else would pay even more.

Alas, Mary is bankrupt. She can no longer make the payments on her debt. There are not enough renters for her buildings. Her land has dropped to a fraction of what she paid for it. There are no buyers. All the people who made mortgage loans, including the bankers and individuals who sold property on a note, are discovering that they no longer have a mortgage—they have the property back. All good things come to an end.

Moral: Don't get strung out with debt. When it is extremely easy to borrow, it's probably not the time to borrow. And learn to recognize an overexcited market. The tip-off is broad participation. Bernard Baruch is said to have sold his stocks prior to the 1929 crash when his shoe-shine man began giving him stock tips. The same concept applies to any market.

Haphazard Harriet

Harriet put some of her assets into bonds because she heard they were paying better than CDs. She learned how bond prices fluctuate, but that didn't seem to matter. She just wanted a better interest rate. When interest rates started up after she invested, she watched the price of her bonds drop 15 percent in value in just a few months' time!

Discouraged, she sold out at just the wrong time, just as interest rates started to decline again. Of course, the best thing she could have done would have been to buy even more good bonds when rates were high and prices low. Her problem was that she wasn't psychologically prepared.

Harriet had no game plan. She should have made the first investment with the attitude that if prices should happen to fall, she would be ready to invest a prescribed amount more. Instead of welcoming the opportunity to increase her holdings at an even better price, she panicked and sold.

Moral: The only way to live with setbacks in life is to make the best of them. Remember the scout motto: Be Prepared. . . . And make the asset allocation strategies described in Chapter 5 work for you!

Tommy Trader

Neat guy—Tom. Studying for his Ph.D. Studious sort. Tom happened to get hold of one of those books on how to trade stocks by the charts. But, guess what? You can't believe everything you read . . . Tom had another problem. He would get EXCITED! I can hear him now showing everyone those "break-outs" on the charts. "Quick! Buy me 500 shares before it's up another point!" he would say.

Tommy never made any decent money. He just firmly believed that the slot machine would hit three cherries sooner or later.

Moral: Forget the short-term trading. Do something productive with your life!

Mad Mr. Mac

Everyone was out to get Mr. Mac. Or at least, so he thought. He had a string of seven brokers. He got pretty good advice most of the time, too. But he seldom took it, thinking he knew everything.

Mr. Mac had his entire portfolio in silver, gold, and copper mining stocks during the period when silver went from $50 per ounce to $5 per ounce. Each of his brokers tried to get him to diversify, but Mr. Mac wouldn't listen. He thought they were just trying to get a commission. Besides, "The federal deficit has to send inflation back up. Natural resources are where it's at!" he said. Mr. Mac waited for each broker to slip up somewhere and give a poor recommendation. That was all it took to initiate a transfer to a new broker.

Needless to say, Mr. Mac never did too well on his investments. But, of course, it was never his fault. . . .

Moral: Well, how about you finishing this story? What would you say to Mr. Mac if you had the chance?

I hope these stories will serve to sharpen the reader's awareness of some of the pitfalls of investing. Investing is a bit like golf. If you stay out of the roughs and sand traps, you increase the likelihood of a good round! The purpose of this book is to give a framework for solid investing—to help you avoid the pitfalls these poor souls experienced.

9

The One Decade Manager: Mutual Funds and Money Managers

"A man cannot be a good doctor and keep telephoning his broker between patients nor a good lawyer with his eye on the ticker."

Walter Lippman

In the space of just a few years, the investment business has moved from a backward industry to a sophisticated world-wide discipline. It is becoming more difficult to compete against the professionals. More important, this is a world of specialization. To excel in your own profession, you must minimize the dilution of your time and mental energy. Managing your own portfolio, as we discussed in Chapters 5 and 6, is desired. But you just may not have the time. Most investors are probably well advised to use full time professional managers for their investment dollars. Selection of these professionals is crucial. The first thing to do if you are hiring someone for a job is to check their past record. The same is true of hiring investment managers. A recent best selling book was called *The One Minute Manager*. For our purposes, one minute ain't enough. We need to evaluate investment performance over a long period—at least five or ten years. Hopefully, your manager will serve you equally well for at least five or ten more years. Let's look at some concepts to help you identify the One Decade Manager.

There are three ways you can get full time professional management

225

for your bucks—a bank trust department, a mutual fund, or a private money manager (also called an investment advisor or investment counselor). These terms are somewhat confusing. In this discussion I will use the term investment manager to include all three categories. I'll refer to the latter of the three categories as money manager. All three can potentially be good—or bad. With a mutual fund, your money is pooled with that of a lot of other investors. With a money manager your funds are segregated, and your account is managed separately, usually on a discretionary basis. (Money managers have high minimum account sizes that can range from $100,000 to $10 million.) With a bank trust department, your funds may either be separately managed or be part of a common trust fund.

Mutual funds, of course, are investment companies in which you buy shares. Mutual funds have this advantage: they are regulated under the Investment Company Act of 1940. This act requires certain things to protect the investor. For example, no more than 5 percent of a fund's assets at cost may be in any one security. All assets must be physically held by a third party custodian in order to eliminate the risk of fraud. And mutual funds have precise reporting requirements. Their track record is public information. And management fees, commissions paid, and other expenses paid by the fund are taken into account when performance records are calculated. (Up front or rear end load, i.e. commission, charges paid by the investor are usually not considered in performance statistics.)

Money managers and banks don't have such requirements. Perhaps the worst thing is the lack of reliable performance figures. There are no industry standards on how their records are reported, and there are many ways they can be fudged (remember lies and statistics). Just to name a couple: Expenses may or may not be figured in. For example, management fees are usually excluded while commissions and other expenses are normally included. In the case of banks, trust fees are ignored in calculating results. Also, money managers and banks may ignore accounts that are no longer under management. Of course, those are likely to be the poorest accounts in performance. They may also give only a representative sample of accounts, perhaps just the largest ones or certain showcase accounts. Results are usually not audited. But even audited numbers are somewhat suspect, because the auditor just takes what the manager provides and then calculates a summation. Investment counselors do have to report their assets to the government, if they manage over $100 million, in a so-called 13F filing document.

There are a few sources for bank and investment counselor performance numbers, but the average investor would have to dig very deeply to find them, if at all. Banks are the least regulated and need not disclose performance numbers to the public unless they choose to. One source for at least limited bank performance statistics is *Pension and Investment Age* magazine. The basic data is merely provided by the banks themselves without any auditing. CDA Investment Technologies of Silver Springs, Maryland, reports on banks and investment counselors, as well as mutual funds. CDA is perhaps the best source for performance statistics on money managers (referred to by CDA as *investment advisors*), but their methodology has been criticized by some. They merely extrapolate information from government filings, which shows quarterly stock holdings. Those filings do not show prices paid or received for purchases or sales of the stocks. It is assumed that the securities held at the beginning of the quarter are held for the next three months. Also, CDA ranks managers based only on their stock portfolios, so a manager's timely use of bonds or cash is not factored in.

Investors normally see only performance figures provided by the manager in a pretty plastic spiral bound booklet. This is what I call the "spiral-bound syndrome." Of all the many I've seen, I've never seen one that showed poor performance! Only about one-fourth of all investment managers have beaten the market in recent years, but you'd think every one was a genius based on these presentation pieces!

It should be noted that money managers are regulated by the Securities and Exchange Commission under the Investment Advisers Act of 1940. As mentioned in the previous chapter, there is a nominal fee, currently $150, to become registered. Managers are subject to periodic unannounced visits by regulators. This regulation helps prevent fraud, but does not prescribe investment performance reporting standards.

However, for many investors, using investment management is the best way to invest in the stock market. Don't confuse the purpose of an investment manager with the purpose for your personal financial consultant. Your financial consultant should be your primary relation-ship person who oversees your whole financial program. He or she is most likely your broker or another person. Investment managers are, in effect, subcontractors to manage portions of your portfolio for certain purposes. But whether your investment managers are with mutual funds, banks, or money management firms, the trick is to select good managers. I believe there are several characteristics that distinguish the outstanding investment managers. These concepts are important to the long term performance ability of a manager. The following is a summary of some of the elements believed to be most critical for an investor to consider when choosing a manager.

Flexibility.   Flexibility is of crucial importance. Even though stocks have shown the highest long-term returns, simply buying and holding stocks is not the answer. One reason is that there has been a great deal of variability in different time periods. For example, the best 10-year period since 1925, according to the Ibbotson studies cited in Chapter 4, was 1949 through 1958, when common stocks averaged 20.1 percent annually. The worst 10-year period was 1929 through 1938, when stocks averaged −0.9 percent in annual return. For comparison, the best 10-year period for corporate bonds was 1977 through 1986, when returns averaged 10.0 percent per annum. But the worst 10-year period for corporate bonds was 1947 through 1956, when returns averaged only 1.0 percent.

Here's a good tip. Avoid managers who work with a narrow, "approved list" of investments. To me, this is the biggest clue to a management style that precludes original thought. It is felt that this approach is an excuse for average or below average performance. Flexibility should not be severely limited.

Specialized approaches or specialized mutual funds (utilities, health care, etc.) should also be avoided; they may be good performers in some periods, but seldom in the long run.

One example of flexibility is the ability to shift from mature blue chip stocks to small company stocks. Most investment managers limit themselves to one or the other. However, history suggests that value relationships between small company shares and large company shares is cyclical. Figure 9–1 shows how valuations of small stocks have fluctuated against valuations of large companies. It plots the relative P/E ratio of the portfolio of the T. Rowe Price New Horizons

FIGURE 9-1　New Horizons' P/E Relative to S&P 500 P/E (12 Months Forward)

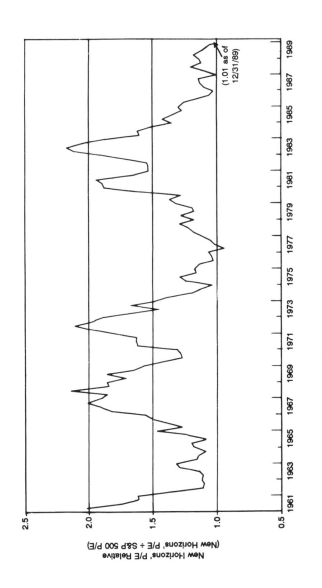

This chart is intended to show the history of the average (unweighted) P/E ratio of the fund's portfolio companies compared with the P/E ratio of the S&P 500 index. Earnings per share are estimated by the fund's investment advisor.

SOURCE: T. Rowe Price Associates, Inc.

fund (which specializes in small companies) to the P/E of the S&P 500 index. When P/Es of small companies have reached double that of the S&P, they were overvalued. When they have gotten to nearly equal the S&P, small stocks were low in value. The ideal investment manager should be flexible enough to invest in small stocks when they appear undervalued, such as in the early 1960s or mid-1970s, but avoid them when they appear very overvalued, such as in 1968 or 1983.

Also, does the manager stay fully invested at all times? To what extent would he/she liquidate a portfolio if a decline were anticipated? Market timing is admittedly a controversial topic. Some successful money managers say that the risk of missing an upward move by being on the sidelines outweighs the possible benefit. However, my view is that there are times to be out of the market to preserve capital, even at the risk of lost opportunities.

With regard to fixed income portfolios, does the manager have a full range of investment opportunities available, for example: zero coupon bonds, mortgage-backed securities, high yield corporate bonds, and hedging techniques such as options and financial futures? The modern portfolio manager should be able to take advantage of all opportunities as they arise.

Philosophy.   Do the investment managers have a defined investment philosophy rooted in empirical evidence? In other words, *can they prove to you that there is historical, factual evidence that their methods of investing are likely to provide above-average results?* Is he/she an independent thinker? Ask him to define his investment philosophy. Don't accept a general statement such as, "We are value-oriented managers." Make them be specific.

There are many different viable investment management styles.

- Growth. The growth stock manager buys companies that display an ability for earnings to increase rapidly or consistently. As we've discussed earlier, one important concept for a growth style manager is earnings momentum. Studies have shown that it takes a fairly long period of time, perhaps weeks or months, for an increase in the rate of growth of a company's earnings to be reflected in the price of its stock. This factor may be more important than identifying consistency of growth. Thus, a good growth style manager looks for companies in the early stages of an increased rate of growth.

- Low P/E. The P/E or price-to-earnings ratio is the price of a stock divided by its earnings per share. As we discussed in earlier chapters, buying low P/E stocks is a viable method of investing.

- Contrary opinion. The contrary opinion manager looks for issues that are out of favor or are unusually cheap due to temporary problems.

- Market timing. The market timer looks at the stock market as a whole rather than individual stocks and attempts to take advantage of cycles to get in and out of stocks at appropriate times.

- Asset allocation. An asset allocation manager is similar to a market timer. However, my definition of a true asset allocator is broader than a market timer. Like a market timer who focuses on when to get in or out of stocks, an asset allocator also uses bonds as an offensive weapon for capital appreciation at appropriate times.

- Income. The income manager focuses on current income or rising future income streams to manage a portfolio.

However, regardless of style, long-term performance records suggest that truly successful managers have some sort of a basic value approach. That is, whatever their style, they have the ability to select the cheapest stocks relative to their future worth. *What managers avoid may be more important than what they buy.* The key is this: unsuccessful managers get caught up in what is popular at the moment (i.e., oil stocks at their peak in 1981, high technology stocks in 1983). Successful managers concentrate on unpopular/undervalued sectors of the market and are emotionally able to avoid overly popular investments.

Risk. Is the investment manager more concerned about risk or reward? It is believed that more attention should be paid to risk. Although there is generally an inverse relationship between risk and reward, portfolio theory suggests that if risk is controlled, the reward tends to take care of itself. To illustrate the mathematical importance of controlling risk, if an investment declines 50 percent, it takes a 100 percent return just to get even. It is important for the client and manager to have a clear mutual understanding of their goals and risk parameters. Warren Buffett, renowned investor and president of Berkshire Hathaway, and reputed to be the third richest person in America, said: "There are two rules for investing: The first rule is, don't lose money. The second rule is, don't forget the first one!"

Managing risk versus reward can be handled through appropriate diversification. Figure 9–2 is very interesting. It depicts standard deviation (a measure of risk) versus annual returns on bonds. A portfolio with 100 percent international (non-U.S.) bond holdings has offered the investor the highest return, but also the highest potential risk. On the other end of the graph, a portfolio with 100 percent U.S. bond holdings has offered the investor a lower return at a lower risk level. However, a portfolio mix of 60 percent U.S. bonds and 40

FIGURE 9–2

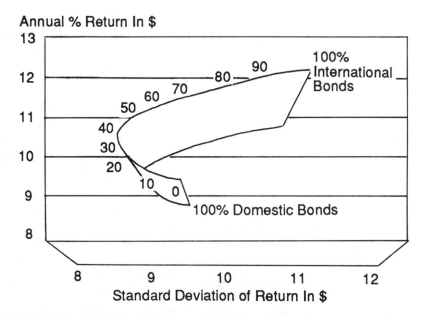

SOURCE: Merrill Lynch/Salomon Bros.

percent foreign bonds has provided the lowest risk, but a higher reward than owning all U.S. bonds! Of course, these parameters will change over time, but a manager understands the importance of balancing risk versus potential reward.

Consistency.   Related to the notion of risk, consistency, or success over time, must be demonstrated. Investment performance should be viewed not as a 100 yard dash, but rather a marathon run (or decathlon)! The managers who are stars in one year are seldom the long-run winners. Performance should be judged over a minimum of a 3- to 5-year period. Better yet, over three economic cycles, which is usually about 10 years. Never look at performance of only one year. Indeed, that is only misleading and would probably be better not evaluated at all! Managers should have demonstrated their ability to make good decisions in a variety of economic climates.

Consider this: If one is aiming for a 15 percent annual return and achieves three straight 15 percent years but in the fourth year loses 15 percent, the annualized return over four years drops to 6.6 percent! Even more instructive is that the fifth year would have to produce returns of 56 percent to get back on a 15 percent track!

The management of Real World Example Fund Number Three likes to tell the story of the hare and the tortoise. You remember the fable. The hare sprinted ahead of the tortoise and, confident of his lead, rested by the roadside. The tortoise, slower but steadier, went on to win the race.

Mutual funds have their hares and tortoises too. Each time one of the rating services comes out with a list of the "best performing" funds, you may be tempted to go with the winner. But what would happen if someone spent a decade investing, on January 1 each year, in the previous year's number one fund? Well, let's assume that on January 1, 1975 you made a $10,000 investment in the growth fund that had been at the top of the charts for 1974. Every January 1st afterward, you switched your total investment to the fund that had the best performance record for the prior year. Disregarding taxes and assuming you reinvested all dividends and capital gains and paid no sales charges, how much do you think your investment would be worth on December 31, 1984, the end of a decade of such investing? Here are the results:

In the Year	The Best Performing Fund Had a Total Return	The Next Year	That Fund's Total Return	The $10,00 You Originally Invested on 1/1/75 Would Be Worth
1974	+10.9%	1975	−24.1%	$7,590 on 12/31/75
1975	+184.1	1976	+47.5	11,119 /76
1976	+72.5	1977	+19.9	13,332 /77
1977	+51.5	1978	+27.6	17,012 /78
1978	+58.9	1979	−23.4	13,031 /79
1979	+187.3	1980	+78.9	23,312 /80
1980	+93.9	1981	−13.2	20,235 /81
1981	+48.2	1982	+81.3	36,686 /82
1982	+81.3	1983	+24.8	45,785 /83
1983	+58.1	1984	−28.0	32,965 /84

Your average compounded annual return would have been 12.67 percent. Note, however, that there were four years that produced very negative results.

Meanwhile, if you had bought and held Real World Example Fund Number Three, an income fund, you would have been better off. The fund would have grown to $44,473 (even after paying the 7.25 percent sales charge), for a return of 16.09 percent compounded per annum. This is particularly interesting as this fund is conservatively managed for income, with most of its investments in bonds and income stocks such as utilities. The tortoise is the winner in the real world.

One question investors often ask is: "Is now the right time to invest?" If you select well managed funds, it should not make that much difference over time. A study of the Real World Example Fund Number Two illustrates this. The study covers the period January 5, 1958, to October 31, 1987. Nine bull and bear markets were identified over this period of time. If one had been lucky enough to have invested a total of $100,000 over this period in equal installments of

$11,111 at exactly the bottom of each bear market low, the value would have grown to $1,856,647 by October 31, 1987 (including reinvested dividends and capital gains reinvested less maximum sales charge). On the other hand, if one had been "unlucky" and invested the $100,000 at exactly the wrong time by buying precisely at the top of each bull market, the value would still have grown to $1,592,934! Unless you think you'll be smart enough to buy at just the right time over the years, it will not make much difference when you begin a long term investment accumulation program. It is more important to pick a good money manager (or mutual fund) than to worry about when to begin.

The best managers are distinguished more in the bad times than in the good times. Humphrey Neill said: "Don't confuse brains with a bull market." The key to long-term success is keeping what you've made through the bear markets. Going back to Real World Example Fund Number One again as the model, this fund has never been the best performer in any one year. And there have been many years when it failed to do better than the market averages. But there has never been a five-year period in which its investors failed to make a profit. The worst period for the market as a whole since the Great Depression was the six-year period 1969–1974. As we discussed, the average stock as measured by the Value Line Index of 1700 issues declined to one fourth of its high point during this period! Even if you had purchased the fund at the beginning of this devastating period in January 1969, you would still have had a 68 percent profit by the end of 1974, even after paying a 7.75 percent sales charge.

A closer look at the Real World Example Fund Number One (Figure 9–3) is instructive. The table shows how a $10,000 investment in the fund would have compared to a like amount invested in a 6 percent interest account. The table covers the period November 29, 1954, which is when the fund began, to December 31, 1989. Notice that there were seven years as indicated by a "D" (1957, 1962, 1966, 1970, 1973, 1974, and 1981) where the fund declined in value from the previous year, assuming reinvestment of dividends and capital gains. This is part of the real world. It takes enough patience to ride through the cycles, even with the good funds, to make money. You need a three-to-five-year time horizon at a minimum, and preferably nine to ten years, to have a high enough probability of success.

FIGURE 9-3 Real World Example Fund Number One Compared to 6 Percent Interest

Year Ended Dec. 31	Cost of Investment			Value of Investment — With All Distributions Reinvested					$10,000 AT 6% INTEREST — With All Interest Compounded Quarterly — 6% Interest		
	Income Dividends Reinvested		Total Cost of Shares	Value of Original Shares	Capital Gains Reinvested	Sub-Total	Income Div. Reinvested	Total Value of Shares	Annual	Cumulative	Total Value
	Annual	Cumulative									
1954	$ —	$ —	$ 10,000	$ 9,296	$ —	$ 9,296	$ —	$ 9,296	$ —	$ —	$10,000
1955	—	—	10,000	9,950	—	9,950	—	9,950	614	614	10,614
1956	—	—	10,000	10,412	—	10,412	—	10,412	651	1,265	11,265
1957	—	—	10,000	8,651	—	8,651	—	8,651 D	691	1,956	11,956
1958	—	—	10,000	12,873	—	12,873	—	12,873	734	2,690	12,690
1959	—	—	10,000	14,675	—	14,675	—	14,675	779	3,469	13,469
1960	—	—	10,000	16,706	—	16,706	—	16,706	826	4,295	14,295
1961	—	—	10,000	19,762	—	19,762	—	19,762	877	5,172	15,172
1962	—	—	10,000	17,091	—	17,091	—	17,091 D	931	6,103	16,103
1963	—	—	10,000	17,969	—	17,969	—	17,969	988	7,091	17,091
1964	238	238	10,238	22,818	—	22,818	287	23,105	1,049	8,140	18,140
1965	352	590	10,590	27,484	—	27,484	738	28,222	1,113	9,253	19,253
1966	357	947	10,947	25,709	—	25,709	1,017	26,726 D	1,181	10,434	20,434
1967	476	1,423	11,423	28,765	—	28,765	1,633	30,398	1,254	11,688	21,688
1968	483	1,906	11,906	39,103	—	39,103	2,773	41,876	1,331	13,019	23,019
1969	692	2,598	12,598	46,057	—	46,057	4,054	50,111	1,413	14,432	24,432
1970	757	3,355	13,355	42,397	—	42,397	4,487	46,884 D	1,499	15,931	25,931
1971	773	4,128	14,128	50,046	983	51,029	6,135	57,164	1,591	17,522	27,522
1972	732	4,860	14,860	81,885	3,527	85,412	10,942	96,354	1,689	19,211	29,211
1973	646	5,506	15,506	67,063	10,216	77,279	9,514	86,793 D	1,792	21,003	31,003
1974	1,362	6,868	16,868	56,999	10,126	67,125	9,193	76,318 D	1,902	22,905	32,905
1975	1,753	8,621	18,621	76,761	14,023	90,784	14,220	105,004	2,019	24,924	34,924
1976	1,502	10,123	20,123	110,064	21,792	131,856	22,227	154,083	2,143	27,067	37,067
1977	2,049	12,172	22,172	123,239	34,969	158,208	27,270	185,478	2,275	29,342	39,342
1978	1,790	13,962	23,962	145,105	42,032	187,137	33,968	221,105	2,414	31,756	41,756
1979	3,346	17,308	27,308	178,683	56,088	234,771	45,677	280,448	2,562	34,318	44,318
1980	5,170	22,478	32,478	208,326	85,210	293,536	59,513	353,049	2,719	37,037	47,037
1981	6,977	29,455	39,455	203,934	83,413	287,347	64,854	352,201 D	2,886	39,923	49,923
1982	9,481	38,936	48,936	207,228	105,363	312,591	77,674	390,265	3,063	42,986	52,986
1983	9,304	48,240	58,240	270,083	137,321	407,404	111,283	518,687	3,251	46,237	56,237
1984	10,015	58,255	68,255	261,574	149,663	411,237	118,698	529,935	3,451	49,688	59,688
1985	13,346	71,601	81,601	311,803	208,723	520,526	156,651	677,177	3,663	53,351	63,351
1986	24,463	96,064	106,064	353,248	265,624	618,872	202,110	820,982	3,887	57,238	67,238
1987	28,068	124,132	134,132	321,958	311,881	633,839	212,639	846,478	4,127	61,365	71,365
1988	35,179	159,311	169,311	377,402	383,884	761,286	284,933	1,046,219	4,379	65,744	75,744
1989	48,114	207,425	217,425	432,571	475,083	907,654	374,596	1,282,250	4,647	70,391	80,381

Initial net asset value is the amount received by the Fund after deducting the maximum sales commission of 8½%. The actual sales commission on an investment of $10,000 is 7¾% as described in the prospectus.
The dollar amounts of capital gains accepted in shares were: 1971—$906; 1972—$1,555; 1973—$8,557; 1974—$1,777; 1975—$370; 1976—$1,377; 1977—$9,094; 1978—$35,840. Total—$254,606.
1980—$16,370; 1981—None; 1982—$16,591; 1983—None; 1984—$15,286; 1985—$26,691; 1986—$26,613; 1987—$68,894; 1988—$18,095; 1989—$254,606.

Stock prices were generally higher at the end than at the beginning of the period shown, and the results are not a representation of the dividend income or capital gain or loss that may be realized from similar investments today. Compared to a fixed interest account, an investment in a mutual fund carries no guarantee as to what the account will be worth in the future, because of the fluctuations in the value of the shares. This fund has been a uniquely outstanding fund. The point is that even the best investment managers have ups and downs, but identifying ones that do relatively well in bear markets can give you an edge.

Just for the record, you may like to look even closer at how various time periods have worked out for the Real World Example Fund Number One. Take a few minutes to study Figure 9–4.

The same concepts hold true for bond funds. Let's look at municipal bond funds as an example. Managed municipal bond mutual funds were established following an IRS ruling in the latter part of 1976. Listed in Table 9–1 are the results of a study of the 15 funds that provided continuous investment data from the inception of such funds—beginning January 1, 1977 through December 31, 1986—a period of 10 years.

Notice especially the year-by-year record of the best performing fund. The portfolio managers for this fund were notably successful in minimizing losses in down years. Perhaps the two worst years we have ever had in the bond market in this country were 1980 and 1981. In these two years, the fund was down only 1.9 percent and 1.8 percent respectively, compared to some horrendous losses by most other funds. Similarly, Real World Example Fund Number One's ability to hold its own in bear markets has been the primary reason why its total return has been the best over the long run. (Total return is change in net asset value assuming reinvestment of dividends.)

Historical perspective.   Does the manager have a sense of history? Those who ignore history are doomed to repeat it. Perspective is wisdom. The hot shot managers right out of business school will always get written up in the magazines. But the true test is time.

Personnel.   Too many people look at track records in a vacuum and never ask whether the individuals who made it happen are still there. Who are the decision makers? It's the bottom line. There are only a handful of people in this country who really know how to manage

FIGURE 9-4 Real World Example Fund Number One—Summaries of Performance on an Assumed Investment of $10,000 (with income dividends reinvested and capital gains distributions accepted in shares)

EVERY 5 YEAR PERIOD

Period covered Jan. 1 to Dec. 31		Cost			Value
		Initial investment	Income dividends reinvested	Total cost	At end of period
1955	1959	$10,000	$ —	$10,000	$14,444
1956	1960	10,000	—	10,000	15,364
1957	1961	10,000	—	10,000	17,370
1958	1962	10,000	—	10,000	18,075
1959	1963	10,000	—	10,000	12,774
1960	1964	10,000	148	10,148	14,398
1961	1965	10,000	323	10,323	15,454
1962	1966	10,000	438	10,438	12,378
1963	1967	10,000	761	10,761	16,271
1964	1968	10,000	970	10,970	21,328
1965	1969	10,000	933	10,933	19,843
1966	1970	10,000	896	10,896	15,196
1967	1971	10,000	1,089	11,089	19,564
1968	1972	10,000	1,035	11,035	29,005
1969	1973	10,000	786	10,786	18,961
1970	1974	10,000	780	10,780	13,934
1971	1975	10,000	1,028	11,028	20,495
1972	1976	10,000	959	10,959	24,656
1973	1977	10,000	694	10,694	17,616
1974	1978	10,000	892	10,892	23,312
1975	1979	10,000	1,252	11,252	33,617
1976	1980	10,000	1,208	11,208	30,763
1977	1981	10,000	1,148	11,148	20,911
1978	1982	10,000	1,320	11,320	19,254
1979	1983	10,000	1,418	11,418	21,469
1980	1984	10,000	1,338	11,338	17,302
1981	1985	10,000	1,273	11,273	17,540
1982	1986	10,000	1,731	11,731	21,329
1983	1987	10,000	1,998	11,998	19,849
1984	1988	10,000	1,961	11,961	18,463
1985	1989	10,000	2,573	12,573	22,130

Thirty-one different 5-year periods —and all thirty-one showed a profit

EVERY 25 YEAR PERIOD

Period covered		Initial investment	Income dividends reinvested	Total cost	Value At end of period
1955	1979	$10,000	17,034	27,034	276,028
1956	1980	10,000	20,670	30,670	324,680
1957	1981	10,000	25,889	35,889	309,575
1958	1982	10,000	41,175	51,175	412,733
1959	1983	10,000	34,294	44,294	368,731
1960	1984	10,000	36,299	46,299	330,227
1961	1985	10,000	39,207	49,207	370,817
1962	1986	10,000	44,489	54,489	380,226
1963	1987	10,000	66,443	76,443	453,085
1964	1988	10,000	81,140	91,140	532,860
1965	1989	10,000	82,039	92,039	507,726

Eleven different 25-year periods —and all eleven showed a profit

EVERY 10 YEAR PERIOD

Period covered Jan. 1 to Dec. 31		Cost			Value
		Initial investment	Income dividends reinvested	Total cost	At end of period
1955	1964	$10,000	$ 234	$10,234	$22,741
1956	1965	10,000	543	10,543	25,955
1957	1966	10,000	832	10,832	23,492
1958	1967	10,000	1,505	11,505	32,148
1959	1968	10,000	1,355	11,355	29,769
1960	1969	10,000	1,617	11,617	31,226
1961	1970	10,000	1,836	11,836	25,673
1962	1971	10,000	1,910	11,910	26,474
1963	1972	10,000	2,601	12,601	51,575
1964	1973	10,000	2,803	12,803	44,206
1965	1974	10,000	2,624	12,624	30,220
1966	1975	10,000	2,602	12,602	34,034
1967	1976	10,000	3,140	13,140	52,735
1968	1977	10,000	3,236	13,236	55,832
1969	1978	10,000	2,633	12,633	48,302
1970	1979	10,000	2,686	12,686	51,205
1971	1980	10,000	3,732	13,732	68,907
1972	1981	10,000	4,051	14,051	56,358
1973	1982	10,000	3,236	13,236	37,066
1974	1983	10,000	4,507	14,507	54,687
1975	1984	10,000	6,160	16,160	63,524
1976	1985	10,000	5,489	15,489	59,006
1977	1986	10,000	5,102	15,102	48,743
1978	1987	10,000	5,523	15,523	41,762
1979	1988	10,000	6,016	16,016	43,304
1980	1989	10,000	6,209	16,209	41,864

Twenty-six different 10-year periods —and all twenty-six showed a profit

EVERY 20 YEAR PERIOD

Period covered		Initial investment	Income dividends reinvested	Total cost	Value At end of period
1955	1974	$10,000	$6,759	$16,759	$ 75,116
1956	1975	10,000	7,927	17,927	96,566
1957	1976	10,000	8,897	18,897	135,434
1958	1977	10,000	12,872	22,872	196,155
1959	1978	10,000	9,926	19,926	157,183
1960	1979	10,000	10,783	20,783	174,761
1961	1980	10,000	12,308	22,308	193,327
1962	1981	10,000	13,640	23,640	163,117
1963	1982	10,000	20,841	30,841	208,893
1964	1983	10,000	24,570	34,570	264,177
1965	1984	10,000	22,972	32,972	209,836
1966	1985	10,000	23,015	33,015	219,489
1967	1986	10,000	32,554	42,554	280,986
1968	1987	10,000	36,938	46,938	254,805
1969	1988	10,000	34,385	44,385	228,552
1970	1989	10,000	37,400	47,400	234,117

Sixteen different 20-year periods —and all sixteen showed a profit

TABLE 9-1

Municipal Bond Fund Performance

Rank 1/1/77–12/31/86	1977	1978	1979	1980	1981	Total Return 1982	1983	1984	1985	1986	1/1/77– 12/31/86
Municipal Fund #1	+7.4%	+0.3%	+0.3%	– 1.9%	– 1.8%	+42.4%	+12.8%	+10.6%	+20.6%	+18.2%	+163.6%
Municipal Fund #2	+6.7	– 6.8	+0.8	– 5.4	– 4.7	+52.5	+13.2	+ 4.5	+23.5	+21.2	+144.0
Municipal Fund #3	+7.6	– 1.7	– 1.2	– 13.7	– 9.9	+43.1	+14.3	+10.3	+21.2	+19.1	+111.5
Municipal Fund #4	+6.2	– 2.1	+2.0	– 5.2	– 0.9	+31.0	+ 7.0	+ 7.1	+16.9	+19.8	+109.8
Municipal Fund #5	+6.3	5.1	3.4	– 14.9	– 9.2	+43.7	+16.9	+10.6	+21.4	+19.7	+103.2
Municipal Fund #6	+7.6	+0.7	0	– 11.5	– 7.1	+32.5	+ 9.9	+ 8.7	+21.4	+19.7	+103.2
Municipal Fund #7	+5.1	– 2.4	+0.3	– 12.0	– 10.7	+43.3	+ 9.2	+10.2	+17.4	+16.8	+ 91.0
Municipal Fund #8	+7.1	– 3.5	– 3.1	– 16.8	– 8.9	+43.9	+ 9.6	+10.6	+23.1	+16.3	+ 89.8
Municipal Fund #9	+7.7	– 3.0	– 1.4	– 14.3	– 10.0	+39.6	+11.6	+ 8.6	+19.4	+17.3	+ 88.6
Municipal Fund #10	+5.4	– 3.8	– 3.3	– 15.8	– 9.1	+41.8	+10.5	+ 9.5	+20.2	+21.0	+ 87.1
Municipal Fund #11	+7.3	– 3.4	– 1.8	– 16.5	– 11.6	+39.5	+ 9.9	+ 9.8	+21.2	+20.4	+ 85.0
Municipal Fund #12	+6.6	– 6.3	– 2.7	– 16.5	– 10.5	+36.0	+ 8.5	+10.0	+24.3	+21.5	+ 77.9
Municipal Fund #13	+7.1	– 5.5	– 3.5	– 17.6	– 10.4	+45.3	+10.7	+ 6.2	+18.3	+20.4	+ 77.3
Municipal Fund #14	+6.2	– 5.1	– 4.6	– 15.7	– 10.2	+44.0	+ 9.0	+ 6.5	+18.5	+20.7	+ 73.9
Municipal Fund #15	+7.5	– 6.2	– 2.0	– 18.1	– 10.2	+39.7	+ 9.3	+ 9.0	+20.1	+19.5	+ 73.6
										Average =	+ 98.5%

SOURCE: Weisenberger Investment Companies Service.

money. Murphy Teigh Bloom once said that "Committees seem to be as poor in selecting stocks as in composing sonnets." At any firm, there is usually one key decision-maker. Find out who he or she is and talk to that person if possible. Or more realistically, be sure your financial consultant has done this for you. Ask your consultant hard questions about the managers he recommends to you. By doing so you may find out as much about your consultant as about the managers! **Global Perspective.**   The U.S. markets are today just one piece of the investment pie. The values of the Japanese stock market and real estate market have now surpassed those in the United States. Many European companies offer superior investment potential. And as many developing countries enter the world of modern technology and ways of life, there will be tremendous investment opportunities. One study, covering the 15-year period between 1978 and 1987, showed total returns at various assets:

    U.S. inflation   +171%
    U.S. bonds   +266%
    U.S. stocks   +306%
    Non-U.S. bonds +467%

Another study covering 1973 to 1989 showed the following:

    U.S. stocks   +468%
    Worldwide stocks +678%

Figure 9–5 shows the performance of worldwide stock markets between 1976 and 1989. Interestingly, the U.S. market was the leader only in one year during this period.

Your portfolio should be represented by worldwide investments. This concept is also important to reduce risk. While some countries' markets are going down in price, others will be going up. Worldwide investing can potentially offer more consistency to your portfolio. Your investment manager should have this attitude: "At all times there are some investments on the globe that are overvalued, and some investments that are undervalued. Our job is to seek out those that are the bargains, wherever they may be." One of the reasons for the success of Real World Example Fund Number One is its international

FIGURE 9–5 Best Performing Equity Markets

	Germany	Switzer-land	UK	Australia	Hong Kong	Japan	Singapore	Canada	US
1976	6.6	10.5	(12.7)	(10.2)	40.7	25.6	13.9	9.7	23.8
1977	25.8	28.7	58.0	11.9	(11.2)	15.9	5.9	(2.1)	(7.2)
1978	26.9	21.9	14.6	21.8	18.5	53.3	45.1	20.4	6.5
1979	(2.2)	12.1	22.1	43.6	83.5	(11.9)	28.5	51.8	18.5
1980	(9.1)	(7.3)	41.2	55.3	72.7	30.3	62.8	22.6	32.4
1981	(8.2)	(9.5)	(10.6)	(23.9)	(15.8)	15.8	18.3	(10.7)	(4.9)
1982	12.3	3.4	9.2	(22.6)	(44.5)	(0.5)	(16.7)	2.4	21.5
1983	25.9	19.3	17.2	56.0	(3.0)	24.9	31.7	33.4	22.2
1984	(3.8)	(11.1)	5.4	(12.6)	46.8	17.1	(26.9)	(7.6)	6.2
1985	139.2	107.4	52.8	20.9	51.6	43.4	(22.2)	15.9	31.6
1986	37.2	34.3	27.1	43.8	56.0	99.7	45.2	10.7	18.2
1987	(23.4)	(8.8)	36.5	10.3	(4.1)	43.2	2.3	14.6	5.2
1988	23.1	7.1	7.1	38.0	28.0	35.5	33.3	17.9	15.8
YTD to 9/89	17.4	23.0	16.6	12.5	6.4	(0.5)	29.7	21.4	28.7

SOURCE: Templeton International

diversification. Figure 9–6 is really interesting. It shows how the fund has shifted its assets over the years.

Top-Down Versus Bottoms-Up Approach

There are two approaches to managing a stock portfolio. One approach is concentrating on individual stocks, i.e., trying to identify which companies appear to offer the best value. This is referred to as the bottoms-up method. Alternatively, some portfolio managers concentrate on identifying general economic trends and industry trends. This is a top-down approach. In reality both approaches may reach the same conclusion. They just use different methodologies. My observation is that most good investment managers tend to recognize major industry developments and concentrate investments by industries. (Mutual funds are somewhat limited in their ability to do this, as any fund that comes under the Investment Company Act of 1940

FIGURE 9-6   Real World Example Fund Number One

1955

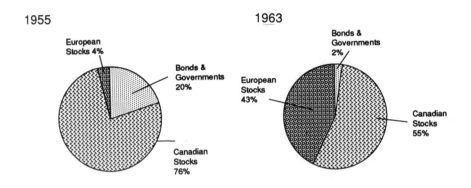

1963

1973

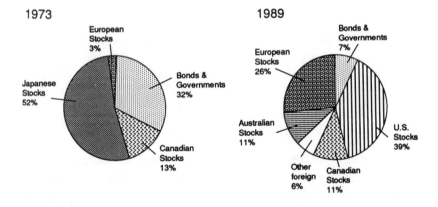

1989

cannot invest more than 25 percent in any one industry.) The idea is that most stocks within an industry tend to move in tandem. If General Motors is doing well, so will Ford and Chrysler, as an example. So the portfolio manager will shift investments from industry to industry. The following study (Figure 9–7) by Danforth Associates, Inc. (Wellesley Hills, Massachusetts) shows that if one could have stayed invested in the correct industry from 1946 to 1961, performance would have been far superior to a buy and hold strategy, and even better than a market timing approach. Of course, no one is smart enough or lucky enough to always know which industry is going to be the next hot mover. But most superior money managers seem to use some form of industry trends analysis.

The founder of Real World Example Fund Number One has made a somewhat different comment on management styles. He says that one can distinguish between a "quantitative" and "qualitative" approach. The qualitative approach focuses in on a company's management ability, its products, and so on. A quantitative approach focuses on what a company is worth. Even a lousy company may be a good investment at the right price. He says that the quantitative approach takes 10 times more study than the qualitative method—which is why most investment managers don't use the quantitative approach and are thus underperformers.

Mario Gabelli is another investment manager who has produced superior returns using quantitative analysis. Gabelli, when analyzing a company, makes a determination of the company's private market value and its public market value. In other words, if someone were to acquire the entire company, what would be a reasonable price? His analysis often finds companies that are undervalued compared to true worth.

There is no one method for successful investing. The very best money managers say that up to 40 percent of their decisions are wrong! They emphasize that investors should be flexible enough to change methods. One method of analysis may work well at some times and not so well at others.

FIGURE 9–7 Two Ways of Perfect Investing

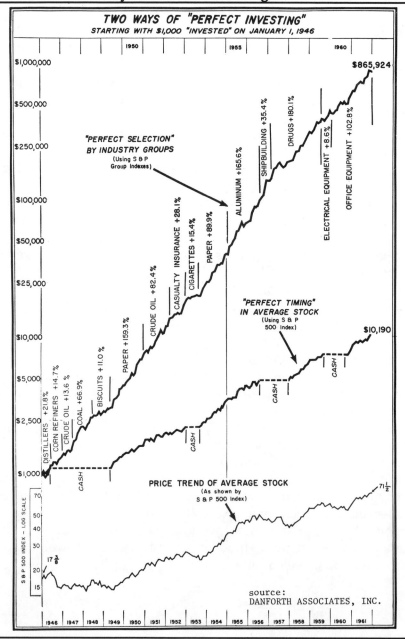

Measuring Performance

Is it okay if we get a bit technical for a minute? If so, let's get a little deeper into the statistical aspects of measuring investment management performance. The object is to analyze how well a manager is doing in light of the risk he is assuming. There are three concepts we will touch on: beta, alpha, and standard deviation. (No, this has nothing to do with a sorority.)

Beta. The beta coefficient measures the volatility of a specific fund relative to the overall market as measured by the S&P 500 stock index. The market is assigned a Beta of 1.00. A fund possessing a beta of 1.5 is 1½ times as volatile as the market; and a fund with a beta coefficient of .75 is only ¾ as volatile as the market. It is important to remember that volatility, as measured by beta, pertains to both up and down market movements. Funds possessing higher than market betas will outdistance the market on the down side as well.

Beta can be used to determine which fund best fits your investment needs and objectives. More specifically, beta should be one of the factors used when making an assessment of your attitudes toward risk. For example, the aggressive growth/capital appreciation funds with an average Beta of 1.19 are more volatile than the growth/income funds group with an average Beta of 0.87. Therefore, growth/income funds would be more suitable for those investors with low risk tolerance levels.

Alpha. The alpha coefficient is a measure of risk-adjusted return. Alpha is the difference between the fund's actual performance and the performance anticipated in light of the fund's risk and the market's behavior. To illustrate, suppose the S&P 500 was up 15 percent, risk-free T-bills earned 9 percent, and the fund advanced 18 percent. Suppose further that the fund had a beta of 1.25. Since the fund was 25 percent riskier than the market, it should have outperformed the market. More specifically, an investor in the overall stock market would have done 6 percentage points better than a risk-free return (i.e., 15 percent for the S&P 500 minus 9 percent for T-bills equals 6 percent). If the market's risk premium was 6 percentage points, then the fund's risk premium should have been 1.25 ÷ 6, or 7.5 percentage points. Actually, the fund outpaced T-bills by 9 percentage points (18 percent minus 9 percent). Accordingly, the fund did 1.5 points better

than expected, and its alpha coefficient would have been 1.5 percent.
Standard Deviation.   This is another measure of risk. It is most often
used to compare one fund's risk against another. If two funds each
had a 36 percent total rate of return over 36 months, and one fund
achieved the 36 percent at a rate of approximately 1 percent each
month, while the second fund was up 10 percent the first month,
down 9 percent the second, up 14 percent the third, then down 7
percent, etc., clearly the second fund is riskier than the first, and,
consequently, its standard deviation would be correspondingly higher.
Time Weighted versus Dollar Weighted Rates of Return.   Here's a
concept that pops up once in awhile. Most investment managers'
results are measured on a time-weighted method. This method
ignores inflows or outflows of money from one year to the next. On
the other hand, to calculate how you actually did on your portfolio a
different method is necessary. You might have been lucky enough to
put a lot more money than usual with a manager during an unusually
good year, as an example. If so, your return would actually be better
than someone else's who happened to invest with a different cash
flow schedule. A dollar weighted return might actually show a truer
result, though in reality it is seldom measured because most investors
want to see how a manager has performed regardless of how much
money he happened to have under management in any one year, thus
eliminating any "luck" involved with timing of contributions. Another aspect to this is that you should not judge a manager's results based
on your own account if you put money in at a bad time.

The difference between the return calculations is illustrated by two
investors, each of whom opens a $100 account with a money
manager. The manager buys two shares of the same $50 stock for each
client. A year later, each share has risen to $100. Client A adds $100,
which the manager uses to buy another share of the same stock.
Finally, after another year, the stock is back to $50. On a time
weighted basis, the return on both accounts is zero because $1
invested at the start of the period was still $1 at the end. But on a
dollar-weighted basis, Client A's account shows a negative 18.1
percent return, as the $150 invested fell to $100. Client B, with $100 at
the start and the end of the period with no cash flows, had a zero
dollar-weighted return.

Market Line Analysis. This is graphic analysis of risk versus reward. It is a terrific tool. Statisticians show risk (usually standard deviation) on the horizontal axis and percentage return on the vertical axis, as in Figure 9–8. On this graph, several points are plotted. Treasury bills represent a "risk-free" point (Point T). The Standard & Poors 500 Index can be used to show stock market returns (Point S). Usually some sort of bond index is plotted (Point B). An index of both stocks and bonds together is plotted (Point C). On the graph the CMI Index (i.e., Capital Markets Index) represents a balanced index of stocks and bonds. And your portfolio is spotted as well (Point A).

Then a line is drawn from the T-bill point connecting either the CMI, the S&P 500, or the bond index. If your portfolio is a balanced portfolio with both stocks and bonds, the comparison should be primarily with the balanced index, so the market line would be connected between T-bills and the CMI.

In this example, point A is your portfolio. It has a good rate of return

FIGURE 9–8   Market Line Analysis

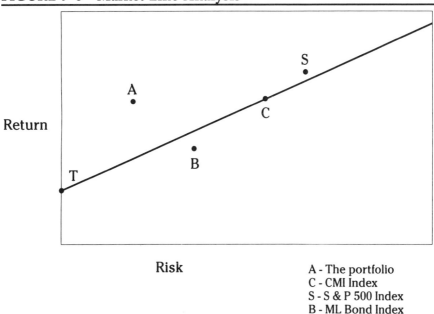

Return

Risk

A - The portfolio
C - CMI Index
S - S & P 500 Index
B - ML Bond Index
T - T-bill rate

SOURCE: Merrill Lynch.

at a fairly low level of risk. What you want to see is your portfolio above the market line. That would indicate that, given the level of risk taken in the portfolio, the return is higher than "average."

Another investment manager might have a higher return than yours, but took a lot of risk as evidenced by being far to the right side of this chart. And if it were below the market line, you might give the manager a failing grade. Why? Because if the manager is too high a risk-taker, he may lose everything he made in the next market cycle. This is a very important concept. A superior investment manager can balance risk with reward.

To get this type of information, you will have to purchase it. Your financial consultant may be able to access a source for this. Usually this performance measurement analysis includes a lot of additional information to help you evaluate how your portfolio or investment managers are doing.

Especially if you are responsible for a pension or profit sharing plan, you should consider using such a service to meet your fiduciary duty to monitor the performance. Based on the information in this chapter as well as in previous chapters, I suggest having some specific written performance standards for your investment managers. The following are some good standards for a fixed income, balanced, or equities (stock) portfolio.

Performance Standards For Fixed Income Accounts

The account should achieve average compound annual results better than at least one of the following standards over a complete market/ economic cycle (usually four years) net of management fees and commissions:

a. Any standardized index of corporate and government bonds, such as the Merrill Lynch Corporate and Government Bond Master Index.

b. The Consumer Price Index plus 4 percent.

c. The top quartile (¼) of other fixed income money managers nationally.

d. Score above the risk adjusted return line on market line analysis.

e. Score better than the Portfolio Policy Index. This is an unmanaged index constructed by your performance analysis firm to reflect a possible unique policy mix of bonds and cash. For example, if you have set a specific policy of 70 percent bonds and 10 percent cash (money market instruments), the Portfolio Policy Index substitutes appropriate unmanaged indexes at these weightings to construct a comprehensive index to compare against your portfolio.

Performance Standards For Balanced Accounts

The account should achieve average annual results better than at least one of the following standards over a complete market/ economic cycle (usually four years) net of management fees and commissions:

a. Any standardized index of stocks plus bonds, such as the Merrill Lynch-Wilshire Capital Markets Index (CMI). This index consists of a market weighting of corporate bonds, government bonds, and 5,000 common stocks. Approximately one-half is stocks.

b. The Consumer Price Index plus 6%.

c. The top quartile (¼) of other balanced money managers nationally.

d. Score above the risk adjusted return line on market line analysis.

e. Score better than the portfolio policy index. This is an unmanaged index constructed by your performance analysis firm to reflect a possible unique policy mix of stocks, bonds, and cash. For example, if you have set a set specific policy of 30 percent bonds, 60 percent stocks, and 10 percent cash (money market instruments), the portfolio policy index substitutes the appropriate unmanaged indexes at these weightings to construct a comprehensive index to compare against your portfolio.

Performance Standards For Growth/Maximum Total Return Accounts

The account should achieve average annual results better than at least one of the following standards over a complete market/economic cycle (usually four years) net of management fees and commissions:

a. The Value Line Composite Index. This index consists of 1700 stocks. It is considered an excellent measure of the individual investor's actual exposure to the stock market.

b. The Standard & Poors 500 Index, including dividends. This is the standard for comparing institutional portfolio performance.

c. The consumer price index plus 8 percent.

d. The top quartile (¼) of other equity money managers nationally.

e. Score above the risk adjusted return line on market line analysis.

f. Score above the Portfolio Policy Index. This is an unmanaged index constructed by your performance analysis firm to reflect a possible unique policy mix of stocks and cash. For example, if you have a set a policy of 90 percent in stocks and 10 percent in cash (money market instruments), the portfolio policy index substitutes appropriate unmanaged indexes at these weightings to construct a comprehensive index to compare against your portfolio.

Of course, you could set more or less stringent requirements. For example, you could say that your investment manager should achieve at least one of these standards every year. However, as we've discussed, even the best managers have off years. So I think the above list is very reasonable.

A couple of comments about stock performance. Most institutions measure versus the S&P 500 Index. However, the Value Line Composite Index sometimes differs considerably from the Dow Jones or S&P 500 measures. The Value Line has approximately 1700 stocks in it. As you can see from Figure 9–9, the Value Line dropped a far greater percentage from 1969 to 1974 than the Dow. However, from 1976 to 1981, the Value Line went up substantially while the Dow went sideways. My experience suggests that the Value Line is a much better representation of how the individual investor is doing, while the S&P 500 or the Dow Jones Industrial Average better reflects how the average institution is fairing over a given time period.

What About No-Load Mutual Funds?

A "no-load" mutual fund is one that has no sales charge (commission). Don't confuse management fees with commissions. Every fund has a fee to the fund's investment manager as well as other internal expenses, including expenses to distribute fund shares. Some funds, however, may have no fee to buy or sell the shares, which is paid to your salesperson. In either case, there is no free lunch. Somebody's

FIGURE 9–9   Value Line Selection and Opinion

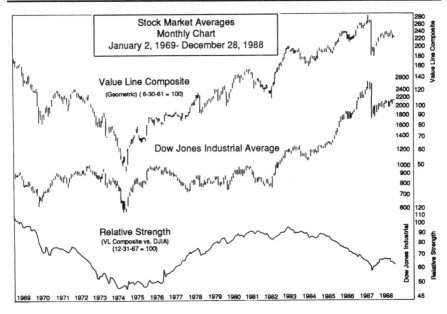

SOURCE: Value Line Publishing, Inc., 711 Third Avenue, New York, NY 10017.

gotta pay the light bill. If you do your own research as we discussed in this chapter and feel comfortable knowing when to buy and when to sell your fund, then if you can find a good no-load fund that has lower internal expenses than a load fund, it makes sense to buy it. However, consider this: If the fund doesn't perform, it certainly wasn't a bargain. On the other hand, if the fund does well, any normal commission fee is a bargain.

According to Michael Lipper of Lipper Analytical Services, one of the premier mutual fund performance measurement companies, in a study covering the 10 years from 1973 to 1983, load funds had the best record. Typically, says Lipper, (*Barron's*, November 14, 1983,) the "load or sales charge is a negative factor for the short term, but irrelevant over five to ten years." Don't be penny wise and pound foolish.

Summary

This writer can pile all his 25 years' experience in investing into this advice: For most people, you need four team members—one financial consultant and at least three investment managers. This is the second part of Meek's Reasonably Reliable Rags to Riches Recipe. (The first, you'll remember from Chapter 2, is to invest regularly and automatically.)

Unless you have a portfolio of hundreds of thousands of dollars, the easiest way for most of us to have three investment managers is to select the three best mutual funds we can find. These three funds should each be of a different management style. For example, you might pick an income fund, an international growth fund, and an asset allocation fund (which can shift between stocks, bonds, and cash). You might also add a small company stock fund, a contrary opinion style fund, a market timing fund, a junk bond fund, etc. With this diversification, your portfolio will be more insulated from the ups and downs of segments of our economy. To illustrate how such diversification can work, Table 9–2 shows performance figures for three mutual funds. One is an income fund, using both bonds and income producing stocks in a balanced portfolio. Another is an international growth fund, which happens to be the Real World Example Fund Number One. The third is an asset allocation type of fund that makes dramatic shifts between stocks, bonds, and cash.

I've taken the performance back to 1973 to show bad times as well as good ones. 1973 and 1974 were the two worst years for the securities markets since the Depression. The asset allocation fund started in 1987.

If you study the year by year statistics, you'll see that the growth fund significantly outperformed the income fund in the late 1970s. However, in several years in the early 1980s the income fund beat the growth fund.

In 1987, the year of Black Monday on October 19, 1987, the asset allocation had a great year, up 34 percent, as they got out of stocks into bonds prior to the crash. The other two funds just eked out a profit for 1987. Then, in 1988 the growth fund was back on top, while the asset allocation underperformed. The managers of the asset allocation fund stayed too long in the bonds that year. Overall, each of the funds produced excellent returns. But by using the three in tandem, the year-to-year cycles were dampened, providing a more consistent return.

The third and final ingredient in the recipe is what I call the "9–9 rule." Over the last century, the average bull market lasted 26 months, with the average bear market lasting 13 months. Thus the average market cycle averaged 39 months, that is 3 years and 3 months. If you set your sights on three market cycles, plan on looking over the hills and valleys to 9 years and 9 months.

Indeed, even the 9–9 rule is an oversimplification. Investing is a life long endeavor. No one is going to give you a date for you to be rich and successful. . . . Aren't you glad that life isn't that simple?

I constantly have people worrying about month-to-month and year-to-year fluctuations. In the real world, that's a waste of mental energy and stress! You've got to let time pass. Give your investments enough time to work out. If you've taken the simple steps outlined in this book, you can have confidence that your portfolio will grow handsomely. Just sit back, relax, enjoy life, and have fun watching the fascinating developments as they occur. Think long term, and let the 9–9 rule work for your portfolio. Here's a summary of what it takes to make mutual funds work for you. I only wish somebody would have told me these things twenty-five years ago. . . .

TABLE 9-2

Performance Figures For Three Mutual Funds, 1973–1989

Year	Income Fund	International Growth Fund	Asset Allocation Fund	S&P 500	Inflation
1973	−9.6%	−9.9%		−14.7%	8.8%
74	−6.7	−12.1		−26.5	12.2
75	35.8	37.6		37.2	7.0
76	35.2	46.7		23.8	4.8
77	−.2	20.4		−7.2	6.8
78	5.1	19.2		6.6	9.0
79	7.6	26.8		18.4	13.3
80	9.9	26.1		32.4	12.4
81	11.5	−.1		−4.9	8.9
82	36.2	10.8		21.4	3.9
83	17.2	32.9		22.5	3.8
84	14.6	2.2		6.3	4.0
85	27.8	27.8		32.2	3.8
86	15.2	21.2		18.5	1.1
87	.7	3.1	34.4%	5.2	4.1
88	14.8	23.6	8.1	16.6	4.6
89	22.7	22.9	25.4	31.6	4.6
Total:	718.2%	1,237.9%	—	608.6%	196.3%
Annual:	13.2%	16.5%	—	12.2%	6.6%

How To Make Mutual Funds Work For You

Well-managed mutual funds have returned 12 percent to 14 percent per year over the long run. Past results do not assure future results, but if the economy and investment results continue approximately the same in the future as in the past, a $10,000 investment will grow as follows in 20 years.

Amount Invested	Type of Investment	Compound Yield	Value in 20 Years	Value in 40 Years
$10,000	CD	8%	$46,000	$217,000
$10,000	Mutual fund	12%	$96,000	$930,000

My experience suggests that there are several crucial factors that the investor must have to achieve success in mutual fund investing, listed in the approximate order of importance:

10-Year Time Horizon. A long-term outlook is absolutely crucial. The short run for the economy is totally unpredictable. Based on a detailed analysis of historical business cycles, a time horizon of two years has a poor probability of achieving a result better than CDs. A time horizon of five years has only a fair probability of achieving a satisfactory result. But a 10-year holding period is a long enough time to average out the inevitable business cycles. Over 10 years, the probability becomes excellent that the investor can achieve a result approaching the 12 percent goal. Patience is a virtue.

B. A Confident Attitude. My observation is that pessimists are seldom successful in business. When applied to investing, an overly fearful person is the one who panics and sells during each inevitable business recession when prices are low. On the other hand, a confident and optimistic investor recognizes that the long term trend for mankind (and thus the world economy) is strongly up. The successful mutual fund investors are thus emotionally (and financially) prepared to buy more of their well-managed mutual funds during periods of bad news and market weakness. This is what separates the winners from the losers.

C. Diversification. I recommend having at least three top mutual funds at all times. And each fund should have a different investment philosophy or approach. By doing this, when one fund lags behind in performance, another may be doing well to take up the slack. Diversification is always a basic tenet of investing.

10

Professional Assistance: How to Choose or Lose a Financial Consultant

Unless you "aced" the quiz at the beginning of the book, maybe you are convinced that you need assistance with your investment program. In fact, in the real world, most of your investments will be made through a third party, individual or institution. It is a world of specialization, and it is the experience of this author that most folks are too busy with their job and their family to give adequate time to their investments. And that's not all bad. Let's put first things first—one's family and job, along with one's religious, charitable, and community endeavors are rightfully priority items. Investments, if done properly, are a full time job by themselves. What's one to do?

They come in all sizes, shapes, and disguises—waiting eagerly to help you with your money. Generally, they earn their living on commissions. You may even have known them in their previous lives—as bankers, stock brokers, insurance or real estate salesmen, or even lawyers and accountants. Today, they are financial consultants (or "financial planners," or "investment executives," or "financial advisors").

They can be worth their weight in gold . . . dead weight if you happen to be trying to swim through the ocean of financial products available today with the wrong advisor as a coach. However, this is the wave of the future and the way financial services will continue to be provided to consumers. And everyone is getting in on the act.

257

One of the most important relationships in your life will be with your financial consultant. How do you find the right one (or ones)? What can you expect from him or her? And what should he or she expect from you? A lot has been written about investments themselves, but very little about these important concepts. And for most Americans, these concepts are really crucial.

Selecting A Financial Consultant

In selecting your consultant, rule number one is to shop around. Recognizing that there are personality differences, look for someone in whom you have confidence and with whom you feel comfortable. There are two things you want to determine:

1.   Is he/she competent?

2.   Does he/she have your best interests at heart?

These items, obviously, can be tough to determine. Relationships are built over time. But don't be afraid to ask questions, as there are some strong clues to look for. Let's consider both of these concepts.

First, is he or she competent?

- Does he have a sense of long-term economic history? Theodore Roosevelt said that "nine tenths of wisdom is being wise in time." This boils down to perspective.

- Does he have the back-up of a good firm? Are the firm's resources strong and deep? Do the products and services cover all areas of possible investment? If not, the advice may be biased.

- Look, however, to see if he only offers "in-house" products. A true professional is constantly on the look-out to find the best investment products for his clients, wherever they may be.

- Does this person have a record of success, both in and out of the office?

- Does he have other clients who are willing to tell you of their experience? If so, talk with them.

- Does he understand risk and value? Or is he always getting caught up in what's popular at the time? A competent investment advisor is an independent thinker.

- Does he have broad capabilities and knowledge? Ask about his licenses and academic background. His knowledge should not be limited to a few areas or products. Be very critical in your evaluation of a potential consultant on this point. Select the person on the basis of his unbiased perspective, available from a varied background and wide product line.

- Does he have the ability to help you with estate planning, tax planning, children's education planning, retirement planning and other important aspects to financial planning?

- But, does he know his limits? Is he too hesitant to use third party specialists for help? This is a common failing. All of us are reluctant to lose control or let others think we don't know something. Don't expect someone with a securities background to practice law. Likewise, don't expect someone with an accounting background to know everything about modern portfolio theory or all the details of the complicated financial instruments being introduced today. A true professional has access to other experts for special problems and is not too proud to use them.

Now, there is more to a good relationship than just competence. You don't pick a spouse, for example, just because he or she is a good cook or is a good provider. There are intangibles.

Here are a few character clues that may help determine if your potential advisor has your best interest at heart:

- Does he or she have a history of family and community involvement? If the person has a well-rounded approach to life and you sense that he cares about the world around him, it's likely that the individual is the quality of person you're seeking.

- Does he have a stable record? Sometimes, though certainly not always, continuous career jumping could be an indication of a short-term outlook. In other words, does the individual really care about your long-term future, or are his customers just a stepping stone to the next location?

- Does he encourage building an overall financial program? In other words, is it a top down rather than a bottoms up approach? Also, do you get the feeling that you could come to this person about a financial concern (or any concern, for that matter) even though it would not involve something that he would be paid for directly? This is a strong clue that he does care.

- Does he help you set goals? If you don't know where you're going, you're certainly never going to get there! Goal setting is a key to financial planning (as well as to human behavior in general). There are many ways to accomplish a given investment objective. It's the goal that is the crucial first step.

- Does he understand "suitability"? What is right for one person may not be right for another.

- Does he encourage adequate diversification? Of course, "adequate" is not a precise notion. Diversification should mean, however, diversifying over various investment mediums as well as diversifying over time. This last one is the one that is most often missed. What is a good investment in one time period may be a poor one in another. Is your advisor willing to forego a current fee or commission, if it would be appropriate to wait on an investment? Don't expect this person to be omniscient about the future, but do expect him to be concerned about controlling risks that could hinder achieving your goals. In general, no single investment should be large enough to stop you from reaching your goals if the investment fails.

- Would he put his money in the same recommendations he makes to you, if he were in your situation? This is the true test.

What about the so-called *financial planner*? This designation purportedly shows certain credentials; however, the investment industry is in a state of flux with this concept. Anyone can call themselves a financial planner as there is no governing body or defined regulation. The two most commonly accepted designations among financial planners are Certified Financial Planner (CFP), awarded by the College for Financial Planning in Denver, and Chartered Financial Consultant (ChFC), awarded by the American College in Bryn Mawr, Pennsylvania. Both of these programs are fairly rigorous correspondence courses that last a year or two. Entry into these programs usually requires a combination of some college education and a few years' experience in a related field such as insurance, securities, or banking. Courses cover estate planning, taxation, retirement planning, investments, insurance, and so on. Classroom exams must be passed. Many people who have these designations have an insurance background. That's especially so with the ChFC designation, which is really for insurance agents who already have their Chartered Life Underwriter (CLU) designation.

There are certain regulations that apply. Anyone who gives financial advice for a fee must be registered with the Securities and Exchange Commission (SEC). The exception to this is someone who is employed by a brokerage firm, or someone who has 15 or fewer clients. However, the SEC registration is next to meaningless—just pay your $150 fee and you're in. In addition, most states require that anyone giving investment advice must register as an investment advisor. Usually no exam is required, so who cares? In fact, studies show that many people practice financial planning without registering as required. There will no doubt be tougher regulation in the future.

In any case, what really matters is the individual with whom you're doing business. Most financial advisors are honest and reasonably competent; however, there are a few wolves in sheep's clothing out there. A survey of twenty states[1] turned up $20 million in actual fraud and other abuses by financial planners. Medical Economics magazine cited some questionable situations they uncovered with doctors:[2]

- Three surgeons in California were told by a financial planning firm that they needed an $800,000 whole-life policy at a cost of more than $100,000 a year, with only a 2.5% return. It was seven months before the doctors realized their mistake and terminated the insurance. The policy had already cost them more than $65,000 in premiums, to say nothing of the interest they could have earned on that money.

- A Kentucky doctor spent $1,000 for what he thought would be an in-depth financial plan. Instead, he got an eight-page computer report with only the most general recommendations. His financial planner was specific about one thing though: life insurance. The planner exhorted the doctor to buy $100,000 of life insurance on his wife to pay for housekeeping expenses if she died, a rather large figure considering the doctor's children were grown and living on their own.

- A physician in Chicago was sold what turned out to be an abusive leasing shelter for $80,000. The firm later tried to sell him more shelters, despite the fact that the doctor had children in college and needed current income to pay their bills. The IRS assessed the doctor at least $36,000 in penalties and also disallowed the tax benefit.

Financial planners can be compensated either through commissions or fees alone or a combination. There are pros and cons to each approach. The fee-only service makes sense on the surface, as the planner theoretically is unbiased. However, one negative of the fee-only planner is that he may be less likely to stay up on the details of all the new investment products available today. And the fee-only planner has less motivation to help you implement the plan, which is where most financial planning fails. Worse, is the fact that you'll probably have to pay commissions anyway to implement the plan—thus paying twice.

One family I know that owns a successful business was approached by a financial planning firm on a fee-only basis. The concept was that they had no ax to grind as they didn't sell products. They were told that another related sister company did have some investment products if they should decide to make any investments, but there was no obligation to use them. The family paid a $12,000 up-front fee—just for advice and a plan. The planners arranged for health physicals to start. When they returned with the plan, the primary recommendation was—you guessed it—a multimillion dollar whole life insurance policy on the father to pay for inheritance taxes when the father died.

Since the father had already taken the physical exam, the planners had the policy ready for them to sign when the plan was delivered. The family bought. Now, there was nothing wrong with the concept. Indeed, the family had substantial illiquid investments that should have been insured for estate planning purposes. But why did they have to pay $12,000 for the privilege of purchasing life insurance? Any decent insurance or brokerage firm could have done the same thing for them—without the twelve grand!

I know another person who spent $20,000 (true!) for a beautiful three volume financial plan from a fee-only planner. It was really a fine document. However, the only recommendation that the person followed (out of several hundred) was to change his will. (That may have been the most expensive will on record.) The planner had no vested interest in helping the client follow through on the plan. The $20,000 was basically for naught. This man died three years later with the plan still sitting on his desk.

The other alternative is to use a commission oriented planner. With the commission-only provider, there is a distinct possibility of conflict of interest. Make no mistake about it. Yet another case I saw was a young couple that went to a financial planner when they received a million dollar settlement from a medical malpractice suit on their young daughter's illness. The planner had them put almost all the money in life insurance. A multimillion dollar life insurance plan seemed a bit ridiculous for a school teacher and his wife who were only earning $23,000 a year. The tip-off should have been when the life insurance companies refused to accept that much insurance on the father and mother. So what did the planner do? He bought most of the life insurance on the grandparents' lives! Anything to make a sale.

I've dwelled on the negatives in these illustrations, which is unfair. For every financial planner or broker that is unscrupulous, there are hundreds that go out of their way to do the right thing.

In the real world there is conflict of interest in just about everything. A cynic says even a preacher will lie about the used car he wants to sell. If you go into a consumer electronics store to buy a TV (or refrigerator, or stereo, or whatever), how do you know that the salesman isn't selling you the model that has the highest commission? How do you know your dentist really needs to cap that tooth, instead of just filling it? And, of course, the medical profession has gotten lots of press about unnecessary surgery.

A doctor group I know was determined to find a pension consultant that was fee-only in order to get unbiased guidelines in restructuring their profit sharing plan. They paid thousands of dollars to receive a report that recommended two money managers. Interestingly, the consultant just happened to be on the board of directors of one of the money management firms, and was crosstown friends of the other money manager. No conflict of interest? . . .

One difference between your family financial consultant or a family physician or other professional compared to an appliance salesman or even a surgeon that you will only need once is the professional's need (or lack of need) for a long-term relationship with you, the consumer. That is, is it just a one-time transaction or an ongoing relationship? The only way the family-oriented professional is going to make it is to treat you right so that you'll do business again and again—and send your friends to do business, too! That's a very important distinction.

But there's lots more to the story. Choosing your consultant is just the first important step. In our society, it seems to be easier to get married than to stay married, just as an illustration. How do you develop the relationship with your advisor?

Getting the Most Out of Your Financial Consultant

Once you've selected your financial consultant, you need to know how to deal with the lucky person. There are a few basic ingredients that you and your consultant have a right to expect of each other that will make this union work:

Communication.   An honest and forthright attitude is crucial. You obviously want this from your advisor. And he has an equal right to expect it of you! You must be willing to share your complete financial situation and to clearly express your goals and risk tolerances. (Oh! How horrifying.) This means that both of you need to be able to express yourselves, but it also means that you need to be able to listen. No two people's concept of risk and reward is the same. This means that both of you will have to give and take in developing an understanding of your true needs.

You should also develop "what if . . . " strategies. As an investor, you need to have contingencies to put into action depending on which way the play may develop. This is part of the communication process, and as much of it as possible should be outlined in advance so that you'll be ready to act.

Do you and your advisor have your goals clearly in mind? You should judge each other by the progress made toward those goals. You should keep your advisor informed—of your thoughts and concerns, the changes in your financial situation, and other investments you hear about from other sources. This latter idea is important. A good consultant learns from his clients and develops ideas and strategies from them as well as from other sources. You ought to be part of this process, sharing your research. It's part of the communication effort.

Normally, it is in your best interest to settle on one advisor. This is because if you really want someone to feel completely responsible for your financial success, you need to put the burden on his or her shoulders. Management by committee usually fails because everyone assumes the next guy is going to do it. The B-school text is correct—it takes both responsibility and authority focused on one person to have effective execution.

However, if your account is large enough, it is not necessarily a sin to have more than one financial advisor. But it is a sin to fail to disclose what you're doing, in my opinion. If you have two sources, inform both parties of your reasons for doing so and also discuss what share of your business you will be doing with each. This may allow you to capitalize on the strengths of two professionals and, if not overdone, can foster a degree of healthy competition. It's even acceptable to discuss the ideas of one consultant with the other—provided that you are not wasting anyone's time without adequate overall compensation to him. He should be glad to give you an unbiased opinion of a competitor's product or service. However, a risk you may run if you use a second consultant is creating resentment in your first consultant. And the more competent the person is and the more pride he has in his work, the more he may feel this resentment. In the real world, such feelings will hurt his ability to serve you. Avoid this situation when possible.

Also, from the standpoint of a consultant, one of the most frustrating occurrences is his having to reach too far to earn your business. For example, some investors put a consultant on the spot by shopping constantly for a little higher rate on an investment. You may be inadvertently telling your consultant to increase the risk quotient on his investment ideas to you, when such is not really in your best interest. In this situation, you've succeeded in turning a consultant into a salesman. Get the picture?

Mark Twain once said that there are lies, damn lies, and statistics. The last is the trickiest in this business, and the most abused. Insist that you get the straight story on investment returns and risks. Be sure that all comparisons are "apples to apples," over the same time frame, with the same investment objectives, etc.

If there are problems or things that bother you, by all means talk to the person about your concerns. Don't just clam up. Good communication is the key.

The Ability to Make a Decision.   This is very important for you as an investor, as well as for your relationship with your advisor. Discipline comes first in achieving a goal. It's what separates the winners from the losers.

From the standpoint of your consultant, it is frustrating to proudly develop a solid strategy for a valued client, then have the client fail to respond due to procrastination. If your consultant becomes convinced that his time is better spent somewhere else, you'll find that you will drop off his list of priority clients. You won't get good service. It's only human nature.

If you need more information before making a decision, ask for it. If you have a good reason for not taking advice, talk it out. But just as you expect your consultant to be disciplined, he has a right to expect the same of you. Make your decision based on your best logic and reasons. Then go with it. It's to your advantage. Perhaps the problem is simply old fashioned procrastination. If you are a chronic procrastinator, there's only one alternative. Change your life, today! Be a winner.

Common courtesy.   The rules are no different from those of any other interpersonal relationship. Both parties should have enough respect for the other to follow through on what you say you'll do—return phone calls, be at meetings on time, respect the other's time, etc. This may seem obvious, but it is extremely important. And it's amazing how far a "thank you" can go!

By the way, your financial consultant appreciates referrals. This may seem crass or commercial, but it doesn't hurt to let your consultant know that if he does you a good job, you'll send him business. Now, don't make it sound like a bribe! Just let him know that you honestly appreciate his help.

Trust.   Once you've decided on your consultant, trust him. And if you've carefully worked out your overall plan together, you should be able to follow your consultant's recommendations on its specific implementation. And let him know that you trust him and that you plan to follow his advice. This is important. Think about it. If someone tells you that they trust you implicitly, human nature is such that the burden is suddenly shifted to your shoulders. You now sense an obligation for that person and will go out of your way to do your absolute best job for that person.

Remember this also and listen closely: If your consultant is truly competent, he will be searching out undervalued investments for you. Such investments usually have the least risk. But almost by definition, such investments are often not the obvious and popular ones! (The obvious and popular ones may not be bargains because public recognition will have pushed market prices to normal valuation or over valuation.) Think about this: Many investors improperly tend to evaluate risk by looking in the rear view mirror rather than looking forward.

This is at the heart of the problem of trust. And it is the reason that most investors are mostly wrong most of the time. The best investments are seldom obvious and usually have more reasons not to buy than to buy. Not that you shouldn't ask questions about recommended investments. We all make mistakes and discussion and healthy skepticism are valuable. But you will get the fullest benefit of your consultant's expertise if you trust his judgment without trying to constantly second guess him. Just as a lack of trust between friends or spouses alters one's behavior toward that person, if your consultant senses a lack of trust, his behavior toward you will be detrimentally changed. Again, it's human nature. Just appreciate this fact.

Let me put this a little more bluntly. The investment industry by its nature pushes what people are most willing to buy. It's up to you to convince your financial consultant that you are different. You want to know what is really a superior bargain, not just what sounds hot.

Show an interest in learning. A good financial consultant should be flattered by your questions. However, don't expect to learn everything at once. This is a world of specialization. You don't expect your lawyer, your architect, or your doctor to teach you the skills they've taken years to develop. Pick your professionals with care, then give them your trust.

Your consultant, likewise, needs to be able to trust you in turn. For example, he may think that it is advisable to wait before investing. Assuming that he is paid by commission, if he is afraid that you may spend the money somewhere else if you wait, he may simply recommend that you invest in whatever is best now. You need to assure him that you will wait indefinitely for the best time. Again, it is a matter of trust and communication.

In the real world, you're dealing with people—more so than with numbers. Dealing with people is much harder than dealing with numbers! It takes considerable effort, skill, tolerance, discipline, compromise, discernment, and empathy. Being a nice guy won't make you rich. But it's a start.

If you are currently working with someone, ask yourself this question: Is it highly likely that you will respond to his suggestions? If the answer is no, there is something wrong. You need to fix the relationship with the person, or get a new consultant—pronto!

Here's another little piece of advice: Beware of well meaning friends. Chances are they don't know as much as they think they do. I can always tell when the market is about to change directions by my "Martha's Brother" indicator. My client, Martha, a widow, gets a call periodically from her brother in Houston, who gives her investment advice. Martha's brother is always wrong. But, of course, Martha calls me in a panic every time she hears from her brother.

You may ask: "How can a small investor like me hope to get a good financial consultant to help me? My account is not big enough to interest anyone." I strongly believe that if you are willing to share your goals (and fears) with your consultant, following the approach outlined in this chapter, you will be able to find many excellent people to assist you. Most people in the investment business are there because they like dealing with people. Their greatest reward is helping people with their long-term goals and working with them to see those goals realized. Give someone a chance to do that for you and you'll be surprised how much service you can get, regardless of the size of your account.

What about using a discount broker? Let me use the illustration again of the salesman in a consumer electronics store. There are some consumers who will go into a store, spend time with the salesman, ask questions, and so forth. Then after they have learned what model TV or camera, etc., they want, they'll purchase the unit by mail order. Even if they didn't talk to the salesman, but just went into the showroom and gathered enough information to decide on what they want, they were still using the facility and inventory that the store owner paid for in order to serve you, the consumer. In my view, it is then unethical business practice for you to turn around and go buy the merchandise from a mail order house. This is especially true if you went into the store knowing you would not do business with them and only planned to use them for information. You can wrestle with this notion all you want and justify it by saying others do it, etc., but I believe it is proper business ethics for you to fairly compensate the business for the value you received from them.

Now, if you go into that store and ask reasonable questions of the salesman and cannot get real assistance (due to lack of knowledge or attitude, etc.)—it's another situation. Or if you find that the store's prices are far out of line with similar stores—it's also a different situation. In these cases, you have given the establishment a fair shot at your business and you are certainly justified in going out and buying the merchandise somewhere else. Can you see yourself in this situation? Think about it. It's an important question of business ethics in our society.

The same thing holds true in dealing with a provider of financial services. A few people maintain an account with a full service institution, but do their business at a discounter. They maintain their account at the full service house for several reasons: to take advantage of certain services such as their central assets account, information bank, a multitude of small services, a feeling of safety, or the comfort of knowing that when a question comes up, their professional account advisor will more likely have an answer than their discounter. They may even do a little business from time to time, perhaps on one of the many specialized investment products that the discounter doesn't offer. The problem is simply that the full service organization has a

huge investment in equipment, people, and backup services support-
ing your account. The account advisor, in your eyes, may spend little
or no time on your account except to sell the occasional investment to
you. The fact is that the information bank at his disposal, which you
comfort in knowing is available to you, if only occasionally, took years
to develop. Even if the individual only occasionally has an idea for
you, he has spent considerable time getting to know you and thinking
about your account and your needs.

That discount, on the other hand, which may appear evident on the
surface, may be eaten up by lack of service, especially when the tough
situations come up. And service is what you really want, isn't it? Have
you ever bought an item in the store, just because it was a bargain?
Then, when you got it home, either it fell apart or you never used it
after all? Right now, consumers are having an affair with bargain
financial services. Those bargains will show their true value when you
get them home—during the next good economic recession.

I believe that discount brokers provide a valuable service. They
make sense for a very active trader that does all his own research or is
very sophisticated. However, if you are going to deal with a full
service consultant at all, and if that individual and his financial
institution meet the criteria we have discussed, you should consider
doing the lion's share of your business through him. You may find that
the true bargain lies in establishing a lifetime relationship with a
financial consultant who cares about you! Again, the answer lies, I
believe, in communication. Work through this with your consultant.
One approach is to agree on the level of service and level of
compensation. Such compensation could be a certain dollar amount
of commission business annually; it could be a certain percentage of
your assets; it could be an assurance that you will do all (or 50% or
some other percentage) of your business with your advisor. This is the
approach that the large institutional investors take with their consultants. I propose the same approach for individual investors.

Not to sound like the TV evangelists, but there is a loosening screw
in the ethical fiber of our society, and it is working its way through the
business sector. Interestingly, there still may be some correlation
between financial success and morality. Many great business and
financial leaders are also ethical leaders. One example, and the hero of
many of us in the investment business is highly successful money

manager John Templeton. He is also a noted philanthropist and religious proponent. His investment committee meetings begin with prayer and he believes his best investments are his religious tithings (giving 10 percent of his earnings to charity). He also takes pride in the fact that in over 50 years of business, dealing literally with hundreds of thousands of people, he has never been involved in a law suit.

. . . Ooops. Better get back on track. My publisher doesn't like these digressions. . . .

Beware of a Partner

I believe you can tell a lot about a potential consultant by the types of products he deals in. Here are a few tips.

Forms of investments.   There are three major forms of investments:

1.   Direct investments, such as deposits with a financial institution or individual ownership of real estate.

2.   Corporate securities, i.e., stock and bonds.

3.   Limited partnerships.

All three have advantages and disadvantages that you should discuss with your consultant. Direct investments, for example, have relatively few hidden charges, but tend to be relatively illiquid. Corporate securities are indirect investments, as you are relying on third party management, that is, the management of the corporation. From this perspective you may be giving up control of your investments, but you have the advantage of excellent liquidity.

Limited partnerships, on the other hand, deserve some extra comments. You have the advantage of being able to participate in some large investments in which you would otherwise be unable to participate. You also have the advantage, at least in some partnership programs, of limited liability. That is, the legal limit of your amount at risk is what you invested—no more.

However, in my opinion, there are many negatives. A limited partnership is both an indirect investment (with lack of control) and an illiquid one. This can lead to numerous abuses. High fees, paying too high prices for partnership investments, and management mistakes are hidden due to the illiquidity. Compare this to a corporate security, where an efficient market tends to automatically reflect the good and bad aspects of the investment. The market price adjusts to its approximate true fair value. Ask yourself this about a partnership deal: If this were listed on the New York Stock Exchange today, what would it sell for? I submit that most limited partnerships would sell at a discount to their issue price.

Here's another criterion you can use when evaluating a partnership investment program: Does the program look like a separate ongoing business? The distinction is that most partnership programs are serial in nature. That is, each few months, the syndicator puts out another program. You may be buying Sure Thing Real Estate Partners XV, that is, the fifteenth program with the same type investment and same management.

In this situation, the issuer's loyalty is dispersed among several deals. And what you find is that this business is a fee driven business. Much of the return comes up front, and thus they need to keep issuing deals to stay in business. The oil industry programs of the 1970s and early 1980s are a classic example. Most of those people weren't looking for oil, they were looking for investors! Nobody ever really made money, even with the honest syndicators.

On the other hand, you and your consultant should look for programs that look like real life business entities, where the management has few if any other businesses. Also, evaluate the structure of the deal to see if the lion's share of the syndicator's compensation comes out of eventual profits (not up front fees)—with a fair sharing with the investors. This will help a lot in showing that the general partner's (managing partner) motivations are in the best interest of the investors.

With corporate stock, as a comparison, corporate management is unified behind the success of one company and is daily responsible to the shareholders. This is especially true in smaller companies where the management is also often the major stockholders, and management objectives are one-and-the-same with the shareholders.

In addition, it is very hard to establish a valid track record and relative value for a partnership. In fact, you may not even know how you are doing for several years after you've invested! This removes the general partner from direct accountability to the investors.

Many limited partnerships have been sold as tax shelters. Too many investors jump at the chance to save taxes without being aware of the ramifications. That write-off looks wonderful until you discover that the true long-run internal rate of return, even reflecting the tax benefits, is no better than that of a municipal bond—with a lot more risk. That's because many partnerships use a lot of debt. And often, such shelters only defer taxes, usually at the expense of investment potential and risk. The 1986 Tax Reform Act rightfully discourages tax shelters by making them more oriented to their true economic benefit.

This is not to say that limited partnerships cannot be desirable investments. However, you have to be careful. They are suitable only for the risk portion of your portfolio. It is my opinion that one should avoid a financial consultant who emphasizes limited partnerships over other forms of investments. As a general rule, no more than perhaps 10% of one's net worth should be in limited partnerships.

Mutual Funds.   In comparison, for most people, mutual funds offer an ideal investment medium. They offer diversification, professional management, liquidity, and an accountable track record. Some funds offer track records of as long as 50 years of superior investment performance.

In summary, one of your best investments will be your effort to develop and nurture a relationship with a top flight investment professional—one who can put to work the concepts in this book and will treat you as a valued friend and client.

Endnotes

[1]*Medical Economics,* April 15, 1985, p. 199.
[2]*Medical Economics,* "Is That a 'Financial Planner' or a Salesman?", July 22, 1985, pp. 70–74.

11

Light Ages for Small Businesses: The Entrepreneur's Guide

Hats off to the business person. It's still the entrepreneur that makes our economy work. It's not the government workers, nor the investment brokers! The success of our economy is based on the new products and services developed, produced, and marketed by business. Hopefully, the people of America will continue to find excitement and profit through an entrepreneurial spirit. This chapter is devoted to a few financial concepts important to people involved in running small businesses, including professional practices as well as any entrepreneurial endeavor.

275

Cash Management

Let's analyze how the finances of a small business are typically handled, and see what new developments are available to help. Typically, a small business operates with three distinct financial systems:

1. *Checking account.* This account is the catchall account for most collections and disbursements. It will not bear interest, since commercial banks are still prohibited from paying interest on checking accounts of taxable businesses.

2. *Savings.* This will be an interest bearing account such as a money market fund, or, more likely, a money market deposit account (limited to a few transactions per month). We can also include in this category various investments such as certificates of deposit.

3. *Loans.* These are typically bank loans secured by equipment, receivables, inventories, or personal guarantees. A loan may be a term loan or it may be a line of credit. A line of credit is an agreement with the lender that, based on potential future needs, the lender agrees in advance to lend the business a maximum amount of money. The business can "draw down the line" any time without making a new loan application. The line of credit may be a legal contract secured by consideration; that is, the business may have paid an up-front fee to the lender to guarantee that the lender will appropriate the funds as needed. This is sometimes referred to as a *committed* line of credit. It is also normal for the bank to require some sort of *compensating balance,* which is money left on deposit with the bank in checking or savings accounts. The purpose of compensating balances is additional security for the loan, but also a source of additional profit for the bank as they can earn more on these deposits than they are paying the depositor.

Now, in the real world this arrangement is not only potentially cumbersome to the business, but also expensive. It is cumbersome because it requires a great deal of management's time keeping everything shuffled from one location to the next. It is expensive because of certain hidden costs on top of the interest rate paid to the lender for the loan.

A good business person is constantly moving money from one account to the next to try to maximize returns. He is trying to determine when to cover checks he has written either by moving money from the savings account or drawing down his line. He is trying to predict his cash flow needs so as to know when he can safely pay back a portion of the loan, and so forth. Remember, the checking account pays no interest, the savings account pays interest, though probably below-the-market rate of interest, while the loan is expensive in terms of posing a high interest rate cost.

This process is probably more costly than it appears on the surface. Not only does it take a lot of the business owner's time, but he is probably paying the lender in four distinct ways:

1.   Loan interest.

2.   Various transaction fees.

3.   Lost interest on idle cash.

4.   Commitment or line fees.

If you as a business person want to know what your true cost of money is, see if your lender will share with you his *account analysis statement* on your account. Most small business people have never heard of this. But your lender probably has one! (Smaller banks may not generate account analyses.) This is not your monthly statement. It is a separate document prepared internally by the lender. Your lender knows exactly how profitable each of his accounts are—yours included.

You can approximate your true cost by yourself. Let's take a hypothetical example. Let's assume a business has an average loan balance through an entire year of $100,000. The loan rate is "prime plus one." With a prime rate of say 9 percent, the loan account is charged one percentage point higher or 10 percent—that is $10,000 per year.

Now let's say that you also have an interest-bearing account that has an average balance through the entire year of $30,000, and you earn 6 percent on it. Further, you have a noninterest bearing checking account. From time to time you may have as much as $50,000 in your checking account or as little as zero. Every business is different, but such deposits can typically fluctuate greatly. You can tell what your average daily balance is by looking at your monthly bank statement. Normally it will tell you specifically. Don't be fooled by the fact that your ledger balance (check book balance) is low. Because of float, your true balance will normally be much higher than you think.

Suppose your average checking account balance, though, through the entire year is $20,000. This would be typical for a business with a million dollars in sales, as studies show that most small businesses have between 2 and 5 percent of sales in their average daily checking account balances. Also, assume you paid $500 in bank fees during the year for such items as check-writing, collections, deposits, and so forth. What is your actual cost of money?

First, in a perfect world, it is fair to say that the $30,000 in the savings account could have been used to pay off part of your loan. Had you been able to do that, you would have saved the difference between the cost of the loan (10 percent) and the actual earnings on the savings account (6 percent). The effective cost to you thus would have been 4 percent.

$30,000 amount in savings
× 4% difference between loan interest paid
and savings interest earned
$1,200 effective cost of savings

Now, that $20,000 you had in your checking account could also have been used to pay off the loan. Your savings could have been the difference between your loan interest rate (10 percent) and your checking account earnings rate (0 percent):

$20,000 amount in checking account
× 10% cost of loan
$2,000 effective cost of checking account

Your total cost, not even counting any commitment fees, is thus:

$10,000 loan interest
1,200 effective cost of savings account
2,000 effective cost of checking account
500 misc. fees
$13,700 total cost

As a percentage of your loan amount, you actually paid 13.7 percent:

$$\frac{\$13,700}{\$100,000} = 13.7\%$$

Thus your true cost was not prime plus one, but rather prime plus 4.7 percent!!

Enter—the *central assets account* for businesses. This account is now being offered by investment firms. It nets loan activities with savings and checking account balances, in effect creating a single unified account. Such accounts automatically use all extra funds to pay down the loan amount. All deposits are used to keep loan balances to a minimum. If the loan account is paid off, excess funds are automatically put into an interest-bearing account. No funds are left idle.

Basically, this automated account uses a computer to be the perfect cash manager. It will keep your loan amounts down as well as increase your investment earnings—automatically. Table 11–1 illustrates this.

With the central assets account, both the savings and checking balances are used to keep the loan down to $50,000, compared to $100,000. At first blush you may ask, "Where do I get the money to pay bills?" The answer, of course, is that it comes out of the loan account automatically as needed.

Note also that there may be an extra fee with the central assets account to guarantee the line of credit. In this illustration I assumed that you lowered your total potential line of credit to $75,000, even though your average loan amount would be $50,000—just to be sure that you had enough loan power in emergencies. The illustration shows an annual fee of one-half percent of the $75,000 potential line of credit, or $375. The bottom line is that with the central assets account your total cost is lowered from $8,700 annually to $5,875!

TABLE 11-1   Cash Management Costs

	Without Central Assets Account		With Central Assets Account	
Average loan amount	$100,000		$50,000	
Loan interest Rate	×____10%		×____10%	
		$10,000		$5,000
Amount in savings	30,000			0
Interest on savings	×___6%			
		(1,800)		0
Line of credit fee		0	1/2% of 75,000 line of credit	375
Misc. fees		500		500
Net cost		$8,7000		$5,875

This type of program brings business financial services out of the Dark Ages. The "Light Ages" are finally here for the small business person. And the business owner can go back to doing more important things than shuffling funds between accounts.

Retirement Plans for Businesses

For many small businesses, a qualified retirement plan may be not only the best available tax shelter, but also the single most important part of a long-range financial life. We won't attempt to cover all the details of retirement plans. The laws change so frequently that the book would be obsolete before it's printed! But, here are some of the most frequently asked questions about retirement plans.

Why Have a Retirement Plan?

There are several important reasons why your business should consider a retirement plan:

1. *To shelter income from taxes.* Contributions to a qualified plan are generally tax deductible, and earnings accrued are tax sheltered until withdrawal.

2. *To provide a real benefit to employees.* A plan can be a competitive advantage to help attract and keep valuable employees. After all, a company is only as good as its people. Further, many employers feel a moral obligation to help employees, as employees look to them for leadership.

3. *To encourage employees to be concerned about company profits.* This is especially valid with a profit-sharing plan.

4. *To create a forced savings plan.* If there exists a magic road to riches, it is most certainly one's ability to save and invest regularly.

What Types of Plans Are Available?

Defined benefit. A defined benefit pension plan guarantees employees a prescribed retirement income, usually a percentage of preretirement income. The amount of annual contributions to be made by the employer is determined by an enrolled actuary, and is based on such considerations as employees' ages and assumed investment results. A key concept of a defined benefit plan is that the risks and rewards of market fluctuations in plan assets rest with the employer. The employer's obligation is to guarantee a specified retirement income for the employee. If the plan's investments do well, the employer needs to contribute less money to provide the employee pensions, and vice versa. Traditionally, large firms provide defined benefit plans for their employees. However, highly profitable small businesses or professional people may find such plans desirable, also. The law allows a pension benefit paid to you from the plan as high as $90,000 per year, or 100 percent of annual pay, whichever is less. The full $90,000 benefit is available only at your social security retirement age, which varies between 65 and 67 as follows:

Year of Birth	Social Security Retirement Age
before 1938	65
1938–1954	66
after 1954	67

If benefits commence before social security retirement age, the benefit must be reduced actuarially, as shown:

Age When Benefits Commence	Social Security Retirement Age		
	65	66	67
65	$90,000	$84,000	$78,000
62	72,000	67,500	63,000
55	39,885	37,392	34,899

These limits are proportionately reduced for participants with less than 10 years of participation in the plan. Beginning with the year 1988, the $90,000 benefit is adjusted upward annually with inflation. For example, in 1990 the figure was $102,587, with all other figures proportionally adjusted.

In order to prefund for this kind of retirement income, the employer may (depending on several variables) be able to "tax shelter" 50–100 percent or more of his/her income through retirement plan contributions, while making modest contributions for other employees. One of the variables is age. If, for example, a self-employed professional establishes a plan within five or ten years of retirement, he will need to contribute quite large tax-deductible contributions in order to build the pension fund up to a size necessary to actuarially guarantee his pension.

Defined contribution. In a defined contribution plan, the contributions are based on a percentage of payroll or a percentage of profits. The maximum annual contribution is the lesser of 25 percent of compensation or $30,000 per employee. A key concept of a defined contribution plan is that the amount to the employee at retirement will depend on the investment return of the plan's assets.

There are two main types of defined contribution plans: *money purchase* and *profit-sharing*. With a money purchase pension plan, the employer sets a mandatory fixed percentage of compensation to be contributed. That percentage may be set as high as 25 percent of compensation. With a profit-sharing plan, the maximum contribution is 15 percent of compensation. However, a profit-sharing plan allows more employer flexibility, as the percentage amount contributed each year may be determined at the employer's discretion. There is merely a requirement of "substantial and recurring" contributions. Many employers choose a combination money purchase and profit-sharing plan. For example, a 10 percent money purchase plan used with a 15 percent profit-sharing plan allows the employer to annually elect a rate between 10 and 25 percent, as the employer is obligated only for the 10 percent money purchase contribution.

A so-called *Keogh* plan is essentially a defined contribution plan for an unincorporated business. "Compensation," for the purpose of establishing contribution limits for a self-employed person, is considered net earnings from self-employment less retirement plan contributions.

Which Employees Must Be Covered?

Generally, all employees 21 years old and employed 2 years must be covered, though the employer may set less stringent standards. Generally, all eligible employees must be covered comparably. Certain rules do allow a slight favoring of key employees. For example, integrating a plan with social security may mean more contributions go to higher paid employees. Also, vesting rules may favor long-term employees.

What Is Vesting?

Vesting is a system in which employees must, in effect, earn by length of service their right to their accrued benefit. If they leave the firm before a certain number of years, they may leave some of their accrued benefit "on the table." Such forfeitures may be used to reduce the employer's future contribution costs or may accrue as an extra benefit to those who remain with the company.

Does the Employer Have to Make All the Contributions?

Yes, with some important exceptions. A so-called thrift or savings plan is a defined contribution plan that allows a portion of contributions to be made by the employee. A modification of a profit-sharing plan is a so-called 401(k) plan. 401(k) plans are currently a popular type of plan approximately $7,000 annually. The $7,000 is annually adjusted upward with inflation. In 1990, the figure was $7,979. The employer may still make contributions. These may be regular profit sharing contributions or amounts as a percentage of employee contributions. For example, the employer may match a portion of any contributions made by employees. Total employer plus employee contributions cannot exceed regular defined contribution limits.

Is It Cost Effective for a Small Business Owner to Establish a Retirement Plan for Employees?

Basically, the employer needs to put a pencil to the tax savings realized versus the costs incurred to fund the plan for nonfamily employees. In some cases the employer may find that his tax savings are actually greater than his required contribution for nonfamily employees.

What Is a Simplified Employee Pension (SEP) Plan?

A SEP is similar to a profit-sharing plan with a 15 percent of compensation maximum contribution. Because a SEP is not a "qualified" plan, no annual report to the IRS need be filed. Also, unlike qualified plans, which must be established prior to the applicable fiscal year end of the employer, a SEP (like an IRA) can be established right up to April 15 with extensions. Note: Even qualified plans need not be funded for the previous year until tax filing time. One form of SEP's, the *salary reduction SEP*, is similar to a 401(k), with employees allowed to make their own before-tax contributions. The salary reduction SEP is limited to companies with 25 or fewer eligible participants. Also, an employee can be required to be employed for up to three years before becoming eligible for the SEP.

There is a disadvantage to a SEP, however. Distributions from a SEP do not qualify for favorable ten-year or five-year averaging tax treatment. But since few people withdraw all retirement plan amounts in a lump sum, this is seldom an important consideration.

What Is Ten-Year or Five-Year Averaging?

This is a nice tax benefit of qualified plans associated with a lump sum distribution of an employee's accrued benefits. When calculating the tax on such distribution, the IRS "pretends" that you had no other income during the year. It also allows you to calculate the tax in a tax bracket that "pretends" you received only one tenth (or one fifth) of the total as a single taxpayer. The resulting figure is then multiplied by ten (or five) to get the full tax. The Tax Reform Act of 1986 generally replaced the former ten-year averaging formula with the five-year method, which is available only on a one-time basis for distributions received after age 59½ (age 55 for some). However, if you were 50 or older on January 1, 1986, you have a choice of using ten-year or five-year averaging on a one-time basis.

Is There a Limit on the Compensation that can be Counted for Plan Purposes?

Yes, no more than $200,000 (as adjusted for inflation) can be counted for any one employee.

Are Pension Assets Protected in Bankruptcy?

Probably so. However, law suits that will further test this issue are pending.

What Fees Can I Expect?

Fees to establish and administer a retirement plan vary tremendously from one financial institution to another and from one type of plan to another. A cost conscious employer can save a bundle by shopping around. However, good plan administration is essential and cheapest is not always best.

May I Borrow from My Plan?

Generally, retirement plans can be written to allow for loans to employees. However, loans to "owner-employees" (as defined by law) of sole proprietorships, partnerships, and Subchapter S corporations are not allowed.

How Does One Establish a Plan?

Banks, brokerage firms, and life insurance companies can establish plans for you. You also can get plans established by plan administration firms, which are a fairly new type of organization that does all annual record keeping for a fee. A lawyer will also draft a retirement plan for you, and if your needs are complicated, a lawyer should definitely be consulted. There are usually only a handful of attorneys in any community who are competent in this area.

What Is the Trustee's Role?

The trustee serves like a board of directors to a plan, overseeing the whole operation. The trustee may be an outside institution, i.e., a corporate trust company—or it may be one or more individuals in the sponsoring firm. Small businesses often choose to go the latter route by "self-trusteeing" the plan, and thus saving the trustee fee. Many attorneys say that you cannot really rid yourself completely of fiduciary liability by hiring an outside trustee, so self-trusteeing is a possible cost saving opportunity. The three primary duties of a trustee are:

1.   Set overall broad investment policy.

2.   Select the investment managers.

3.   Monitor the performance of the investment managers.

You, as owner of your company and thus the sponsor of your retirement plan are responsible for doing these things thoroughly anyway, even if you have an outside trustee.

Besides Trustee, What Other Functions Are Necessary?

1. *Plan administrator.* This is the record keeper. Included in the administrator's duties are filing the annual tax returns and keeping track of "allocations" (i.e. monitoring how much money in the plan belongs to each employee).

2. *Investment manager.* This is who makes the day-to-day investment decisions.

3. *Custodian.* The custodian safe-keeps all the plan assets.

4. *Broker.* The broker executes the trades.

5. *Investment performance analyzer.* This is who tracks the investment results.

6. *Communications provider.* Someone has to provide ongoing written and oral information to all employees as to their rights and options under the plan.

Sometimes one firm provides all of these functions. However, I would recommend that you be flexible enough to seek out the best without limiting yourself to only one firm. This is especially true of the investment manager function. Don't get locked into a retirement plan company that won't let you seek nationwide for the best investment managers, as we discussed in Chapter 7.

What Is a "Self-Directed" Plan?

This arrangement for defined contribution plans is one in which each participant has his or her own separate account and can select his own investments. It is excellent, especially for businesses with fewer than 10 or so employee participants. 401(k) plans, regardless of the number of employees, normally are structured to offer employees a choice of investments.

What Kind of Performance Can I Expect?

That depends on what investments you or your investment manager choose. Based on publicly available performance statistics for mutual funds and bank common funds, the top plans have had annual returns in excess of 15 percent in recent years—the poorer ones less than 5 percent.

Retirement plans should be managed conservatively to minimize fluctuations because, in the case of defined contribution plans, one's retirement income may be based on the account value at retirement. You don't want to get caught retiring just when the markets are at a low point. Beware of veiled or misleading illustrations of past performance. However, there is no need to settle for average performance. Growth should be an important element in retirement plan investments. A small increase in performance can make a huge difference over a working lifetime, as we discussed in earlier chapters.

For a defined contribution plan, above average performance can significantly enhance an employee's retirement income. Even a 2 percent difference in performance over a working lifetime can increase one's retirement income by 60 percent. For a defined benefit plan, above average performance will greatly reduce the employer's contribution requirements.

What Other Elements of a Retirement Plan Should I Look For?

Personal service is important to most employers, but this can mean many things. It may mean comprehensive and timely record keeping and monthly statements, willingness to hold employee meetings to encourage participation, and to help employees with personalized employee financial planning as part of the important communication process. It also means investment flexibility, administration service at a reasonable cost, lack of biases in plan design, investment research capability, automatic investment of dividends, other business services such as insurance and corporate loans, or it may mean having access to people who really care about your long-range goals.

Take time to shop around for your retirement plan provider. Ask tough questions. Your financial future deserves it.

What Is a Nonqualified Deferred Compensation Plan?

A nonqualified deferred compensation plan gets its name from the fact that it is not "tax qualified," and the business receives no tax deduction for contributions. However, such a plan has significant advantages to some businesses. There is no statutory limit on contributions or benefits, so highly paid employees may defer substantial income from taxes compared to the limits on a qualified plan. Also, the firm can selectively cover employees without the discrimination rules of qualified plans.

A nonqualified deferred compensation plan is an arrangement where an employer agrees to withhold salary or other compensation for a key employee so the employee doesn't have to pay taxes on current earnings. Taxes would be due when he finally receives the money. From the standpoint of the company, the contributions are not tax deductible until paid out to the employee.

The legal aspects of such a plan can be tricky, but recent court decisions strengthen the viability of such plans (9th Circuit Court of Appeals case of the Snohomish County Washington Physicians Corporation). However, the courts have put certain restrictions on such plans. For example, plan participants cannot have a vested interest in the plan assets. If a plan allowed an employee to use the money in the account as collateral for a loan, a court would find that he had "constructively received" it. Some authorities believe that one- or two-person corporations may be precluded from such a plan because as owner and employee they may possess too much control and thus vested benefit of the assets. Also, the assets must be at risk to claims from the corporation's creditors. The employee's claim on the assets are as a general creditor, and the funds could be forfeited in the event of bankruptcy of the company. For example, with a small doctor plan, malpractice suits could wipe out the employer's ability to pay the doctor his benefits in the plan. Further, the court would also look at other forfeitability considerations. Thus, the employee cannot get the money except under a strict contractual agreement with the company—such as retirement, disability, or other specified constraints.

Interestingly, the company need not fund the plan at all, but merely promise to pay the employee. In this case, the company can use the money for general corporate purposes and is a source of financing. However, the employee may be able to purchase insurance to guarantee his eventual benefits.

The assets of a funded plan do not receive tax sheltered status as does a qualified plan. However, there are certain things a company can do with the assets to shelter the income—such as buy municipal bonds or dividend stocks, which are 70 percent tax free to corporate investors. Investment based life insurance is an excellent vehicle for this purpose.

Here's a related problem. A corporation generally can't accumulate more than $250,000 ($150,000 for a professional corporation) without being subject to an "excess retained earnings tax." However, those limits don't apply if the corporation can show it has a valid business purpose for accumulating more. Some authorities believe a nonqualified deferred compensation plan is a valid business purpose; however, this has never been tested in court. Life insurance, however, has been tested in court as a valid business purpose, and universal life insurance or variable life is a good tax sheltered investment alternative. Thus, life insurance can help to offset potential excess retained earnings tax as well as provide an excellent funding vehicle for a deferred compensation plan.

Overall, a deferred compensation plan can be a good alternative to consider, either by itself or as an addition to a qualified plan, if you want a vehicle to save more for retirement than the law allows for a conventional plan alone. Recommendation: Because of its complexities, get the advice of a lawyer.

What Is an Executive Bonus Retirement Plan?

This is similar to a nonqualified deferred compensation plan, except that funds are placed in an investment account for the employee and the employee becomes the immediate owner of the assets. In this case, the contributions are tax deductible to the employer but are taxable to the employee in the year of the contributions. Typically, the employer will "gross up" the contribution to cover the income taxes due. Usually, investments are made annually into an investment based life insurance contract. Because of the special tax advantages of life insurance contracts, all earnings accrue tax sheltered and the employee may make tax free loan withdrawals. Further, the eventual death benefit is income tax free. Single premium (lump sum) life insurance no longer qualifies for tax free loans, so these plans must be set up with ongoing contributions over several years.

Buy-Sell Agreement

Though there are many other financial aspects of a business that could be covered, let's touch on one more investment related concept—the *buy-sell agreement.* This contractual agreement between business partners is designed to provide a smooth transition of ownership upon the death, disability, or retirement of any partner. A buy-sell agreement allows the living partner to buy the deceased partner's share of the business at a prearranged price, preventing forced liquidation or interference of the heirs. A disability clause can be added to the agreement to become operative if a partner becomes disabled.

A buy-sell agreement must be funded so that money is available if the agreement is utilized. These investments are usually life insurance programs. It is important to update buy-sell agreements regularly so the current value of the business is maintained.

Summary

Running your own business can be an exciting and rewarding way of life. There are many financial and investment considerations for the business owner. We only highlighted some of the important ones. Our hats are off to the entrepreneur, who means so much to our country's economic health!

12

For Letter or Worse

In addition to your estate plan, there's one more thing you ought to do for your family. Write a letter of instruction on how to handle family affairs after your death. This is really important. The vast majority of spouses are left out in the cold when the primary bread winner dies. Do your loved ones a favor, put everything down in writing for them!

The following is a copy of a great sample. It is reprinted with permission of *Medical Economics* magazine. It was written by Richard H. McDonald, M. D. and appeared in the August 5, 1985, issue of *Medical Economics*.

The Last Good Deed You Can Do for Your Spouse

I wrote a long letter to my wife before I retired. She knows about it, but she probably won't read it thoroughly for a while—long while, I hope. Its message: what to do when I die. Lawyers call it a testamentary letter. Although such a letter has no legal force, it ties up the loose ends of your estate planning, disposing of things that just don't belong in a will but can cause your spouse anguish if not taken care of while you're alive.

It's not an easy letter to write. The job doesn't exactly brighten your evenings. And you'll be amazed at how many odds and ends need to be addressed. But now that I've finished my letter, I heartily recommend writing one. You'll feel you've left a final note of appreciation for your loved ones, and you'll experience a sense of relief that you've done what you can to make a saddening time easier for them.

I started thinking about writing such a letter after a colleague died.

293

Apparently, he'd never told his wife where documents were located, what kind of funeral he wanted, or how his trust arrangements would work. Under the pressures of time and grief, she ended up making a lot of expensive mistakes that could have easily been avoided.

After I wrote a first draft of the letter, I had my lawyer look at it. I didn't want anything in it to lead to complications. He had a couple of suggestions, such as changing some wording that described our trust. Then I showed it to my wife, and she had some questions that hadn't occurred to me—did I want to donate any organs to research, for example? After providing answers to her questions, I signed and dated the letter, and we put it in my top desk drawer, where it can be found easily.

The letter (minus such details as names and addresses) follows. You may find it useful as a model.

To my beloved wife,

Thanks for a wonderful life together. You've got still more wonderful years ahead with our family and friends, and the sooner you start enjoying them the better. These words are my effort to get you off to a smooth start. They're simply guidelines; your own good judgment should make the ultimate decisions, but I hope this will help.

Death instructions. I've tried to keep up the records you'll need immediately, and I've put them where you can get them readily. You'll find the details in the addendum to this letter. Here's what needs to be done first.

Call our estate lawyer, CPA, financial planner, and insurance agent. Their names, addresses, and numbers are listed on the attached sheets. Arrange to meet soon after the funeral. You'll need some ready cash for immediate expenses. There's a list of our checking and savings accounts, along with a money-market fund. I've made sure there's enough in your personal checking account. There's also a list of investments held in your name that can be quickly sold, if necessary. Our current financial statement is attached. It will tell you what my estate includes, and which long-term bills are still outstanding.

I've stored most of our important documents in my home safe. The key is in my top center desk drawer. You'll find copies of my will and trust papers (our lawyer has the originals), life insurance policies, birth and marriage certificates, armed-services discharge papers, and pension plan papers. Securities are held by our broker, and his name is listed on the attached sheet. Submit claims for my life insurance as soon as possible, and apply for other death benefits you're entitled to: Social Security, veterans,' and pension plan.

My funeral: I wish to be cremated and have my ashes scattered at sea. Keep the ceremony simple and modest—just family and close friends. Serve champagne and lots of shrimp. On second thought, serve lots of champagne, too. Play '40s swing. Maybe you won't feel up to that, but you get the idea that I don't want solemnity. I had a good life. Should you want to have a simple memorial service, fine. I'd prefer donations to the American Cancer Society instead of flowers. Speaking of donations, I'm afraid my old organs are beyond use to anyone, so I don't think science would be interested.

My practice: I've made arrangements so that you won't have to shop around for a buyer for my practice. My partner and I formulated a "buy-sell agreement," which pays the family of the first of us to go a fair price for his share of the practice. Since we're incorporated, the agreement is in the form of a stock redemption plan. The corporation has purchased and paid the premiums on $150,000 of life insurance for each of us. The corporation is the beneficiary. If I die first, the corporation will get the money and will pay you this total amount. You, in turn, are obligated to accept this amount as full payment for my share of the practice. This plan frees you from having to concern yourself with patients, accounts receivable, records, the office lease, and almost everything else involved in shutting down a practice.

One thing you must do, though, is notify the state board of medical examiners and the Drug Enforcement Agency of any death. Because as executor of my estate, you must comply with all regulations concerning narcotics, check the exact regulations with my partner and our lawyer.

Our wills and trust: Remember what our aims were when we devised this plan: I wanted to make sure you were comfortably fixed for life, and we wanted to make sure the estate was divided clearly upon your death, according to our wishes. We also wanted to make sure the children inherited the maximum amount possible, while protecting the estate from unnecessary taxes, charges, and fees.

Whatever you are left outright is estate-tax-free under present federal law. Therefore, about half of our assets go to you. The exact amount depends on what goes into the bypass trust we've set up for the children, with you as trustee. The trust will receive the maximum allowed free of estate taxes. Under present law, the maximum will be

$600,000. You will receive the income from this trust until your death, after which it will pass to the children, but without the tax consequences that would result if the money were in your estate.

Advisers and counsel: Fortunately, over the years we've managed to find a few trusted people upon whom you can rely for advice and help on taxes, legal advice, investments, and the like. I recommend using our CPA and/or financial planner whenever problems arise in managing your assets. Again, your own good judgment is what you should ultimately rely on. Whatever you do, however, don't give anyone discretionary power over the assets; nothing should be withdrawn from your accounts without your informed consent and signature.

Remaining obligations: As you can see in the attached financial statement, we have only a few outstanding obligations. There's a $4,000 home-improvement loan, and the new-car loan. I suggest paying these off from the life insurance proceeds. The home mortgage has about 10 years to go, and it's up to you whether or not you want to stay in the house. Since you're over 55, you will be eligible to receive up to $125,000 in sale profits tax-free. Unless I've already managed to do so, I think you should get rid of the lots we own in Arizona and on the lakefront in Oregon. I think both lots are clunkers, so why pay the taxes on them?

I hope this letter helps you. If you have any questions about financial arrangements, please don't hesitate to ask the advisers I've listed.

My love and thanks to you again.

Richard

My letter can serve you only as a rough guide, and yours will have to be updated periodically, like a will. The letter can include whatever suggestions you want to include, on anything from the care of your cat to what to do with artworks you may have. I don't care about cats, but I do have a couple of paintings that are alleged to be valuable. My wife and I don't like them enough to display them prominently; I think they were gifts from my cousin. When I update my letter, I'll tell her not to feel guilty about getting rid of them. I just never got around to it.

13
Summary

My hope is that the concepts presented in this book truly are helpful to a large number of Americans. If but a few get on the right investment foot as a result of the book, the effort will have been worth it. Let me simply summarize the major points in the book and add a few comments:

1. First, the don'ts:

   - Don't take unnecessary risks.
   - Don't borrow to excess.
   - Don't invest with emotion or hope that is not based on sound thought.

2. Have a plan for your financial life. Put your goals in writing. I recommend that you keep a monthly log that tracks how you are doing compared to your goals. But at the same time, do not be concerned with short-term ups and downs. It takes patience to make money and to build a successful investment program. This is a life-long process.

3. Be skeptical. Develop the ability to lean against the wind. Beware of the obvious. Shun the majority and the popular press. Remember that the best time to invest is during periods of disappointment, concern, and bad news. Every superior buying opportunity, I guarantee you, will be loaded with distressing thoughts seemingly never encountered before! The best time to sell is when forecasts are rosy and the "experts" predict good things. Ask yourself these questions: What is the easiest opinion to form? Or, is this course of

action the one that a majority of the people I know take at this time? Then ask yourself all the reasons why the opposite view is more likely the correct one!

4. Control your emotions. Be cold, calculating, unemotional, nimble, and flexible in your attitude toward your portfolio.

5. Diversify. I don't care who you are or how confident you are in any one investment notion. Diversify.

6. Remember that preservation of principal means preservation of purchasing power. Invest for the best total return prudently possible—not just for growth alone or income alone.

7. Remember Meek's Reasonably Reliable Rags to Riches Recipe Part One: Invest regularly and automatically.

Part Two of the Recipe: Have four pros working for you—the best financial consultant plus at least three top money managers with different investment approaches.

Part Three: Remember the "9–9 rule." It takes patience—and perseverance!

8. Develop a sense of history.

9. A word of warning: There will be bad times, bear markets, panics, financial dislocations, worldwide epidemics and catastrophes, recessions and depressions. Don't get caught completely by surprise.

10. A word of optimism: Setbacks will be temporary. The outlook for worldwide investments is glorious. Never before have businesses been more sophisticated. Never has technology been so poised to provide benefits for health, welfare, and standard of living for mankind. This means new levels of growth and opportunity for people worldwide as never before. Invest for the future.

11. Have fun investing. Life is too short to worry.

On a final philosophical note, in order to put all of this into perspective, let me offer this prayer:

Dear Lord,
Thank you for the opportunity to have experienced the beauty and excitement of life. May I accept the full honor of this glorious gift. May I take hold of today's moment, to use it, to enjoy it in the most exciting, creative way I can.

Help me to have an open mind to Your will. I pray for wisdom, a calm mind, and the courage of conviction to make good decisions that will benefit all parties. With excellence as my watchword, help me develop my abilities to be the best parent, child, spouse, friend, and business person possible. Help me avoid getting stuck in too deep a rut. May I strive to expand my horizons: physical, academic, and spiritual.

May I look for the good in everyone, with love and forgiveness in my heart. Help me open my heart to others' feelings and search for ways to make those around me a little bit happier. May my life be a daily example of high values.

Today offers a wonderful challenge. Grant me strength and persistence to achieve my goals and set new ones. May disappointments be met with a fighting spirit. As procrastination is an obstacle to a full life, help me develop the ability to "do it now." May thoroughness in thought and action be my modus operandi.

Help me to relax, letting nature's basic success motivations come through. Balance my mind with perspective. Keep me aware that it is not what happens to me in life that matters but rather how I react to what happens. Yet may I not take myself too seriously as I learn the meaning of "lighten up" and the benefits of relaxed concentration. No one reacts to things as they are, but to one's own mental images. As life can be seen as a game in the world of illusion, help me develop my sense of humor and keep a twinkle in my eye. For whatever is troubling me, let me ask "Is this worth keeping me from being happy?" Certainly, if happiness is not my companion today, it never will be, and I have no one to blame but myself.

It is not my life that I am living, but rather Yours, the Creator. We are merely brief visitors to Your place. May we be good stewards. And when I have gone to Your care, let them say that the world around me is a little better place because I did my small part to Your glory.

Amen

We sincerely hope that you enjoyed this book. If you have any questions or comments about the contents, or would like assistance with your own investment program, the author welcomes your phone calls. Mr. Meek may be reached at (512) 397-1854 or (800) 937-0418.

If you wish, you may request additional information from the author by completing the form below and mailing to:

Charles Meek
1900 Franklin Plaza
111 Congress Avenue
Austin, Texas 78701

Please send me information on:

_____ Updates to the Meek Market Model.

_____ Updates to Mr. Meek's bond market timing model.

_____ Investment management services.

_____ Financial planning information.

_____ Other:_____

_____

Name:_____

Address:_____

City/State/Zip:_____

Phone:_____

Index